EMIGRANTS
TO PENNSYLVANIA,
1641-1819

A Consolidation of Ship Passenger Lists
from the Pennsylvania Magazine of
History and Biography

Edited by Michael Tepper

Baltimore
GENEALOGICAL PUBLISHING CO., INC.
1979

Excerpted from selected volumes of
The Pennsylvania Magazine of History and Biography
Reprinted with an added Introduction and Indexes by
the Genealogical Publishing Co., Inc.
Baltimore, 1975, 1977, 1978, 1979
© 1975
Genealogical Publishing Co., Inc.
Baltimore, Maryland
All Rights Reserved
Library of Congress Catalogue Card Number 75-18530
International Standard Book Number 0-8063-0682-3
Made in the United States of America

CONTENTS

INTRODUCTION

Ship passenger lists are the delight of the genealogist because they are the first records of an ancestor on American soil and provide conclusive evidence of his emigration. In one simple act of discovery the genealogist is able to bridge the Atlantic, the passenger list yielding insights into national origins, dates of emigration, and ports of embarkation and arrival, and frequently even admitting of references to a passenger's age and physical description, occupation, religion, and reasons for emigration. Happy the researcher who lights upon the object of his study in a ship passenger list! Where other records founder on insights, passenger lists suggest flesh and personality and summon to mind an inventory of the political, economic, and religious forces that inspired European emigration. Small wonder that the genealogist divines an echo of history in a list of names.

Whether they may be considered the premier tool of genealogical research, ship passenger lists, commencing with the list of passengers aboard the good ship *Mayflower,* have provided a basis for study and serious debate for considerably more than a hundred years. Impressive in their reach, embodying the names of hundreds of thousands of emigrants of a wide variety of national origin, passenger lists have been so often shorn of information and transcribed in books, monographs, and articles, that there exists today a considerable literature on the subject. Published lists that come first to mind, dominating the field, are the *Hotten List*[1] and Ralph Strassburger's formidable *Pennsylvania German Pioneers*[2], both landmark works in their respective areas of coverage. Dozens of less familiar works are near rivals in breadth and importance. Periodical literature, the workhorse of genealogical research, encompasses hundreds of

---

[1] *The Original Lists of Persons of Quality; Emigrants; Religious Exiles; Political Rebels . . . and Others Who Went from Great Britain to the American Plantations, 1600-1700,* ed. John Camden Hotten (London, 1874). Reprinted by the Genealogical Publishing Co., Inc., Baltimore, 1974.

[2] Subtitled *A Publication of the Original Lists of Arrivals in the Port of Philadelphia from 1727 to 1808,* ed. William J. Hinke, 3 vols. (Norristown, Penna., 1934). Reprinted in two volumes, omitting the volume of facsimile signatures, by the Genealogical Publishing Co., Inc., Baltimore, 1975.

contributions on the subject and lays parallel claim to importance. It is by no mere coincidence that the first number of the first American periodical devoted exclusively to genealogy, *The New England Historical and Genealogical Register* (January 1847), contains a list of the *Mayflower* passengers compiled by the noted genealogist Nathaniel Shurtleff. Contributions in the form of periodical literature and book-length monographs continue to this day to attract the enterprise of conscientious students.

Over the course of a century the literature on ship passenger lists grew to unwieldy proportions, but in 1937 Harold Lancour reduced it to order in his *Passenger Lists of Ships Coming to North America, 1607-1825: A Bibliography*, which united hundreds of disparate threads and established a permanent bibliographical organization. Lancour's *Bibliography* not only gave form to an incoherent body of printed material, it also created the opportunity for discursive research in "fugitive lists" (i.e. lists buried in articles devoted principally to other topics), for as many such lists as could be identified were now conveniently enumerated in this one splendid reference work. The current edition of Lancour's *Bibliography*, the third, revised and enlarged by Richard J. Wolfe (1963) and entitled *A Bibliography of Ship Passenger Lists, 1538-1825*, identifies several hundred ship passenger lists in learned journals and monographs and extends the period of coverage to 1538-1825, with an Appendix citing published lists of emigrants to America after 1825.[3]

In common with other bibliographies, the research possibilities of the Lancour work can be extended by permutation. For present purposes it is sufficient to note that one can assemble a comprehensive list of passenger list publications by periodical, determine continuity in the total output, and proceed by method to reduce the labor of research. With prolific contributions from at least a half dozen leading journals and isolated papers from scores more, periodical literature would appear to be best served by some form of consolidation. Articles in the leading periodicals, in fact, have multiplied to the extent that they not only invite consolidation but demand it. This is especially true of *The New England Historical and Genealogical Register, The New York Genealogical and Biographical Record,* and *The Penn-*

---

[3] The New York Public Library, publisher of the Lancour *Bibliography*, maintains a current list of additions and corrections in the Local History and Genealogy Division.

sylvania Magazine of History and Biography, where longevity and editorial policy have favored the proliferation of articles on ship passengers. While there is considerable variation in scope and content—some articles constituting extensive lists of names, others invoking only a few tantalizing references—articles in these periodicals generally meet the highest tests of scholarship. The majority were contributed by genealogists; some by dilettantes or enthusiastic academics. A few run to a couple lines of type, others to several pages, and still others to over a hundred pages in series. In practical terms, consolidation would provide convenient access to an indispensable body of research material.

The rationale of the work in hand is to provide in a single volume a consolidation of the entire body of literature on passenger lists as found in the multiple volumes of one of the outstanding periodicals named—*The Pennsylvania Magazine of History and Biography.* The first number of this quarterly appeared in 1877, and although flourishing still, discontinued genealogical contributions in 1935. Between 1877 and 1934 the *PMHB* published twenty-six articles on ship passenger lists, fourteen of which constituted articles in series. The figure is not remarkable in itself except that it may be cited as evidence of subscriber interest and editorial continuity. In this consolidation all the articles in the *PMHB* identified by Lancour, with the single exception of Louis Middlebrook's article "The Ship *Mary* of Philadelphia, 1740," have been excerpted in entirety and, not counting three very brief articles assembled under the heading "Miscellaneous Lists," all have been arranged chronologically by date of arrival in Pennsylvania.

In their original form, the passenger lists derive from ships' manifests, cargo bills, and Captains' Lists and, in the majority of cases, are located in the holdings of the manuscript collection of the Historical Society of Pennsylvania, publisher of the *PMHB.* All the lists, with minor exceptions, document arrivals in the port of Philadelphia between 1682 and 1819. Two short articles on the expeditions to New Sweden, however, identify passengers of a considerably earlier period. Founded by the indefatigable Peter Minuit, plenipotentiary of a company of Swedish and Dutch speculators, the short-lived colony of New Sweden (1638-1655) here gives up the names of members of the third and eighth expeditions, 1641 and 1649 respectively. Virtually nothing is known of the passengers on board the ships *Kalmar Nyckel* and *Gripen* of the first expedition, save that they were probably company shareholders and adventurers. It is known, however, that subsequent voyages, including the third and the eighth, brought Finns as well as Swedes to New Sweden. Notwithstanding the sacrifices and perseverance of these early colonists, New Sweden did not fulfiill the expectations of the entrepreneurs and in 1655, after years of disagreement with the Dutch over jurisdiction, was absorbed by New Netherland.

Somewhat surprisingly for a journal devoted to Pennsylvania history, the number of German emigrants identified in the passenger lists is comparatively slight. Presumably, publications like the *Proceedings and Addresses* of *The Pennsylvania-German Society* and the *Yearbook* of the *Pennsylvania German Folklore Society* were more suitably disposed to treat the subject and monopolized contributions. Of course the *PMHB* did not eschew articles on German emigration, and did, in fact, publish several lists of substance. John Jordan's article on "Moravian Immigration to Pennsylvania, 1734-1765" identifies several hundred of the founding members of the Moravian Church in America in their original "sea congregations" and obtains a standard of considerable merit. Kelker's "Lists of Foreigners Who Arrived at Philadelphia, 1791-1792," another list of German emigrants, is an article of nearly equal magnitude. The Kelker list is duplicated in part in Strassburger's *Pennsylvania German Pioneers*, but omissions, differences in interpretation, and discrepancies in spelling necessitate a careful comparison of the two lists. It is of some interest to note that the Kelker work derives from the so-called "Captains' Lists" which were drawn up in compliance with a provision of the Order in Council of 1727 requiring ships' masters to maintain lists of foreign passengers, their occupations, places of origin, and reasons for emigration. The "Captains' Lists" seem to have been indifferently kept, but other lists deriving from the same Order in Council of 1727, which directed that foreigners, i.e. non-British subjects, swear an Oath of Allegiance to the English King and declare fidelity to the Proprietor of the Province, constitute the basis of the Strassburger work and, indeed, the basis of almost all that is known of "foreign" emigration to Pennsylvania between 1727 and 1808.

The two articles headed "Partial Lists" are founded on lists which were assembled in compliance with yet another law, this one, enacted in 1684, directing inhabitants then in the Province as well as those who should thereafter arrive, to register with the authorities in their respective counties of residence. This statute does not appear to have been actively enforced and penalties for non-compliance were abolished in 1690, leaving us with only these two incomplete lists of arrivals.[4]

Cardinal interest in this work centers on the pair of articles on indentured servants and apprentices bound and assigned before the mayors of Philadelphia. The two articles run to nearly 200 pages together and name approximately 3,000 persons, not only emigrants, but masters and bondsmen as well. The list for 1745-46, "Servants and Apprentices Bound and Assigned Before James Hamilton Mayor of Philadelphia, 1745," contributed by George W. Neible, is far the most extensive and originally appeared in nine separate numbers of the *PMHB* between 1906 and 1908. Unlike the 1745-46 list, composed predominantly of Irish emigrants, the list for 1772-73, "Record of Servants and Apprentices Bound and Assigned Before Hon. John Gibson, Mayor of Philadelphia . . .," comprises an almost equal proportion of German and British arrivals. It is significant that both lists are apparently based on official documents, and by inference they must be accounted authoritative. While some entries in the first list are specific in their references to places of origin, a detail generally missing in ship passenger lists, the majority indicate only the port of embarkation or that the emigrant is "from Ireland," etc. Still, this list is invaluable for its dates of arrival and references to places of residence in America. From internal evidence it would appear that most who bound themselves out as servants did so in consideration of their passage, and that those who articled themselves to a trade did so as much for the opportunity of passage as the rewards of apprenticeship. Not surprisingly, judging by contemporary accounts in *The American Weekly Mercury* and *The Pennsylvania Gazette*, to name only two early Pennsylvania newspapers, servants and apprentices absconded in droves from their indentures.

By an odd coincidence the list for 1772-73 is almost wholly duplicated in a work of somewhat greater scope, the "Record of Indentures of Individuals Bound Out as Apprentices,

[4] See, however, Hannah Benner Roach, "The Philadelphia and Bucks County Registers of Arrivals, Compared, Corrected and Retranscribed" in *Publications of the Welcome Society of Pennsylvania*, Volume I: *Passengers and Ships Prior to 1684*, for an improved transcript of these two lists. See also Volume II: *The Welcome Claimants, Proved, Disproved and Doubtful*, by Dr. George E. McCracken, for a full discussion and exploitation of the lists. (Both volumes were published in 1970 by the Genealogical Publishing Co., Inc., under the series title *Penn's Colony: Genealogical and Historical Materials Relating to the Settlement of Pennsylvania*.)

Servants, Etc. and of German and Other Redemptioners in the Office of the Mayor of the City of Philadelphia, October 3, 1771, to October 5, 1773."⁵ The *PMHB* list for 1772-73, published here, was transcribed from the original record book in the manuscript department of the Historical Society of Pennsylvania, but the Pennsylvania-German Society list for 1771-73 was compiled from a volume in the possession of the American Philosophical Society. Neither, apparently, is a copy of the other, there being serious discrepancies between the two, so it is assumed that the compilers worked from different records of the same source. The data in our list for 1772-73 is by no means as complete as that in the list published by the Pennsylvania-German Society, even for the parallel months of coverage, because it fails to include, in most instances, the port of embarkation, occupation, and term of indenture. However, our list includes one feature of manifest genealogical importance peculiar to itself: in the instance of a minor's indenture, it supplies the name of the consenting parent or guardian.

Among the incentives for using this collection of passenger lists is the fact that official U.S. government lists, those that exist—customs passenger lists, immigration passenger lists, and customs lists of aliens—cover a later period of emigration, usually post-1820, and provide no opportunity for research in the area of Colonial emigration. So here is a void profitably filled. Moreover, even when they can be turned to account, the government lists defy practical use. They are indexed by date and subject and are therein only loosely alphabetized by passengers' surnames. The arrangement of this collection is also chronological, but the indexes of names and ships reduce searching to seconds. It is hoped that the search will bear fruit and that consolidation will have proved instrumental to success.

⁵ Published in *The Pennsylvania-German Society Proceedings and Addresses*, Vol. XVI, 1907, and reprinted with an added index in 1973 by the Genealogical Publishing Co., Inc.

EXPEDITIONS TO NEW SWEDEN

THE THIRD SWEDISH EXPEDITION TO NEW SWEDEN.—The following names of persons, who embarked in Sweden, in 1641, for the colony of New Sweden (as related on page 407), are obtained from copies of lists, preserved in the Royal Archives at Stockholm, in the possession of the Historical Society of Pennsylvania, one of which, comprising thirty-three individuals, is headed "*Des Secretarij Beijers Musterrul auf die Persohnen so mitt der Floijten Charitas auf Gottenburgh sein gefahren, und von dennen nach Nova Suecia sollen übergeführt werden,*" and the other, mentioning thirty-five emigrants, is entitled "*Lengde der Persohnen so mitt der Floijten Charitas von hier den 3 Maij A° 1641 auff Gottenburgh sein gefahren,*" etc. :

Måns Kling, with his wife, a maid, and a little child, to serve as lieutenant on the pay of 40 *riksdaler* a month, beginning May 1, 1641, granted 50 *riksdaler*, expectancy-money, by Clas Fleming, as a present. June 20, 1644, he was the officer on the Schuylkill.

Herr Christoffer —— (no surname in the original), a priest, going on the recommendation of the *Riksamiral*, from whom he received a present of 100 *daler*, copper money, stipulating for nothing but maintenance, since he joins the expedition to gain experience. This person and the two following are not named in the Lists of 1644 and 1648, and probably either did not reach New Sweden, or made but a short sojourn with the colony.

Gustaf Strahl, a young nobleman, sailing also on the recommendation of the Admiral for a similar purpose, receiving nothing, therefore, from the Company but maintenance.

Michel Jansson, the burgomaster's son, from Gefle, also an adventurer, receiving no compensation for the same reason.

Måns Svensson Loom (according to Beyer's *Musterrul*, Larsson), a tailor, formerly lieutenant, to engage in agricultural pursuits, paid at the start 5 *riksdaler*, but drawing no wages nor monthly allowances; accompanied by his wife, with two young daughters, and a little son. He is not mentioned in the List of 1644, but was still living in New Sweden, a freeman, in 1648.

Olof Persson Stille, of Penningsby Manor, Länna Parish, Roslagen, a millwright, to engage in agriculture, paid at the start 50 *daler*, copper money, drawing no additional wages, but to be paid for whatever work he does for, and for whatever he furnishes to, the Company; accompanied by his wife and two children, one seven, the other one and a half years old. He is not mentioned in the List of 1644, but his place of residence in 1655 is indicated on Lindström's Map. In 1658, and subsequently, he was one of the magistrates on the Delaware. He was still living in July, 1684, when he obtained confirmation of a grant of land in Passyunk, in Philadelphia County, Pa., (ceded to him June 3, 1664, by d'Hinojossa, the Dutch Governor on "South River,") but died before May, 1693, leaving as heir an only son, John Stille, born in America in 1646, the ancestor of a well-known Philadelphia family.

Mats Hansson or Jansson, to serve as gunner for the new fort, and at the same time engage in agricultural pursuits, or the cultivation of tobacco; accompanied by his wife. In 1644 he acted as gunner at Fort Christina, and is described in 1648 as "freeman."

Anders Hansson or Jansson, the gunner's brother, engaged by Måns

Kling as a servant of the Company, to cultivate tobacco, to receive as yearly wages 20 *riksdaler* and a coat; a freeman in 1648. This name and the one which follows do not appear in the List of 1644.

Axel Stille, *ditto*, with 15 *daler* copper money at the start; likewise a freeman in 1648. He was naturalized in 1661 in Maryland, but probably returned to the Delaware, since the name occurs among those of persons residing in Passyunk, in Philadelphia County, in 1683.

Olof Pålsson, *ditto*, with 20 *daler* copper money at the start. This name and the one which follows do not occur in the Lists of 1644 and 1648.

Per Jöransson, the same as Pålsson.

Jan Ericsson, from Ångermanland, *ditto*; a labourer, cultivating tobacco on the plantation at Upland in 1644, in 1648 a soldier.

Jacob Sprint, from Nyland, the same as Axel Stille; occupied in 1644 and 1648 like Ericsson.

Pål Jöransson or Jönsson, from Jemtland, *ditto*; in 1644 a labourer, cultivating tobacco at the plantation on the Schuylkill, in 1648 a soldier.

Evert Hindricsson, a Finn, the same as Pålsson; in 1644 occupied like Jan Ericsson; in 1648 still a labourer. Banished from Upland in 1663, he settled afterwards at Crane Hook, and became captain of the company there. He was a participant in the insurrection of the "Long Finn," for which offence he was fined 300 guilders. For some reference to him see THE PENNSYLVANIA MAGAZINE, vol. ii. pp. 329–30.

Lars Markusson, the same as Anders Hansson. Possibly the person called Carl Marckusson, who died at Elfsborg July 10, 1643.

Hindrich Matsson, a lad, to receive 10 *riksdaler* as yearly wages, with 10 *daler* copper money at the start; occupied in 1644 and 1648 like Pål Jöransson.

Johan Andersson, a lad, *ditto*; occupied in 1644 and 1648 like Jan Ericsson.

Olof Ericsson, a lad, *ditto*; in 1644 a labourer at Tinicum, appointed to make hay for the cattle, and to accompany the Governor on the little yacht; still a labourer in 1648.

Pål Smaal, a lad, a baker's son, from Norrmalm, receiving no wages from the Company; served as a soldier, and set out from Christina for Sweden, on the *Fama*, June 20, 1644.

Carl Jansson, to accompany the expedition for punishment. Printz speaks of this person in his Report to the West India Company, dated February 20, 1647, as follows: "The bookkeeper Carl Johanson, who chanced to get into a difficulty through some misdemeanour in Kiexholm [in Finland], and for that reason was sent over to New Sweden, has been here six years, and behaved very well the whole time. Three years ago I not only appointed him to take care of the storehouse, but also trusted him to receive and audit the Commissary's monthly accounts, giving him a salary of 10 *riksdaler* per month (to be ratified graciously by the Right Hon. Company), which service he ever since has faithfully performed. Now he requests," proceeds the Governor, "by Her Royal Majesty's and the Rt. Hon. Company's favour, to be allowed, with the next ship, to go home to the Kingdom for a while, so long as it may please Her Royal Majesty, to settle his affairs there. His purpose for the future is willingly to serve Her Royal Majesty and the Rt. Hon. Company to the best of his judgment and ability, so long as he lives, either here in New Sweden, or wheresover else he may be ordered."

Mats Hansson, formerly Clas Fleming's servant, drawing no wages, only to be supplied with needful apparel, because he committed an offence and must accompany the expedition for punishment; in 1644 occupied like Jan Ericsson, in 1648 a freeman.

Peter Larsson Kock, born in 1611, " *ein gefangener Knecht,*" out of *Smedjegården,* to serve, as punishment, for necessary food and clothes, paid at the start 2 *daler* copper money; in 1644 occupied like Pål Jöransson, in 1648 a freeman. He held several offices under the government of the colony, and died at Kipka, in Philadelphia County, Pa., by March, 1688–9. He had, at least, six sons and as many daughters, and left numerous descendants. For some reference to him see a foot-note on page 94.

Eskil Larsson (in Beyer's *Musterrul*, Michel Hindrichson), a deserter from the army, sent by the War Office for punishment; not named in the List of 1644, in 1648 a labourer.

The persons mentioned above were joined by others at Gottenburg, and the *Rulle* of 1648 (referred to on page 402, note 2) supplies their names:

Clement Jöransson, a courier ("*brefswijsare*") and "forest-destroying" Finn, of the Parish of Sund, in Vermland, enlisted for punishment in the soldiery; permitted by a royal mandate to Governor Olof Stake, dated July 29, 1640, to emigrate to New Sweden, where in 1644 he cultivated tobacco as a labourer on the plantation at Upland, and by 1648 became a freeman.

Eskil Larsson, or Lars Eskilsson, *ditto.*

Bartel Eskilsson, son of the preceding, *ditto.*

Hans Månsson, from Skara (most likely the trooper spoken of on page 407), occupied like Clement Jöransson in 1644, in 1648 a freeman.

Hindrich Matsson, a Finn, *ditto.*

Lars Biörsson, in 1644 the same as Jöransson, in 1648 still a labourer. He had a son Laurence (born in New Sweden in August, 1648), who lived in Dublin Township, Philadelphia County, Pa., and left issue known by the surname of Boore.

Sivert or Evert Sivertsson, who came as a freeman on the *Charitas,* not named in the List of 1644, but still living in New Sweden in 1648.

Måns-Jöransson, a Finn, sent out on the *Kalmar Nyckel,* who afterwards (by 1648) became a freeman. Neither this nor the following name occurs in the List of 1644.

Mats Olofsson, who came on the *Kalmar Nyckel* as a sailor, in 1648 a wood-sawyer.

Claes Claesson, a Dutch carpenter, who came on the *Charitas,* residing in 1644 on the island at Christina.

Laurens Andriesson Cuyper, a Dutchman who came in the *Kalmar Nyckel,* in 1644 making tobacco-casks, etc., at Christina.

Lucas Persson, who came as a sailor on the *Charitas,* in 1644 engaged like Cuyper, in 1648 a sailor on the sloop at New Sweden.

Lars Thomson, from Vedding, who came as a sailor on the *Charitas,* in 1644 and 1648 a sailor on the sloop.

Anders Christiansson Dreyer, a miller, in 1644 at Christina.

Knut Mårtensson Vasa, who came as a sailor, in 1644 cultivating tobacco for the Company on the plantation at Christina, in 1648 a freeman.

Olof Thorsson, in 1644 engaged like Vasa, in 1648 still a labourer.

Lars Andersson Ulf, from Gottenburg, in 1644 engaged like Vasa, in 1648 cook on the sloop.

Gottfried Hermansson, who came as a steward on the *Charitas,* in 1644 and 1648 assistant to the commissary.   G. B. K.

THE EIGHTH SWEDISH EXPEDITION TO NEW SWEDEN.—The following is translated from a copy, in the Library of the Historical Society of Pennsylvania, of the original Swedish MS. document in the Royal Archives at Stockholm entitled *Rulla som meedh H. Commandanten Hans Amundson åter affordighe till Nye Swerige så wel Mann som Quinn Personen den 3 Julij* 1649:

List of Persons, Male and Female, who set out with Commandant Hans Amundson for New Sweden, July 3, 1649.

The Commandant Hans Amundson, with his wife and children, in all seven.
The preacher Mr. Matthias Rosenlecchig.
The bookkeeper Joachim Lucke.
Gunner Jöran Duffua, with his wife and two children, a boy and a little daughter, in all four.
Johan Jönson, with his wife, two.
Hans Pärson, with his wife, two.
The barber, with his wife and two children, in all four.
Guune Turckelson Timmerman (carpenter), with his wife and children, in all four, born in Sivedaheiat.
Gunnar Olufson Roth, born in Giöteborg.
Pär Larsson Bryggiare (brewer), born in Reduegs district.
Swen Hockeson Bråd, born in Iland.
Tolle Anderson Kiempe, born in Uddewal.
Pär Anderson Snickare (joiner), born in Giöteborg.
Oluf Benckson Hiort, born in Swedish "*hysing.*"
Oll Hakeson Buur, born in Mandaal.
Pär Johanson Rutare (trooper), born in Kynna district.
Olff Swensson Repslagare (ropemaker), born in Uddewal.
Måns Josephson Falcke, born in Ångermanland.
Beria Pärson Ugla, born in Tesberg parish.
Haken Larson Skoster, born in Kynna district.
Erik Anderson Drake, born in Ångar parish.
Gösta Pärsson Krabbe, born *ibidem.*
Anders Carlson Gedda, born in Giöteborg.
Lars Oluffson, with his wife and a daughter and two boys, born in Nerikie, in all five.
Jon Olffson, born in Wermerland.

BOYS.

Daniel Olufson Buurman, born in Stockholm.
Biörn Toolfson Flygare, born in Vesberg parish.
Börje Hakensen Reunare, born in Tuffur parish.
Anders Pärson Kiärna, born in Vesberg parish.
Oluf Tiörberson Sachtmodig, born in Siö parish.
Hendrich Benckson Buller, born in Danish "*hysing.*"
Printe Nielson Jeagare, born in Giöteborg.

WOMEN.

Ingrij Pär's daughter, born in Lundby parish.
Sigrij Oluff's daughter, born in Borg parish.
Britha Oluff's daughter, born *ibidem.*
Karin Pär's daughter, born in Österbåtn in Vasa.
Sigri Niels's daughter, born in Langland parish.
Margaretha Hans's daughter, born in Bolnes parish.
Annika Hans's daughter, born in Finnland.

Maria Benck's daughter, born in Arbåga.
Margaretha Niels's daughter, born in Vesberg parish.
Karin Niels's daughter, born *ibidem*.
Cristin Jöns's daughter, born in Bongsund.
Ingrij Lars's daughter, born *ibidem*.
Brita Suen's daughter, born in Mariestadh.
Anna Lars's daughter, born in Siöö parish.
Wife Elie Oluff's daughter, with a little child born in Skara, two.
Ingebår Bänc's daughter, born "*på hysing.*"

HANS AMUNDSON.

G. B. K.

A PARTIAL LIST OF THE FAMILIES WHO ARRIVED AT PHILADELPHIA BETWEEN 1682 AND 1687.

WITH THE DATES OF THEIR ARRIVAL.

From the original in the possession of the Historical Society.

[The paper here printed gives the names of some few of the persons who arrived at Philadelphia between 1682 and 1687. It is not entirely a contemporaneous document; if such were the case the entries would appear in chronological order. Nor is it, judging from what we know of the extent and character of the emigration of the period, as complete as a list of that kind would have been. It is, however, of early origin and of great interest, and we may well inquire into the circumstances under which it was prepared.

The importance of registering servants was patent to Penn when he prepared the laws agreed upon in England in 1682, and statutes providing for such a record, as well as for the registration of births, marriages, burials, wills, and letters of administration form a portion of that code. Provisions of like character are found in The Great Law or Body of Laws passed at Chester in 1682. These acts were re-enacted in 1683 and 1684. Up to the last year, however, no provision was made for registering arrivals, which is evident from the absence of legislation on this point as well as from the list of fees which the Register was allowed to charge.

In 1684, a law was passed directing inhabitants then in the province, and all who should thereafter arrive, to register in their respective counties. A similar law was enacted the same year in New Jersey, showing that the necessity for such legislation was more than local. In Pennsylvania it was probably called forth to give effect to a statute already existing requiring persons who intended to depart from the province to give public notice of the fact, and to another which made it obligatory on any unknown person who should presume to travel without the limits of the county in which they resided to have a pass or certificate under the seal of that county— measures which would obviously require that all the inhabitants should be known to the county authorities.

It does not appear that the law for registration was ever carried into effect. The following list, and one almost as imperfect of Bucks County, are too meagre to be looked upon as other than attempts in that direction. Nor are the names in the Philadelphia list confined to those who actually settled in the county as required by law. Some we know took up land in Chester County and others in Bucks. Occasionally the Bucks County list repeats the names given in the Philadelphia list. The penalty for not registering was repealed in 1690.

The entries in the list were made between May, 1684, and August, 1687, with the exception of the 4th dated 28th of 11th month, 1687. This is shown by the fact that all those in the handwriting of James Claypoole, Sr., who was appointed Register in 1686, and who died in August, 1687, are either on what were the waste leaves of the book, or are interpolations, and, therefore, the body of the manuscript must have been written before it came into his hands.

It may surprise some of our readers to learn of the number of servants brought out by the early settlers. This was no doubt greatly increased by the liberal terms which Penn offered to emigrants. The advantages offered to those who would bring servants and those who would come as such were equal. Each was to have fifty acres when the servant's time should expire. Nor did the word servant as used here necessarily imply a person who was to perform menial duties. On the contrary, they were often farm hands or skilled mechanics, in some cases of the same social position as their masters, in others they were no doubt overseers to act for purchasers who remained in England, a measure suggested by Penn in his first proposals to purchasers and which he subsequently found reasons to regret.—ED.]

1682. 9 $\frac{10}{mo.}$ The Antelope of Bellfast arrived here from Ireland.

James Attkinson arrived here and Jn° Ashbrooke his servant p. $\frac{2}{7}$.

The Morning Starr Thomas Hayes mast^r. Arrived from Leverpoole in England about the 20th $\frac{2}{mo.}$ 168 [3].

Henry Atherly shoemaker a freeman John Loftus Husbandman a freeman from Leverpoole.

William Morgan & Elizabeth his Wife both free arrived at Philadelphia in the same ship from Leverpoole in y° 9th Month 1683.

The Jeffries Thomas Arnold m^r from London Arrived 20 $\frac{1}{mo.}$ 1686.

Johannes Cassel a German his children Arnold, Peter, Elizabeth, Mary, Sarah.

Sarah Shoemaker of the Palatinate Widdow, George, 23 years old, Abraham 19, Barbary 20, Isaac 17, Susauna 13, Elizabeth 11, Benjamine 10 all her Children.

Joseph Ransted Gardner from London.

28th _{mo.} 1687. The Margeret from London arrived here from London John Bowman commander.

Pasco [or Pasro] Beliteg Servant to John Tizack bound at London for four years next ensueing his arrival in this province & Registered in the now [or new] office in London erected by Letters patent for that purpose.[1]

John Colly late of Sauiour Southwork in old England ffeltmaker came came in the Eliza & Mary, John Bowman M^r arrived here ye 22^d ^{mo.}⁄₇ 1683.

in the Endeavour of London, A Ketch George Thorp M^r.

Fran. Rosell late of Maxsfield in Cheshire in old England Millin^r came in endeav^r of London Geo: Thorp M^r arrived here the 29 ^{mo.}⁄₇ 1683.

Michaell Rosell late of the same place Husbandman came in the same vessell.

Thomas Janeway & Margaret his wife late of Poonnall in Cheshire Husbandman came in ditto shippe. [Children] Jacob, Thomas, Abell, [and] Joseph Janeway. [Servants] John Neild [or Wild], Hanah ffalkner [?].

Jos. Milner, Ann his mother late of Poonnell blacksmith in ditto. [Children] Sarah, [and] Ralph Milner.

Ralph Milner & Rachell his wife late of ditto, carpenter came in ditto vessell. [Children] Robt Milner.

Tho Pierson & Marg^t his wife late of ditto mason came in ditto shipp.

John his Brother & Mary Smith his sister all of the same place came in ditto vessell.

John Nixon & Margery his wife late of Powell Cheshire husbandman came in ditto vessell. [Children] John, Thom, James, Nehemiah, Joseph, ffredrick, Mary, Jane Margery [and] Eliz: Nickson. [Servant] James Witaker.

John Clone & Mary his wife late of Gosworth in Cheshire husbandman came in ditto shipp. [Children] W^m, Margery [and] Rebeckah Clone. [Servants] Joseph Charley, John Richardson, Sam: Hough.

---

[1] This entry is the only one which appears to have been made after the book passed out of the hands of James Claypoole.

Richard Hough late of Maxfield in Cheshire husbandman. Ditto ship. [Servants] Fran. Hough, Jam: Sutton, Tho. Woodhouse, Mary Woodhouse.

Fran: Stanfield & Grace his wife late of Garton in Cheshire Husbandman in ditto shipp. [Children] Jam: Mary, Sarah, Eliz: Grace, [and] Hannah Stanfield. [Servants] Dan: Browne, Tho: Marsey, Isa: Brookesby, Rob. Sidbotham, John Smith, Robt Bryan, Wm Rudway, Tho. Sidbotham.

John Maddock, Joyner. Richard Clone, Joyner. John Clous, shoemaker, Chas: Kilbeck. all of Nantwich in Cheshire came in ditto shipp.

Servants to Henry Madock. George Phillips, Ralph Duckard.

Daniell Sutton, Taylor. John Presoner [?] blacksmith, both of Maxfield in Cheshire came in ditto shipp. & Jo: Charlesworth, Taner, of the same place.

John Oudfield, Tayloer, of the same place in ditto ship.

John Howell & Mary his wife late of Budworth in Cheshire, Husbandman, came in ditto vessell. [Children] Hannah his daughter.

Mary Taylor late of Clatterwitch in Cheshire came in ditto ship. [Children] Isaack, Tho: Jona: Phebe, Mary [and] Martha Taylor.

Anne Robothan servt to the mr of the sd Ketch.

in Capt. Jefferies' Shipp.

Leonard Aratts & Agnistan his wife late of Crêvelt near Rotterdam in Holland came in the ——— of Lond. Wm. Jefferies com{der} arrived here the 6{th} of $\frac{mo.}{8}$ 1683. Leonard Teison his Brother a freeman.[1]

James Claypoole, Merchant, & Helena his Wife with 7 children and 5 servants vis Hugh Masland and his Wife to serve 4 years. Sissilla Wooley 4 years and Edward Cole Junr to serve 7 years.[2]

---

[1] This name is given under the heading of *Servants*, but as he was a freeman, it was an error to have entered it there.

[2] This entry is in the handwriting of James Claypoole.

The Providence of Scarbrough Rob* Hopper M*.

Joshua Hoopes & Isabell his wife late of Cleveland York-shire husbandman came in ditto ship. [Children] Dan: Mary, [and] Christian Hoopes.

John Palmer & Christian his wife late of Ditto place came in ditto ship.

William Preeson M* of the Vine of Leverpoole arrived the 17th day of the 7 mo. 1684 At Philadelphia ffrom Doly-serne near dolgules in Merionothshire.

Robert Owen & Jeane his wife and Lewes their sone, one serv* Boy named Edward Edwards for 8 years & 4 serv't Maids named Loury Edwards for 4 yrs. Margaret Edwards for 4 ye^{rs}. Ann Owen for 12 ye^{rs} and Hannah Watt for 3 ye^{rs}.

From Derbyshire.

David Davis & Katherine his sister & Mary Tidey her daughter and one serv't man named Charles Hues for 8 ye^{rs}.

From Manhinleth in Montgomeryshire.

Hugh Harris & Daniell Harris.

John Rechards & Susan his wife & their daughters Hannah & Bridget and one servant named Susan Griffith for 8 years.

Margaret the wife of Alexander Edwards and her daughters Margaret & Martha and 2 sones Alexander & Tho:

From Radnershire.

Rees Rees & his wfe Ann & their daughters Mary, Sarah and Phebe, and two sons Rich: & John.

Jane Evans Widdow and her 4 daughters Sarah, Mary, Alice and Eliza: & one sone named Joseph.

From Merionithshire.

Res Jones & his wife Hannah & their sones Rich. & Evan, and one daughter named Lowry.

From Carmarthenshire.

Ane Jones & her daughter Ane Jones.

From Shropshire.

Rechard Turner and Margaret his wife & Rebecca their Daughter.

From Prescoe in Lancashire.

Griffith Owen & his wife Sarah and their sone Rob* & 2 daughters Sarah & Elenor & 7 servants named Thos Armes,

John Ball 4 years, Robert Lort for 8 years, Alexander Edwards; Jeane, Bridget & Eliz Watts 3 years.

From Walton in Lancashire.

Henry Baker & Margaret his wife & their Daughters Rachell, Rebecca, Phebey & Hester and Nathan & Samuel their sones. Mary Becket & 10 servts named John Siddell for 4 years, Hen: Siddell 4 ye^{rs}, James Yates 5 ye^{rs}, Jno Hurst 4 ye^{rs}, Tho: ffisher 4 yrs, John Stedman 4 years, Tho. Candy for Joseph Feoror 4 yr^s, Deborah Booth 4 yrs, Joshua Lert 4 yrs.

From Lancashire.

Wm. Hatton & Eliza his wife. Rebecca, Martha & Elenor Hall; their servants Thos. Harrison for 2 years, John Cowp for 4 years, Lawrence Parker for 5 years, Katherine Owen 4 years, Mary Hall for 8 years, Eliz: Stedman, Sarah & Judeth Buller her Daughters, Joseph Stedman her sone; Rebecca Barrow.

The Ship Providence from old England Capt. Robert Hopper commander arrived here in Delaware River the 29th of 7 mo. 1683.

William Carter, John Lash.

The ship called the Bristoll Comfort from Old England. John Read Master arrived here in Delaware River the 28th of the 7th month & in the same came 1683.

Alexander Beardsly & Margaret his wife & his Daughter Mary the said Alexander is a glover and he came from Worcester.

Tho: Boweter out of Wostershire a servant to ffrancis ffisher out of Woster City Glover for three years they came in the ship aforesaid.

Richard Hillyard and Mary his wife and Rich. and Philip his sons and John Witt his servant.

Christianus Lewis late of Dudley in Worstershire in old England. Schoolmaster came in the Comfort of Bristol Capt Reed arrived here the 1 $\frac{mo}{7}$ 1683.

Geo Painter & Ellinor his wife late [of] Haverford west in Pembrookshire in Southwales, Husbandman, came in the Unicorne of Bristol Tho: Cooper M^r arrived here ye 31 $\frac{mo}{8}$ 1683. [Children] Susan [and] Geo: Painter. [Servahts] Lewis ——— time of service 4 years; payment in money £ 2, Acres of land 50: time of freedom 31 $\frac{mo}{8}$ 1687. Matthew ——— time of service 2 years & wages ye last 2 years at 8. Jannet Umphries time of service 4 years 2 [?] for ye 2 last years. Time of freedom 31 $\frac{mo}{8}$ 1687.

Dennis Rothford son of William Rothford who was Born in Emsstorfey in the county of waxford in Ireland about the year 47: and through the goodness and Mercy of the Lord was Convinced of gods blessed truth About the year 62: Went into England and Landed in Whitehaven in Cumberland the 30th of 3^d mo. 1675. Dwelt in Brighthelmston in Susex 3 years & kept a grocers shop And came into this Province of Pennsilvania with Mary his wife, Daughter of John Heriott of the Parish of Hostperpoynt in Sussex in old England she was Born 14th of the 3^d month 52) in the ship called the Welcom Robert Greenway Commander with two servants Tho: Jones & Jeane Mathewes, the said Dennis two Daughters Grace & Mary Rutherford dyed upon the Sea in the said ship Grace being about 3 years old and Mary being 6 Months old the said Dennis Rutherford Landed wth his family in Pennsilvania about the 24th day of the 8th month 1682.

Mary Rutherford the Second Daughter of Dennis & Mary Rutherford was born in the Province of Pennsilvania at Egely poynt in the County of Philadelphia the 22^d of the 8th Mo. 1683 between 10 & 11 at night she being their second Daughter of that name.

In the Lion of Leverpoole.
Robert Turner late of Dublin in Ireland, merch^t came in ye Lion of Leverpoole, John Crumpton M^r arrived here the 14 $\frac{mo}{8}$ 1683. [Children] Martha Turner.

Servants.			Time of service.	Payment in money.		Acres of land.	Time of freedom.
Robt. Threwecks	.	.	. 4 years.	£8		50	
Henry Furnace	.	.	. 4	3		50	
Robt. Selford	.	.	. 4	6	10	50	
Ben : Acton	.	.	. 4	3		50	
John Reeves	.	.	. 4	6	10	50	14 $\frac{mo.}{8}$ 1687
Row: Hambridge	.	.	. 4	...		50	
Richard Curlis	.	.	. 4	3		50	
John Furnace	.	.	. 4	3		50	
Daniel Furnace	.	.	. 9	...		50	14 $\frac{mo.}{8}$ 1692
Robt. Threewecks	.	.	. 13	...		50	14 $\frac{mo.}{8}$ 1695
Lemuel Bradshaw	.	.	. 4	2	10	50	
Robt. Lloyd	.	.	. 4	4		50	14 $\frac{mo.}{8}$ 1687
Wm. Longe	.	.	. 4	3		50	
Hen. Hollingsworth	.	.	. 2	...		50	14 $\frac{mo.}{8}$ 1685
Aiolce Cales	.	.	. 4	3		50	14 $\frac{mo.}{8}$ 1687
Kath: Furnace	.	.	. 6	...		50	14 $\frac{mo.}{8}$ 1689
Jos. Furnace	.	.	. 4	3		50	14 $\frac{mo.}{8}$ 1687

Joseph Fisher & Elizabeth Fisher his wife late of Stillorgin near Dublin in Ireland, yeoman, borne in Elton in Chesshire in old England came in ditto ship. [Children] Moses, Joseph, Mary, [and] Marth Fisher.

Servants.			Time to serve.	Payment in money.		Acres of land.	Time of freedom.
Edward Lancaster	.	.	. 4	£4	10	50	
Wm. Robertson	.	.	. 4	...		50	
Ed Doyle	.	.	. 4	...		50	14 $\frac{mo.}{8}$ 1687
Ben: Clift	.	.	. 4	...		50	
Tho: Tearewood	.	.	. 4	...		50	
Robert Kilcarth	.	.	. 8	...		50	14 $\frac{mo.}{8}$ 1691
Peter Long	.	.	. 2	6		50	14 $\frac{mo.}{8}$ 1685
Phill Packer	.	.	. 4	...		50	
Wm. Conduit	.	.	. 4	3		50	14 $\frac{mo.}{8}$ 1687
Mary Toole	.	.	. 4	3		50	
Elez: Johnson	.	.	. 4	...		50	

Marg^t Colvert late of Dublin came in ditto ship.

The Rebecca of Liverpoole James Skinner commander Arrived at Philadelphia the 31st of the 8 mo. 1685.

The passengers names are as followeth.

John Cutler Edmond Cutler, Issabell Cutler Elizabeth Cutler Thomas Cutler William Cutler. Freemen. They came from Bullandin Yorkeshire.

Rechard Mather, Cornelious Netherwood, James Myrriall, William Wardle, James Molenex, Eliz: Wingreene, Servants to said John Cutler.

Thomas Bates [?] a freeman.

James Ratclife, Mary Ratclife Richard Ratclife, Edward Ratclife, Rebecca Ratclife, Rachell Ratclife, free persons from Monsebury in Lancashire.

James Heyworth, Robert Hewet James Rothwell servants to the said Ratclife.

Richard Cureton & Margaret his wife, William Cureton his sone & Jane Cureton his Daughter free persons.

James Holgate and Ann Dugdale servants to the said Cureton.

Matthew Holdgate & Mary his Daughter free persons.

John Lathum, Ann Lathum his wife, John Jennings his wifes son. John Lathum his sone Aron Lathum his sone, Moses Lathum his sone & Ann Lathum his Daughter, free persons.

James Scoles, John Scoles, Hester Rothwell free persons.

The Bristoll Merchant John Stephens Commander Arrived here the 10th of 9th Month 1685.

The Passengers names are as followeth viz.

Jasper Farmer, Senior, his Family.[1]

Mary Farmer, widdow, Edward Farmer Edward Batsford, Sarah Farmer, John Farmer, Robert Farmer, Katherine Farmer, Charles Farmer.

Jasper Farmer Juniors family.[1]

Thomas Farmer, Katherine Farmer, widdow, Elizabeth Farmer, Katherine Farmer Junior.

---

[1] The will of Jasper Farmer, Sr., is dated 7 mo. 25, 1685, and was proved second of 11th mo. 1685. Letters of administration to the estate of Jasper Farmer, Jr., were issued 19th day of 11th mo. 1685. It is probable that they both died on the voyage.

Their Servants are as followeth viz.:

Joane Daly, Philip Mayow and Helen his wife, John Mayow, John Whitloe, Nicholas Whitloe, Thomas Younge & his wife, William Winter, George Fisher, Arthur Smith, Thomas Alferry, Henry Wells, Robert Wilkison, Elizabeth Mayow, Martha Mayow, Sarah Binke, Shebe Orevan, Andrew Walbridge.

Thomas Webb and Danniell his son.

Thomas Webbs servants are as followeth:

John Beltshire, John Robinson, Richard fford, James Banbury, Thomas Case, Henry fford, John ffox, Derby Haley, Joseph Case, Thomas Burke, John Garrett, John Mehone, David Quinn, Mary Widdam, Prudence Stuart, Katherine Robinson, Richard Muske.

Nicholas Scull, free.

his servants are as followeth:

Samuell Hall, Cornelious Davye, George Gooding, Miles Morin, Daniell Morin, John Ward, Mary Cantrell.

Tho: Carters family.

Thomas Carter senior, Frances his wife, Thomas his sonn, Henry his sonn, John his sonn, Ann his Daughter.

Jonathan Thatcher.

Arrived here the 29th of the 7th month 1682, the Ship called the Elizabeth, Ann & Catherine from old England Thomas Hudson Commander.

Robert Kent serv^t to Phillip Oxford.

Arrived here the 6th of the 6th month 1685 the ship Charles from London, Edmund Payne Commander.

John Marlton serv^t to Robert Kent.

The ffrancis and Dorothy ffrom London Richard Bridgeman Commander Arived at Philadelphia the 16th of the 8th months 1685.

The Passengers names are as followeth:

Isaac Sheepeard and Gertrude his wife and Margaret his Daughter.

John Peter Umstat and Barbara his wife, John his sonn
Margaret and Eve his Daughters.

Garret Hendrix and Mary his wife and Sarah his Daughter. Henry Fry his servant.

Peter Shoemaker and Peter his sonn Mary his Daughter
& Sarah his cosen, Frances and Gertrude his Daughters.

Henry Pookeholes and Mary his wife.

Aron Wonderley.

John Saxby and Eliz: his wife & John and Thomas his
sons and Elizabeth Lucy and Ester his Daughters.

The Unicorne from Bristoll Arived here the 16th of the
10th month 1685.   Thomas Cooper Commander.

The Passengers Names are as followeth:

Daniel fflower, Mary Bradwell, Mary Bradwell Juner,
Sarah Bradwell, Thomas Nixon, Thomas Nixon Juner. Philip
Doling, Mary Townsend, Hannah Smith. Tho: Martin, Margery Martin, Mary Martin, Sarah Martin, Hannah Martin,
Rachell Martin, Tho: Hopes, John Hopes, Moses Mendinhall,
Godden Walter, Joshua Chart, Jane Chart, Sam Chart, Jane
Chart Juner, John Roberts, Joseph Morgan, Benjam: Morgan, Tho Tutlin [or Tuslin], Anne Morgan, Faith Notten,
Eliza: Philpot, Henry Laking, Sarah Laking, Susanna
Laking, Moses Laking, John Ironmonger.

The ship the Desire from Plymouth in old England
Arived here the 23th of June 1686 James Cook Commander.

Francis Rawle Senᵉʳ, Francis Rawle Junᵉʳ—his servants
are Thomas Janveiries als January, ffrancis Jervine, John
Marshall, Samuel Rennell, Isaac Garnier, Elizabeth Saries.

Richard Grove,—his servants are, David Savanplane,
David Bonifoye.

Nicholas Pearce—his servants are Richard Weymouth,
John Fox.

James ffox & Elizabeth his wife, George & James his sonns,
Elizabeth and Sarah his Daughters—his servants are Richard
ffox, Stephen Nowell, Christopher Lobb, Richard Davis,

Nathaniell Christopher, Abraham Rowe, Mary Lucas, Sarah Jefferies.

John Shellson & Naomie his wife—his servants are: John Hart, John Cocker, Justinian ffox, Mary Welsh.

James Shaddock and Jane his wife—his servts are Jacob Coffin, Eliz: Gibes.

John Holme—his serv^ts are: William Hayes 5 years, Richard Bestitraser 9 years, George Gwinop 5 years from the arrival of the Desire afores^d.

The America Joseph Wasey M^r from London Arrived 20th of 6th mo. 1683.

Jacob Shoemaker borne in ye Palatinate in Germany servant to Danel Pastorius & comp^a.

Joshua Tittery servant to ye Society broad Glass maker from New Cassle upon Tine to serve four years at £ 88 ℔ an.[1]

The Wellcome Rob Greenway master from London arrived at Upland about the end of ye 8th month 1682.

Richard Townsend, Carpenter servant to ye Society for 5 years to have £ 50 ℔ ann. salary.

Ann Townsend his Wife & Hannah their Daughter. Wm Smith, Natha: Harrison, Barthol: Green, his servants each for 7 years.

The ship Delaware From Bristol in Old England John Moore Comander Arrived here the 11th of the 5th Month 1686.

Thomas Greene (Husbandman)& Margaret his wife, Thomas and John Greene his sons, Mary Guest his servant for 7 years to come from the third day of May 1686.

---

[1] Until we met with this entry we were not aware that definite steps had been taken towards the manufacturing of glass in Pennsylvania in the 17th century. That the Free Society of Traders proposed establishing such an industry, and selected a site for the works, and possibly built a house upon it, is evident from Penn's letter to the Society, dated August 16, 1683. He writes: " The Glass house [is] so conveniently posted for Water carriage." But we were unaware that workmen were employed to develop the scheme. It is not likely that anything practical resulted from the effort. See Weeks's Report on the Manufacture of Glass, U. S. Census, 1880, p. 79.

Richard Moore (Brickmaker) & Mary his wif & Mary his Daughter & John Moore his sone, Sarah Searle his servant for 4 years to come from the 3ᵈ of May 1686.

Henry Guest (sawyer) & Mary his wife & Henry his sone.

The Amity Richard Dymond mastr. from London arrived in Pennsylvania the 15ᵗʰ 5 month 1686.

David Lloyd born in the year 1656 in ye Parish of Manavan in ye County of Mount Gomery in North Wales, Sarah Lloyd his Wife borne in ye year 166[] at Cirensister in Glosester in England.

Christofer Sibthorp & Barbara his wife of London, Brasier, Tho: Peppitt & Barbara Peppitt the Children of Christopher Sibthorps Wife Barbary and Wᵐ Pike their Servant bound in London for 7 years and had about 4 year to serve when they arrived here which was in Ship above written ye 23 3d month, 1685.

A PARTIAL LIST OF THE FAMILIES WHO RESIDED IN BUCKS COUNTY, PENNSYLVANIA, PRIOR TO 1687, WITH THE DATE OF THEIR ARRIVAL.

[In volume VIII. of the Magazine (p. 382) we printed a partial list of the families who arrived at Philadelphia between 1682 and 1687. In introducing it to our readers we explained that it must not be looked upon as a "List of Arrivals," made up of entries recorded at the time the several families mentioned in it landed. It was, in fact, a record made in conformity with a law passed in 1684, directing the inhabitants then in the province, and those who should thereafter arrive, to register in their respective counties. The following list is a similar one relating to Bucks County. It was prepared under the same statute, and while not a complete record, is probably nearer so than the Philadelphia list. In printing we have followed a certified copy of the original in possession of the Historical Society.]

GEORGE POWNALL and ELLENOR, his wife, of Layloch, in the County of Chester, in old England, yeoman. Came in the ship the "Friend's Adventure." The Master, Thomas Wall. Arrived the 28th of the 7th Month, 1682. *Children*, Reuben, Elizabeth, Sarah, Rachel, and Abigail Pownall. *Servants*, John Brearley, Ro. Layler, Martha Worrall. *Time of Service & Freedom*, To serve 4 years; loose the 29th of the 7th Month, 1686. *Wages & Land*, 50s. at the end of their time, and 50 Acres of land apeice.

WILLIAM YARDLEY and JANE, his wife, of Ransclough, near Leeke, in the County of Staford, in old England, yeoman. Came in the ship called the "Friend's Adventure." The Mr., Thomas Wall. Arrived in Delaware River the 28th of the 7th Mo., 1682. *Children*, Enoch, Thomas, & William Yardley. *Servant*, Andrew Heath. *Time of Servitude & Freedom*, to serve 4 years; Loose the 29th of the 7th Mo., 1686. *Wages & Land*, 50 acres of land.

LUKE BRINLEY, of Leeke, in the County of Staford, mason. Came in the ship aforesaid. Arrived the 28th of the 7th Mo., 1682.

JOHN CLOWS, JR., of Gosworth, in the County of Chester, and JOSEPH, his brother, & SARAH, his sister. Came in the ship aforesaid. Arrived the 28ᵗʰ of the 7ᵗʰ, 1682. *Servant,* Henry Lingart, to work his passage money at — p. the day, and then to be free.

JOHN BROCK, near Stockport, in the County of Chester, in old England, yeoman. Came in the ship called the "Friend's Adventure." The Mʳ., Thomas Wall. Arrived in the Deleware River the 28ᵗʰ of the 7ᵗʰ Mᵒ., 1682. *Servants,* Job Houle, Eliza Eaton, to serve 4 years; Loose the 29ᵗʰ 7ᵗʰ Mo., 1686, and William Morton, his servant. Came in the ship called the "Freeman." The Mʳ., Jon Southren. To serve 4 years; Loose the 6ᵗʰ of the 6ᵗʰ Mᵒ., 1686. Each to have 50 acres of land apeice.

ANN MILCOM, of Armaugh, widow, in Ireland. Came in the ship called the "Antilope." The Mʳ., Edward Cooke. Arrived the 10ᵗʰ of the 10ᵗʰ Mᵒ., 1682, in this river. *Children,* Jane, Grace, and Mary Milcom. *Servant,* Francis Sanders, to serve 4 years; loose the 10ᵗʰ of the 10 Mᵒ., 1686. To have 50 acres of land.

WILLIAM VENABLES and ELIZABETH, his wife. Came in the ship the "Friend's Adventure." Arrived in Deleware River the 28ᵗʰ of the 7ᵗʰ Mᵒ., 1682. He came from Chatkill, in Eccleshill parish, in the County of Staford, husbandman. *Children,* Joyce and Francis Venables.

JOHN HEYCOCK, of Slin, in Eccleshill parish, in the County of Staford, husbandman. Came in the "Friend's Adventure." Arrived in Deleware River the 28ᵗʰ of the 7ᵗʰ Mᵒ., 1682. *Servant,* James Morris, to serve 4 years; loose the 28ᵗʰ 7ᵗʰ Mᵒ., 1686. To have 50 acres of land.

HENRY MARJORUM and ELIZABETH, his wife, of Cheverell, in the County of Wilts, husbandman. Arrived in the "Bristol Merchant," the Mᵐ. name Wᵐ. Smith, in the 12ᵗʰ Mᵒ., 1682.

WILLIAM BEAKES, husbandman, of the parish of Backwill, in the County of Summerset. Came in the "Bristol Merchant," the 12ᵗʰ Mᵒ., 1682. *Children,* Abraham Beakes.

ANDREW ELLET, a Seller of small wares, and ANN, his

wife, of the parish of Fifed, in the County of Summerset. Arrived in Deleware River in the ship called the "Factor," of Bristol. The M^r., Roger Drue. *Servants*, John Roberts and Mary Sanders.

JOHN WOODS, of Atterclife, in the parish of Sheafield, in the County of York, husbandman. Arrived in Deleware river in the "Shields," the M^r., Daniel Foos, in the 10th M^o., 1678. *Children*, John, Joseph, Esther, Mary, and Sarah Woods.

JOHN PURSLOW, of Dublin, in Ireland, husbandman. Arrived in Deleware river in the "Phenix," the M^r., Mathew Shaw, in the 6th M^o., 1677.

JOHN ROWLAND, of Billingshurst, in Sussex, husbandman. Arrived in Deleware river with his wife, PRISCILLA, in the "Welcome," the M^r., Robert Greenaway, in the 8th M^o., 1682. *Servant*, Hannah Mogdridge; loose in the 3^d M^o., 1684. To have 50 Shillings P. Annum, & 50 acres of land.

THOMAS ROWLAND, of Billinghurst, in Sussex. Came in the "Welcome," at the time abovesaid.

JOSHUA BOARE, of Drainfield, in Darbyshire, husbandman. Arrived in Deleware river in the "Martha," of Hull, the M^r., Thomas Wildbuys, the 7th M^o., 1677. *Children*, Joshua Boare, born the 29th 4th M^o., 1681. MARGARET, his wife, of Horton, Barent in Wiltshire. Arrived in the "Elizabeth and Sarah" the 29th of the 3^d M^o., 1679.

WILLIAM BUCKMAN, of the parish of Billinghurst, in the County of Sussex, carpenter. Arrived in the Deleware river in the "Welcome," the M^r., Robert Greenaway, with his wife, SARAH, in the 8th M^o., 1682. *Children*, Sarah and Mary Buckman.

GIDEON GAMBELL, of Hevizes, in the County of Wilts, Slator. Arrived in Deleware River, in the "Bristol Factor," the M^r., Richard Drue, in the 10th M^o., 1681.

WILLIAM BILES, of Dorchester, in the County of Dorset, vile monger, and JOHANNAH, his wife. Arrived in Delaware river in the "Elizabeth & Sarah," of Waymouth, the 4th of the 4th M^o., 1679. *Children*, William, George, John, Elizabeth, Johanah, Rebecca, and Mary Biles. *Servants*, Edward Hancock, to serve 8 years; loose the last of the 3ᵈ Mº., 1687. To have 50 acres of land. Elizabeth Petty, to serve 7 years; loose the last of the 3ᵈ Mº., 1686. To have 50 acres of land.

CHARLES BILES, of the town and County above. Arrived in the ship aforesaid, the time aforesaid.

THOMAS JANNEY,[1] of Shiall, in the County of Chester, yeoman, and MARJORY, his wife. Arrived in Deleware River the 29ᵗʰ of the 7ᵗʰ Mº., 1683, in the "Endeavor," of London. The Mʳ., George Thorp. *Children*, Jacob, Thomas, Abel, & Joseph Janney. *Servants*, John Nield, to serve 5 years, and have 50 acres of land. Hannah Falkner, to serve 4 years; loose 29ᵗʰ 7 Mº., 1687. To have 50 acres of land.

JOHN CLOWS, of Gosworth, in the County of Chester, yeoman, and MARJORY, his wife, arrived in the aforesaid ship, the time aforesaid. *Children*, Marjory, Rebecca, and William Clows. *Servants*, Joseph Chorley, to serve 2 years; loose the 29ᵗʰ 7ᵗʰ Mº., 1685. To have 50 acres of land. Samuel Hough, to serve 4 years; loose the 29ᵗʰ 7ᵗʰ Mº., 1687. To have 50 acres of land. John Richardson, to serve 4 years; loose the 29ᵗʰ 7ᵗʰ Mº., 1687. To have 50 acres of land.

GEORGE STONE, of Frogmore, in the parish of Charlton, in the County of Devon, serge wavor. Arrived in Maryland in the " Daniel & Elizabeth," of Plymouth, the Mʳ., William Ginney, in the 9ᵗʰ Mº., 1683, and from thence transported to this river. Arrived here in the 10ᵗʰ Mº., 1683. *Servant*, Thomas Dyer, to serve 4 years; loose the 9ᵗʰ Mº., 1687. To have 50 acres of land.

GILBERT WHEELER, of London, fruiterer, and MARTHA, his wife. Came in the ship " Jacob & Mary." The Mʳ., Danˡ. Moore. Arrived in this river the 12ᵗʰ 7ᵗʰ Mº., 1679. *Children*, William, Briant, & Martha Wheeler. *Servants*, Charles Thomas, Robert Benson, & Cathrin Knight.

RICHARD HOUGH,[2] of Macclesfield, in the County of Chester, chapman. Arrived in Deleware river in the " Endeavor," of London, George Thorp, Mʳ., the 29ᵗʰ 7ᵗʰ Mº., 1683. *Servants*, Francis Hough, to serve 2 years, and to

[1] See Vol. VIII. p. 330.   [2] Ibid., p. 331.

have 50 acres of land; loose the 29th 7th M^{o}., 1685. Thomas Wood and Mary Wood, his wife; he to serve 5 years, and she 4 years, and each to have 50 acres of land. James Sutton, to serve 4 years, to have 3£ 15s. per Annum, and 50 acres of land at the expiration of the term.

JOHN CHAPMAN, Aged about 58 years, and JANE, his wife, about 42 years. Came from Stangnah, in the parish of Skelton, in the County of York, yeoman. Came in the ship the "Shields," of Stockton. The M^{r}., Daniel Foos. Arrived in Maryland in the beginning of the 8th M^{o}., 1684, and arrived in this river the latter end of the same Month. *Children*, Marah, born the 12th 2^{d} M^{o}., 1671; Ann, born 18th 3^{d} M^{o}., 1676; John, born the 9th 11th M^{o}., 1679; Jane, his daughter, came at the same time, and died at sea.

ELLIN PEARSON, of Kirklydam, in the County of York, aged about 54 years. Came at the aforementioned time in the abovementioned ship.

ANN PEACOCK, of Kildale, in the County of York. Came at the same time in the same ship abovementioned.

HENRY PAXSON, of Bycot house, in the parish of Slow, in the County of Oxford, aged about 37 years. Came in the ship the "Samuel," of London. The M^{r}., John Adee. Arrived in the Middle of the 7th M^{o}., 1682. His wife came at the same time, and died at sea in the last of the 5th M^{o}., 1682. His son, Henry, died at sea the day before his Mother. John Paxson died about the middle of the 5th M^{o}. aforesaid.

THOMAS PAXSON, brother of the said Henry. Came in the said ship, and died at sea about the beginning of the 7th M^{o}., 1682. Elizabeth, daughter of Henry, born about the 5th 9th M^{o}., 1675.

JOHN PALMER, of Cheadland, in Yorkshire, husbandman, and CHRISTIANA, his wife. Arrived in this river in the "Providence," of Scarborough, the M^{r}., Robert Hopper, the 10th of the 9th M^{o}., 1683.

RICHARD RIDGWAY and ELIZABETH, his wife, of Welford, in the County of Bark, Taylor. Arrived in this river in the ship "Jacob & Mary," of London, in the 7th M^{o}., 1679.

Children, Thomas, born the 25ᵗʰ 5ᵗʰ M⁰., 1677, and Richard, born the 27ᵗʰ 2ᵈ M⁰., 1680.

SAMUEL DARK, of London, Callenderer, arrived in this river in the ship the "Content," of London, the Mʳ., William Jonson, in the 8ᵗʰ M⁰., 1680. *Servants*, James Craft, to serve 4 years. Had in hand 10 Bushels of Corn. At the expiration of the time to have one cow and calf and 50 acres of land. Mary Craft, to serve one year. To have 4£ wages.

ANN KNIGHT arrived in the ship "Society," of Bristol, the Mʳ., Thomas Jordon, in the 6ᵗʰ M⁰., 1682.

JOSHUA HOOPS, of Skelton, in Clunland, in Yorkshire, yeoman, and ISSABEL, his wife. Came in the abovementioned ship, the "Providence," the 10ᵗʰ 9ᵗʰ M⁰., 1683. *Children*, Daniel, Margaret, & Christian.

WILLIAM BENNET, of Hammondsworth, in the County of Middlesex, yeoman, and REBECCA, his wife. Arrived in this river the 9ᵗʰ M⁰., 1683, in the ship the "Jeffery," of London. The Mʳ., Thomas Arnold.

LYONEL BRITTAIN, of Alny, in the County of Bucks, Blacksmith, and ELIZABETH, his wife. Arrived in this river in the "Owner's Advise," of Barmoodes, the Mʳ., George Bond, in the 4ᵗʰ M⁰., 1680. *Child*, Elizabeth, his daughter, died as they came up the bay, and was buried at Burlington.

THOMAS FITZWATER, of Hanworth, in the County of Middeson, near Hampton Court, husbandman. Arrived in this river the 28ᵗʰ 8ᵗʰ M⁰., 1682, in the "Welcome," of London. The Mʳ., Robert Greenaway. MARY, his wife, and Josiah and Mary, his children, died at sea coming over. *Children*, Thomas and George. *Servants*, John Hey, to serve six years; loose 28ᵗʰ 8ᵗʰ M⁰., 1688. To have 50 acres of land.

ROBERT LUCAS, of Deverall, Longbridge, in the County of Wilts, yeoman. Arrived in this river the 4ᵗʰ of the 4ᵗʰ M⁰., 1679, in the "Elizabeth and Mary," of Waymouth. ELIZABETH, his wife, arrived in the ship the "Content," of London, the Mʳ., William Jonson, in the 7ᵗʰ M⁰., 1680. *Children*, John, his son, born the 11ᵗʰ 11ᵗʰ M⁰., 1654, Giles, Edward, Robert, Elizabeth, Rebecca, Mary, & Sarah.

DANIEL BRINSON, of Membary parish, in the County of Devon. Arrived in this river the 28th of the 7th M°., 1677, in the " Willing Mind," of London. The Master's name was Lucome. Married, the 8th of the 8th M°., 1681, to Frances Greenland, of East Jersey.

JOHN HOUGH, of Hough, in the County of Chester, yeoman, and HANNAH, his wife. Arrived in this river in the 9th M°., 1683, in the ship " Friendship," of Liverpool, the Mʳ. Robᵗ. Crosman *Child*, with John Hough, their child. *Servants*, George Glaire and Issabel, his wife, to serve 4 years; George Glaire, their child, till 21 ; and Nathaniel Watmough & Thomas Hough to serve 4 years each.

WILLIAM DARK, aged about 58 years, of Rysing, Camden, in the County of Gloster, glover. Arrived in this river about the middle of the 4th M°., 1680, in the " Content," of London. The Mʳ., William Jonson. ALICE, his wife, aged about 63 years, came in the ship the " Charles," of London. The Mʳ., Edward Paine. Arrived in this river the latter end of the 6th M°., 1684. *Child*, John Dark, their son, born the 4th 3ᵈ M°., 1667. Arrived with his mother.

RANDULPH BLACKSHAW, of Hallingee, in the County of Chester, and ALICE, his wife, arrived in Maryland the 2ᵈ of the 9th M°., 1682, in the ship " Submission," of Liverpool. Randulph arrived in this province at Appoquinimine the 15th 11th M°., 1682. Alice, his wife, arrived at Apoquinemene the 9th 3ᵈ M°., 1683. *Children*, Phebe arrived in this province with her father. Sarah, Jacob, Mary, Nathaniel, Martha, arrived in this province with their mother. Abraham died at sea the 2ᵈ 8th M°., 1682. *Servants*. These servants below came in the ship the " Friend's Adventure." The Mʳ., Thomas Wall. Arrived in this river the 28th 7th M°., 1682. *Servants to Randulph Blackshaw*, William Beasy, Ralph Nuttall, and Ralph Cowgill, each to serve 4 years, and to have 50 acres of land apiece. Roger Bradbury, Sarah Bradbury, to serve 4 years, and have 50 acres of land. These arrived in this province with Randulph. Elenor, the wife of the said Roger Bradbury, and Roger, Jacob, and Joseph, sons to the said Roger and Elenor, the said Ran-

dulph sold in Maryland. Martha Bradbury arrived with his
wife, to serve 4 years, and to have 50 acres of land.

JAMES HARRISON, of Bolton, in the County of Lancaster,
aged about 57 years, Shoemaker, and ANN, his wife, aged
about 61 years. Sailed from Liverpool for this province in
the ship the "Submission," of Liverpool, the M^r., James
Settle, the 5th of the 7th M^o., 1682, and arrived at Choptank,
in Maryland, the 21st 9th M^o., following, being brought
thither through the dishonesty of the Master, and arrived
at Apoquinemene, in this province, the 15th of the 11th M^o.
following. ROBERT BOND, came at the same time. AGNES
HARRISON, his Mother, came at the same time, aged 81 years.
Children, Phebe, his daughter, wife of Phineas Pemberton.
Servants, Alice Dickerson and Jane Lyon, each to serve 4
years, and to have 50 acres of land.

PHINEAS PEMBERTON, aged 33 years, of Bolton aforesaid,
Grocer. Came at the same time with PHEBE, his wife, aged
23 years, and arrived at the same time as above, in Maryland. Phebe, his wife, arrived at Apoquinimene, in this
province, the 9th of the 3^d M^o. following, 1683. *Children*,
Abigail, born the 13th 11th M^o., 1679; Joseph, born the 11th
3^d M^o., 1681. *Servants*, Joseph Stew, William Smith. Came
in the "Friend's Adventure." Arrived the 28th 7th M^o., 1682.
To serve 4 years, and to have 50 acres of land, being the
Governor's allowance. Joseph Mather and Elizabeth Bradbury, to serve 4 years, and to have 50 acres of land each.

RALPH PEMBERTON, Father of the said Phineas, aged 72
years. Arrived at the same time abovesaid, in Maryland
and in this province 9th 3^d M^o., 1683.

ROBERT BOND, Son of Thomas Bond, of Waddicar Hall,
near Garstang, in Lancashire. Came aboard the ship "Submission," of Liverpool, at the time aforementioned. Aged
about 16 years, being left by his father to the tuition of
James Harrison. The said Robert Bond died, and was
buried at a place betwixt Jon. Clows & W^m. Yardley. The
time will appear in the record of burials.

ELLIS JONES, of Wales, in the County of Denby, or Flint,
and JANE, his wife. Came in the said ship "Submission,"

and arrived at the time aforesaid. *Children*, Barbara, Dorothy, Mary, and Isaac. *Servants* to the Govérnor these came.

JANE MODE and MARGERY MODE, daughters to Thomas Winn, of Walley. His wife came and arrived at the time aforesaid. Harriet Hodges, servant to the said Thomas Winn.

LYDIA WHARNBY, of Bolton aforesaid. Came in the said ship " Submission," at the time aforesaid. Aged about 42 years.

JAMES CLAYTON, of Middlewitch, in the County of Chester, blacksmith, and JANE, his wife. Came in the said ship "Submission" at the time aforesaid. *Children*, James, Sarah, John, Mary, Joseph, & Lydia.

DAVID HALL, of Maxfield, in the County of Chester, shoemaker, and MARY, his wife, arrived in Maryland the 3ᵈ day of the 12ᵗʰ Mᵒ., 1684, in the "Friendship," of Liverpool, the Mʳ., Edmund Croston, and afterwards transported to this river, where his family arrived the 28ᵗʰ 3ᵈ Mᵒ., 1685. *Children*, Jacob, born the 8ᵗʰ 12ᵗʰ Mᵒ., 1679, Sarah, and Joseph. *Servants*, Ephraim Jackson, to serve 4 years, and to have meat, drink, washing, & lodging, and £6 per annum. John Reynolds, to serve 4 years, and to have meat, drink, washing, & lodging, and 2£ 10s. per annum. Joseph Hollinshead, to serve 4 years, and to have necessaries as above & 4£ per annum. Jno. Evans, to serve 2 years, and to have necessaries as above and 6£ per annum. William Fowler, to serve 4 years, to have for 3 of the last years 5£ 6s. 8d. per Ann., and otherwise necessaries as above during the term. Isaac Hill, to serve 4 years, to have necessaries during the time. Jon. Jackson, to serve 7 years, to have necessaries during the time. Jane Gibbons, to serve 4 years, to have meat and drink, washing & lodging, and 35s. per annum. *Servants of Jacob Hall aforesaid & Thomas Hudson*, John Bolshaw, to serve 4 years, died, and was buried at Oxford, in Maryland, the 2ᵈ Mᵒ., 1685. Thomas Rylands, to serve 4 years, died, and was buried at Oxford aforesaid the 1ˢᵗ Mᵒ., 1685. *Servants to the said Thomas Hudson and Jacob Hall*, which arrived in the ship the " Amity," of London, Richᵈ.

Dyamond, M^r., in this river the 28th 3^d M^o., 1685. Joseph
Hull, to serve 2 years, to have one new suit of apparel and
other necessaries during the term, and at the expiration
thereof to have one new suit of apparel and 100 acres of
land. William Haselhurst, to serve 3 years, and to have
apparel and necessaries during the term, and the land
allowed by the Governor. Randulph Smallwood, to serve
3 years, to have necessaries during the term, and land as
above. *More Servants to the said Thomas Hudson & Jacob
Hall* came in the ship " Richard & William," of Boston, and
arrived in this river the 24th July, 1685. William Thomas,
to serve 4 years, to have necessaries and land accustomed.
Daniel Danielson Vanbeck and his wife, Ellenor Brand
Vanbeck, to serve three years and an half a peice, to have
necessaries and land accustomed. *More Servants to the said
Hudson and Hall* came in the " Francis & Dorothy," of London. Arrived in this river the 10th of the 7th M^o., 1685.
Polycarpus Rose, to serve 4 years, to have necessaries during
the term and land accustomed.

RICHARD LUNDY, of Axminster, in the County of Devon,
son of Sylvester Lundy, of the said town, in old England.
Came in a Catch from Bristol (the M^r., William Browne) for
Boston, in New England, in the 6th M^o., 1676, and from
thence came for this river the 19th of the 3^d M^o., 1682.

ELIZABETH BENNET, daughter to William Bennet, late of
this County of Bucks, and now the wife to the aforesaid
Richard Lundy. Came from Longford, in the County of
Middlesex, in the ship the " Concord," of London. The
M^r., William Jefferay. Arrived in this river the 8th M^o.,
1683.

EDMUND CUTLER, of Stateburn, in Bowland, in Yorkshire,
webster. Came in the ship the " Rebecca," of Liverpool.
The M^r., James Skiner. Arrived with his wife, ISABLE CUT-
LER, in this river the 31st day of the 8th M^o., 1685. *Children*, Elizabeth, born the 14th of the 3^d M^o., 1680 ; Thomas,
born the 16th of the 9th M^o., 1681; William, born the 16 of
the 10th M^o., 1682. *Servants*, Cornelius Netherwood, to
serve one year, and to have necessaries during the term.

Richard Mather, to serve 2 years, and to have necessaries during the term. Ellen Wingreen, to serve 4 years, to have necessaries and 16s. wages at the expiration of the term.

JOHN CUTLER, brother of the said Edmund Cutler. Came at the time aforesaid, in the ship aforesaid, and at the time aforesaid. *Servants*, William Wardle, to serve 4 years and a half; loose the 30th of the 2d M°., 1690. James Molinex, son of James Molinex, late of Liverpool, about 3 years of age, and is serve to the age of 22 years. Looke the Court roles.

[I have given C. Taylor an acct. thus far 1st 3d M°., 1686.[1]]

DAVID DAVIS, Son of Richard Davis, of Welchpoole, in the County of Montgomery, Chirurgeon. Came in the ship the "Morning Star," of Liverpool. The Mr., ——. Arrived in this river the 14th day of the 9th M°., 1683.

RICHARD AMOR, of Buckebury, in Barkshire, husbandman. Came in the ship "Samuel," of London, John Adee, Mr. Arrived in this river the 22d day of the Seventh Month, 1682.

JAMES DITWORTH, of Thornley, in Lancasshire, husbandman. Came in the ship the "Lamb," of Liverpool. The Master, John French. Arrived in this river in the 8th M°., 1682, with William, their son. *Servant*, Stephen Sands, to serve 1 year, and to have 50 acres of land.

EDWARD STANTON, Son of George Stanton, of Woster, Joyner. Came in the ship the "Francis & Dorothy," of London. The Mr., Richard Bridgman. Arrived in this river the 10th 8th M°., 1685.

PETER WORRAL, and MARY, his wife, of North Witch, of the County of Chester, Wheelright. Came in the ship the "Ann & Elizabeth," of Liverpool. The Mr., Thomas Getter. Arrived in this river the 7th day of the 8th M°., 1687.

[1] Christopher Taylor was Register-General. The above entry is no doubt a memorandum made by the Register of Bucks County.

WELSH EMIGRATION TO PENNSYLVANIA.

AN OLD CHARTER PARTY.

COMMUNICATED BY W. F. CORBIT.

Articles of ffreightment, covenanted, indented, and made the seventh day of March, 1697–8, between Owen Thomas, of the County burrough of Carmathen, mercer, owner of the good shipp called the William Galley, now riding in the river of Towy, of the one part, and David Powell, of the parish of Nantmell, in the county of Radnor, and John Morris, of the parish of Karbadamfyneth, in the said county of Radnor, yeomen, of the other part: Witnesseth that the said David Powell, John Morris, and several other persons hereunto subscribed, being desirous to goe beyond seas for Pensilvania, have covenanted and agreed to and with the said Owen Thomas, owner of the said shipp, and Samuel Haines, master thereof, for a voyage or passage in the said ship by God's grace, in manner and form following (vizt.).

The said Owen Thomas, owner of the said ship, and the said Master, covenant and grant by these presents, to and with the said David Powell and John Morris, that the shipp with the first and next good wind and weather that God shall send after the tenth day of May next ensuing the date above written, shall depart from the said river of Towy, and directly sail for Philadelphia in Pensilvania, with the said passengers and such goods and wares as they shall sett aboard, or lay in the said shipp, on the River Towy, and being arrived or come to the sd. port of Philadelphia, or so nigh to the same as she safely and conveniently may come, shall there tarry for the space of ffive days next after her arrival, there to discharge and unload the said passengers, with all the goods and wares that shall be freighted and laden in her by them, freely on shore, upon the Key of Philadelphia.

And it is further covenanted and granted between the sd. parties, that the sd. David Powell and John Morris as well for themselves as also for all others the passengers hereunto subscribed, do hereby promise and engage to pay for themselves and all other passengers from 12 years of age and upwards unto the said Owen Thomas, the sum of ffifty pounds, in manner and form following (vizt.) ffifty shillings for each of them att or upon the sixth day of April next, at the town of Rhayader upon the River Towy, and the other ffifty shillings att or upon the day of their entering aboard the sd. shipp, and for every passenger under 12 years of age the sum of ffifty shillings each, before the day of their going aboard for the sd. voyage, and that all sucking children have free passage, and ffreight free of and for all wares and goods for said passengers, not exceeding twentie tunns weight, and that the sd. goods be unloaded at the charge of the said owner and master of the said shipp at the port of Philadelphia aforesaid.

And it is further covenanted and agreed between the sd. parties, that in concideracion of the payments aforesaid by the sd. passengers, the sd. owner and master of the sd. shipp do covenant and grant to and with each and every of the said passengers, to find them during the time of their being aboard for the said voyage with sufficient meat, drink, and cabins, and all other necessaries, at the proper cost and charges of the said Owen Thomas, owner, and Samuel Haines, master of the said shipp.

And it is further covenanted between the said partys, that the said David Powell and John Morris, together with the other passengers hereto subscribed, shall make themselves ready to appear before the owner or master of the sd. shipp att the Burrough of Carmathen, upon the said tenth day of May next, and in case the wind and weather do not then serve to hoist sailes for the sd. voyage, that the sd. passengers do covenant and grant to find and maintain themselves with meat, drink, and all other necessaries, for the space of ffive days, next after the said tenth day of May, and in case the passengers be forced to stay longer after the said five days for wind, then the owner or master of the sd. shipp covenant and grant to find them with meat, drink, and other necessaries for fourteen days next after, and no longer.

Provided, also, that the said shipp be not in readiness for the sd. voyage, att the sd. tenth day of May, that then the

owner or master of the sd. shipp do find and maintain the sd.
passengers with meat, drink, and necessaries until the sd.
shipp be fully ready.

And it is further covenanted and agreed between the said
parties that every master of a family among the sd. passengers having a wife and children, or a considerable family, shall
pay att the time of their going aboard, ffive shillings encouragement to the Doctor belonging to the said shipp, and all
single persons, except servants, pay one shilling apiece.

And also it is agreed by the sd. partys, that the said David
Powell and John Morris shall bring to the said owner or
master the sd. shipp a positive account of the number of passengers intended for the sd. voyage, by the twentieth day of
this instant, March; and it is further covenanted between the
said parties that the sd. Owen Thomas will find cellars, free
without any hire, for the goods and wages of the passengers
to abide until they be sett aboard the sd. shipp.

And finally and lastly, it is mutually covenanted and
agreed by and between the said parties, for themselves, their
heirs, executors, and administrators, to observe, fulfill, and
accomplish all and singular the grants, articles, and agreement herein before specified or mencioned to be observed, fulfilled, and accomplished by virtue of these presents.

In witness whereof, both the sd. Partys have hereunto their
hands and seals interchangeably sett the day and year first
above written.

OWEN THOMAS [SEAL].

SAMUEL HAINES [SEAL].

Sealed and delivered in the sight and presence of us.

DAVID WILLIAMS.
THOMAS OSBURNE.

David Powell,	for 11 passengers.		Thomas Jerman,	for 3 passengers.	
John Morris,	" 6	"	John Powell,	" 2	"
Margaret Jones,	" 3	"	James Price,	" 2	"
Edward Moore,	" 4	"	John Vaikaw,	" 1	"
Thomas Powell,	" 3½	"	Lymley Williams,	" 1	"
Thomas Griffith,	" 2	"	Ann Lewis,	" 1	"
Rees Rees,	" 4½	"	Thomas Watts,	" 1	"
Edward Nicholas,	" 4	"	Waiter Ingram,	" 1	"
Winnifred Oliver,	" 5	"	Benjamin Davis,	" 2	"
Evan Powell,	" 5	"			

NOTE.—The above agreement was probably carried out in good faith by
the captain and owner of the ship, as the passengers named were in Philadelphia in March, 1699.

MORAVIAN IMMIGRATION TO PENNSYLVANIA, 1734-1765.

BY JOHN W. JORDAN.

[The compiler has also prepared a list of the immigrants from 1765 to 1800, which may be consulted in the Manuscript Department of the Historical Society of Pennsylvania.]

Moravian immigration to the British Colonies of North America [1] dates from the year 1735, when, in March, the ship *Two Brothers*, Capt. Thompson, landed at Savannah, Georgia,

Augustus G. Spangenberg,	Peter Rosa,
Anton Seyffert,	Michael Haberland,
John Toeltschig,	George Haberland,
Gottfried Haberecht,	Frederic Reidel,
Gotthard Demuth,	George Waschke.

On February 16, 1736, the *Simonds*, Capt. Frank Cornish, landed at Savannah the second colony:

Bishop David Nitschmann,	Rosina Haberecht,
Christian Adolph von Hermsdorf,	John Martin Mack,
Henry Rascher,	Matthias Seybold,
Andrew and Anna Dober,	Jacob Frank,
David and Rosina Zeisberger,	Judith Toeltschig,
David Tanneberger,	Gottlieb and Regina Demuth,
John Tanneberger,	Catherine Riedel,
David Jag,	Anna Waschke,
Augustine Neisser,	Juliana Jaeschke,
George Neisser,	John Boehner,
John Michael Meyer,	Matthias Boehnisch.

---

[1] The first Moravian to come to America was George Boehnisch, in September of 1734, who accompanied the Schwenkfelders to Pennsylvania. See *Erläuterung für Herrn Caspar Schwenkfeld*, for a narrative of the voyage.

They had as fellow-passengers General Oglethorpe, Charles and John Wesley, Benjamin Ingham, and Charles Delamotte. The Moravians, who had been granted by the Georgia Trustees, in 1734, a tract of 50 acres near Savannah, and in 1735, two lots "in the new town," began to clear the land and erect dwellings. The prospects of these small colonies, however, received a sudden check in 1737, for when the Spaniards of Florida endeavored to expel the English from Georgia, the latter called upon the Moravians to join in taking up arms against them. This they refused, having declared in London, "that they neither could nor would bear arms on any consideration," and eventually those who had not returned to Europe were transferred to Pennsylvania, and the mission abandoned. The Georgia estates were not sold until 1801.

On July 21, 1740, Christian Henry Rauch arrived at New York, and October 26, 1741,

> Gottlob Buettner,   John C. Pyrlaeus,
> J. William Zander.

December 2, of the latter year, Count Zinzendorf and suite landed at New York, and on the 10th inst. arrived in Philadelphia, where a house on the east side of Second Street above Race had been rented for him. With him came

> Benigna von Zinzendorf, his daughter,
> Rosina Nitschmann, wife of Bishop David Nitschmann,
> John Jacob Mueller,
> Abraham and Judith Meinung,
> David Bruce,
> John Henry Miller.

Following closely after the first purchases of land by the Church, in the present Northampton County, Pennsylvania, in the year 1741, two colonies were organized in Europe, which are known as the "First" and "Second Sea Congregations," followed by four at later dates, the most conspicuous in that interesting period in the history of Moravian immigration, which falls in the interval between 1742 and 1765. Individuals and small companies occasionally arrived on vessels from England, and from Holland, through which country the Rhineland sent her Palatinates for transportation to the New World. When, however, the Church organized colonies, she invariably provided vessels of her own, from considerations of economy and out of regard for their comfort, but more particularly from a reluctance to expose her members, for whose spiritual welfare she was concerned, to the hurtful influences of promiscuous association during the tedious weeks and months of a sea voyage.

There were four vessels, the *Catherine, Little Strength, Irene,* and *Hope,* owned by the Church and afloat at different dates, and their crews, with but few exceptions, were members of or connected with the Church. In build they were snows, the largest of all two-masted vessels engaged in commerce. The ensign of the *Little Strength, Irene,* and *Hope* was a lamb passant with a flag, in a blood-colored field, and notwithstanding the peaceable character of these vessels, they carried an armament of from two to four cannon and small arms.

The *Catherine* was purchased in London in the spring of 1742, and on her the " First Sea Congregation " arrived at Philadelphia, July 7. The following day the German colonists were landed and taken to the Court House, at Second and Market Streets, where they took the usual qualification. The following is a list of the colonists :

Henry and Rosina Almers,
David and Ann Catherine Bischoff,
Peter and Elizabeth Boehler,
John Brandmiller,
John and Mary Barbara Brucker,
Paul Daniel and Regina Bryzelius,
George and Elizabeth Harten,
Robert and Martha Hussey,
Adolph Meyer,
Michael and Anna Johanna Miksch,
Samuel and Martha Powell,
Joseph and Martha Powell,
Owen and Elizabeth Rice,
Joachim and Anna Catherine Senseman,
Michael and Ann Rosina Tanneberger,
John and Elizabeth Turner,
David and Mary Elizabeth Wahnert,
Thomas and Ann Yarrell.

Single Men.

Andrew, a negro,	William Okely,
John George Endter,	Christian F. Post,
Hector Gambold,	Gottlieb Pezold,
John C. Heydecker,	John R. Ronner,
John Michael Huber,	George Schneider,
George Kaske,	Leonard Schnell,
Jacob Lischy,	Nathaniel Seidel,
John Philip Meurer,	Joseph Shaw,
Joseph Moeller,	George Weisner,
John Okely,	Christian Werner,

Matthew Wittke.

A number of the English colonists were first settled at Bethlehem, and then at Nazareth, whence they were transferred to Philadelphia, where they formed the nucleus of the Moravian congregation in that city.

After the colonists had been disembarked and the cargo discharged, the vessel and her stores were sold, under instructions from England.

During the month of September, the following colonists arrived on a vessel not owned by the Church:

> Daniel and Hannah Neubert, with an adopted child,
> Jacob and Anna Margaret Kohn,
> Christopher and Christina Franke,
> Martin and Anna Liebisch,
> Anna Liebisch,
> Maria Brandner,
> Michael Schnall.

Maria Dorothea Meyer, wife of Adolph Meyer, died off the Banks of Newfoundland, and was buried at sea.

For the transportation of the colony organized in Germany for peopling the settlements on the Nazareth tract, and known as the "Second Sea Congregation," the *Little Strength* was purchased in England, and Capt. Nicholas Garrison appointed her Master. Late in August of 1743, she was dispatched to Rotterdam, where the colonists were taken on board, and on September 17 sailed for New York, where she arrived after a passage of eighty-seven days. The names of the colonists were:

Gottlieb and Johanna C. Anders,
John Henry and Rosina Biefel,
Martin and Margaret Boehmer,
John David and Gertrude Boehringer.
George and Anna Mary Christ,
Thomas and Agnes Fischer,
John C. and Anna Margaret Fritsche,
Peter and Anna Barbara Goetje,
John Godfrey and Anna Mary Grabs,
Matthew and Elizabeth Hancke,
Abraham and Anna Mary Hessler,
John Tobias and Mary Hirte,
John C. and Mary M. Hoepfner,
John and Anna M. Jorde,
Matthew and Christiana B. Krause,
Andrew and Rosina Kremser,
George and Anna Mary Kremser,
Daniel and Anna Mary Kunkler,
John and Barbara Michler,
John Henry and Rosina Moeller,
John and Mary Philippina Mozer,
John Michael and Catherine Muecke,
Jonas and Margaret Nilsen,
George and Susan Ohneberg,
John G. and Susan L. Partsch,
David and Elizabeth Reichard,
Matthew and Magdalen Reutz,
John and Anna C. Schaaf,
John and Divert Mary Schaub,
Andrew and Hedwig Regina Schober,
Matthew and Anna M. Schropp,
John C. and M. Dorothea Weinert,
Matthias and Margaret C. Weiss.

The following are the names of the colonists fitted out at Herrnhut:

Andrew and Anna E. Brocksch,
Christopher and Anna Mary Demuth,
John G., Senʳ, and Regina Hantsch,

Christopher and Elizabeth Hencke,
John Henry and Barbara E. Hertzer,
John and Rosina Muenster,
George and Johanna E. Nieke,
Christian and Anna D. Schutze,
George and Anna D. Zeisberger.

Single Men.

John Jacob Doehling,	Conrad Harding,
John G. Hantsch, Jr.,	Christian F. Oerter,

John G. Nixdorf.

Single Woman.

Anna Regina Hantsch.

Names of the colonists fitted out in England :

Elizabeth Banister, widow,	John and Sarah Leighton,
David and Mary Digeon,	Andrew and Jane Ostrum,
James and Elizabeth Greening,	Jasper and Elizabeth Payne,

Richard and Sarah Utley.

With Bishop David Nitschmann, David Wahnert (cook of the *Catherine*) and wife, George and Elizabeth Harten, George Weber and wife, and Samuel and Mary (Indian converts), as passengers, the *Little Strength*, on March 24, 1744, sailed from New York for Amsterdam—a port she was never destined to reach. On the morning of May 1, when in the chops of the English Channel, she was captured by a privateer, a prize crew put on board, the passengers robbed, and six days later they were landed at St. Sebastian. The *Little Strength* proved a total loss to the Church. Four years elapsed before the Church again had a vessel of her own afloat.

The demand from Pennsylvania for more colonists becoming urgent, Captain Garrison, who had returned from captivity at St. Sebastian, was dispatched to New York to superintend the building of a transport vessel. On Oct. 25,

Bishop A. G. Spangenberg and wife,
Capt. Nicholas Garrison,
Abraham and Sarah Reincke,
Andrew and Dorothea Horn,
Christian Froelich,
George Neisser,

on the ship *Jacob*, arrived at New York. The day following his arrival, Capt. Garrison called on Timothy Horsfield,
with reference to building the projected vessel, and also on
Thomas Noble, who was to act as financial agent. Finally
they decided that a "snow" should be built, and contracted
with Jan Van Deventer, a reputable ship-builder of Staten
Island, to build the hull, make and set the masts and rig the
vessel. The rigging, cables, and anchors were to be purchased in England, these articles being cheaper there than
in the colonies. The building of the vessel progressed
slowly, and it was not until the spring of 1748 that she was
ready for launching. Accordingly on Tuesday, May 29, at
eleven o'clock A.M., in the presence of about one thousand
spectators, the *Irene*, as she was christened, was successfully
launched, after which a lunch was served to the workmen.
In honor of the event, Bishop Spangenberg presented the
builder's wife with a new gown. Three days later, the new
transport was docked at Old Slip, Captain Garrison put in
command, and she was registered in the name of Henry
Antes. Securing a cargo and a few passengers (not Moravians), on September 8, the *Irene* cleared from New York on
her maiden voyage for Amsterdam. While the *Irene* was
being built, several small companies of Moravians arrived
at Philadelphia and New York. In September of 1745, the
following persons landed at Philadelphia:

William P. and Hannah Knolton,
Eve Mary Meyer (a widow).
Jarvis Roebuck.

On December 28, 1746, the snow *John Galley*, Captain
Crosswaite, arrived off Lewes, Delaware, and navigation

being closed, her passengers were landed and continued their journey by land to Bethlehem, *via* Philadelphia.

Bishop J. C. F. Cammerhoff and wife,
Esther, wife of Christian Froelich,
Matthias Gottlieb Gottschalk,
Vitus and Mary Handrup,
Judith Hickel, a widow,
Sven and Anna Margaret Roseen,
John and Johanna Wade,
John Eric Westerman.

In June of 1748, there arrived at New York,

J. G. Bitterlich,   Paul Paulson,
Andrew Broksch,   Christian Pfeiffer,
John G. Geitner,   Godfrey Roemelt,
Bernhard Adam Grube,   Jeremiah Schaaf,
Joseph Hobsch,   Christian Schmidt,
Gottfried Hoffman,   Paul Schneider,
Matthew Kunz,   John Seyffert,
                Samuel Wutke.

In September there also arrived at the same port:

Baron John and the Countess Benigna von Watteville,
Anna Rosina Anders,   Catherine B. Keller,
—— Hasselman,   Elizabeth Lisberger,
                Elizabeth Palmer.

During the nine years the *Irene* was in the service of the Church, she crossed the Atlantic twenty-four times, sailing between New York and ports in England and Holland, and made one voyage to Greenland. She was always rated a staunch vessel and an excellent sailer, and at the time of her capture and loss had never met with any serious mishap. The large number of colonists she brought over from Europe for settling the estates of the Church in Pennsylvania, and the fact of her never entering or clearing from the port of Philadelphia, caused Governor Hamilton in a personal interview with Bishop Spangenberg to ask for an explana-

ion. " We wish we could use the port of Philadelphia,"
stated the Bishop, " but since our captain is a native of New
York, and has a large acquaintance with the merchants of
that city, he can more readily obtain freight there than in
Philadelphia, passengers alone not being sufficient. Another serious objection is, the merchants of Philadelphia
own their own vessels." As already stated, the *Irene* sailed
from New York for Amsterdam September 8, 1748, and
arrived at the Texel November 1. She cleared from London, March 1, 1749, and arrived at New York May 12,
with the "John Nitschmann Colony," with whom came
Christian David, of Herrnhut, Matthew and Rosina Stach,
missionaries to Greenland, and three converts, who had
been on a visit to Europe.

The "John Nitschmann Colony " was the largest ever
brought over on a Moravian transport. The following is a
roster of the colonists :

> John and Juliana Nitschmann,
> David and Rosina Nitschmann,
> Michael and Anna Helena Haberland,
> Samuel and Rosina Krause,
> Joseph and Verona Mueller,
> Christian J. and Anna M. Sangerhausen,
> Matthew and Rosina Stach,
> John and Anna Stoll,
> David and Mary Wahnert,
> Christian F. and Anna R. Steinman,
> Christian David, widower,
> John Schneider, widower,
> Magdalena E. Reuss, widow.

Single Men.

Gottlieb Berndt, clothier, Upper Silesia,
Wenzel Bernhard, baker, Bohemia,
Joachim Birnbaum, tailor, Brandenburg,
Peter Drews, ship carpenter, Glueckstadt,
J. Philip Duerrbaum, Mittelhausen,
Evert Eversen, joiner, Norway,

J. Godfrey Engel, tailor, Brandenburg,
Elias Flex, farmer, Upper Silesia,
Henry Fritsche, tailor, Silesia,
Paul Fritsche, carpenter, Moravia,
J. Leonard Gattermeyer, blacksmith, Bavaria,
George Gold, mason, Moravia,
John P. Hohman, shoemaker, Brandenburg,
Daniel Kliest, blacksmith, Frankfort,
Andrew Krause, weaver, Brandenburg,
Christopher Kuehnast, shoemaker, Prussia,
David Kunz, farmer, Moravia,
Peter Mordick, farmer, Holstein,
John B. Mueller, clothier, Württemberg,
Michael Muenster, carpenter, Moravia,
Martin Nitschmann, cutler, Moravia,
Carl Opitz, shoemaker, Silesia,
George Pitschman, weaver, Upper Silesia,
John G. Renner, farmer, Swabia,
John C. Richter, joiner,
Andrew Rillman, stocking-weaver, Saxony,
Frederick Schlegel, weaver,
John Schmidt, furrier, Silesia,
J. Christopher Schmidt, fringe and lace maker, Saxony,
Melchoir Schmidt, carpenter, Moravia,
Melchoir Schmidt, weaver, Moravia,
Martin Schneider, mason, Moravia,
Carl Schultze, mason, Posen,
Godfrey Schultze, farmer, Lower Silesia,
John Schweisshaupt, stocking-weaver, Württemberg,
Andrew Seiffert, carpenter, Bohemia,
Thomas Stach, book binder, Moravia,
Rudolph Straehle, mason, Wurtemberg,
David Tanneberger, joiner, Upper Silesia,
John Nicholas Weinland, farmer.

Greenlanders.

John,   Matthew,   Judith.

Single Women.

Rosina Arndt,   Anna Rosina Beyer,
Rosina Barbara Arnold,   Maria Beyer,
Margaret Ballenhorst,   Elizabeth Bieg,

Catherine Binder,
Rosina Dietz,
Maria Dominick,
Sophia M. Dressler,
Margaret Drews,
Charlotte Eis,
Maria E. Engler,
Catherine Fichte,
Catherine Fischer,
Rosina Galle,
Margaret Groeszer,
Helena Gruendberg,
Juliana Haberland,
Anna M. Hammer,
Rosina Haus,
Margaret Heindel,
Maria B. Hendel,
Anna R. Kerner,
Anna M. Koffler,
Anna M. Krause,
Barbara Krause,

Martha Maans,
Magdalena Meyerhoff,
Magdalena Mingo (negress),
Anna M. Nitsche,
Dorothea Nuernberg,
Helena Nusz,
Elizabeth Oertel,
Maria E. Opitz,
Catharine Paulson,
Anna Ramsburger,
Margaret C. Rebstock,
Anna C. Renner,
Anna M. Roth,
Anna M. Schmatter,
Rosina Schuling,
Magdalena Schwartz,
Juliana Seidel,
Dorothea Uhlman,
Divert Vogt,
Susanna Weicht,
Catherine Wentzel.

Loading lumber and other material for the mission in Greenland, the *Irene* sailed on her second voyage from Staten Island June 21, 1748, with Christian David, the missionary Stach and wife, and the three converts, and arrived at New Herrnhut, Greenland, on July 30. She was back again in New York, August 29. In the summer of 1749, the following single men from Yorkshire, England, arrived at Bethlehem, who were to carry on the manufacture of woolen goods:

William Dixon,
Joseph Haley,

John Hirst,
Richard Popplewell.

On October 15, 1749, the *Irene* sailed on her third voyage from New York, and arrived at London November 21, making the quick passage, as her log states, of " thirty days from land to land." She sailed from Dover, May 11, 1750, and arrived at New York on June 22, making a remarkable westward passage, with the following colonists on board:

John A. Albrecht,
Marcus Balffs,
George Baumgarten,
Henry Bergman,
John A. Borhek,
Zacharias Eckhard,
Just Erd,
Walter Ernst,
Claus Euler,
Henry Feldhausen,
J. Christopher Feldhausen,
Godfrey Foeckel,
Samuel Foeckel,
Andrew Freyhaube,
Henry Friz,
Lucas Fuss,
Christian Giersch,
John George Groen,
Abraham Hasselberg,
Balthasar Hege,
Jacob Heydecker,
John Henry Herbst,
Samuel Herr,
Jacob Herrman,
John G. Hoffman,
Thomas Hoffman,
Christian H. Hoepfner,
Eric Ingebretsen,
Andrew Jaecke,
John T. Kornman,
John G. Lange,
John S. Lauck,
Henry Lindenmeyer,
Christian H. Loether,
Carl Ludwig,

Jacob Lung,
John G. Masner,
Christopher Matthiesen,
Nicholas Matthiesen,
Christopher Merkly,
Jacob Meyer,
John S. Meyer,
Philip Meyer,
John Muensch,
Melchior Muenster,
John Jacob Nagle,
—— Neilhock,
John M. Odenwald,
John Ortlieb,
John Matthew Otto,
Peter J. Pell,
Hans Petersen,
Frederick J. Pfeil,
John M. Pitzman,
Jacob Priessing,
John Henry Richling,
John Richter,
Godfrey Roesler,
Daniel Ruenger,
Michael Sauter,
Paul Jansen Sherbeck,
Henry Schoen,
George Schweiger,
Christian Schwartz,
Gottfried Schwartz,
Abraham Strauss,
John D. Sydrich,
—— Theodorus,
John A. Wagenseil,
Andrew Weber.

From Zeyst.

Christopher Feldhausen,
Henry Gerstberger,
Andrew Gross,
John C. Haensel,
Paul Hennig,
Frederick E. Herrman,
Susan M. Herrman,

London (a negro),
John Henry Merck,
Martin Presser,
Paul C. Stauber,
John Thomas,
Francis Steup,
Sophia Steup.

The *Irene* left her dock in New York, 28 August, 1750, on her fourth voyage, and during a severe storm lost both topmasts and narrowly escaped from foundering. On her return voyage, she sailed from Dover, and arrived at New York, 26 September, 1731, with the following passengers:

Joachim and Elizabeth Busse,   John Jacob Schmick,
John Christian Christiansen,   David Zeisberger,
John Michael and Gertrude Graff.

On her fifth voyage, the *Irene* sailed from New York, 22 November, 1751, and was again in port (last from Dover), 17 May, 1751, bringing as passengers:

Rev. Francis and Ann Catherine Boehler,
Rev. Andrew Anton and Anna Maria Lawatsch,
Rev. Jacob Rogers (widower),
Jacob Wahnert   (do),
Rosina Pfohl (widow),
Margaret Wernhamer (single).

About a month after the sailing of the *Irene* on her fifth voyage, there arrived unexpectedly at New York, Bishop A. G. Spangenberg with

Rev. Philip C. Bader,
Rev. Nicholas H. Eberhardt,
Rev. Matthew and Anna M. Hehl,
Matthew Kremser,
Carl Godfrey Rundt,
Henrietta Peterman.

The *Irene* sailed from New York on her sixth voyage, July 6, 1752, and from London on her return, reaching her dock November 20, having on board a number of single women and others:

Anna Maria Beyer,   Margaret C. Klingelstein,
Maria C. Dietz,   Anna Mann,
Margaret Ebermeyer,   Agnes Meyer,
Dorothea Gaupp,   Johanna D. Miller (wife of
Catherine Gerhardt,   Henry Miller, the printer,
Inger Hyde,   of Philada.),

Christina Morhardt,	Anna Sperbach,
Regina Neuman,	John Toeltschig,
Linet Redderberg,	Juliana Warkler,
Catherine Ruch,	—— Schultz (widow),
Felicitas Schuster,	David Wahnert.
Margaret Seidner,	

On April 5, 1753, the *Irene* sailed from New York, on her seventh voyage, and from London on her return, June 13, and was docked September 9.   Her passengers were:

Rev. Peter and Elizabeth Boehler,
Rev. Jacob and Elizabeth Till,
    Susan Till,
    Rebecca Till,
George Stephen and Susan Watson,
Ludolph Gottlieb Backhof, student, Luneberg,
Christopher Henry Baehrmeyer, writer, Brandenberg,
Frederick Beyer, carpenter, Silesia,
Ludwig Christian Daehne, tailor, Weringerode,
Jacob Eyerle, blacksmith, Württemberg,
George Christian Fabricius, student, Denmark,
Jacob Fries, student, Denmark,
George Wenzeslaus Golkowsky, surveyor, Silesia,
Joseph Haberland, mason, Moravia,
Jacob Herr, mason, Württemberg,
Samuel Hunt, clothmaker, Yorkshire, England,
Jacob Jurgensen, purse-maker, Denmark,
Hans Martin Kalberlahn, surgeon, Dronthheim,
Henry Krause, butcher, Silesia,
Otto Christian Krogstrup, student, Denmark,
Joseph Lemmert, tanner, Brisgau,
Jacob Rogers, Yorkshire, England,
Albrecht L. Rusmeyer, student, Luneberg,
George Soelle, student, Denmark,
Christian Frederick Toellner, tailor, Pomerania,
Christian Wedsted, carpenter, Denmark,
Peter Weicht, farmer, Silesia,
Peter Worbass, carpenter, Denmark,
Curtius Frederick Ziegler, student, Pomerania.

It is worthy of mention, that the *first steam engine* operated in the colonies was brought over on this voyage, and taken to the copper mine near the present town of Belleville, New Jersey.

On November 3, 1753, the *Irene* sailed from New York on her eighth voyage, and from Gravesend, March 15, 1754, reaching her dock April 15, the quickest western voyage she ever made, "being but three Sundays at sea." The following is a list of her passengers:

> Bishop Augustus G. Spangenberg,
> Rev. Francis Christian Lembke,
> David Nitschmann, Senr.,
> Andrew Schoute,
> C. T. and Anna Maria Benzien,
>   Anna Benigna Benzien,
>   Christel Benzien,
> Rev. Paul D. and Regina Dorothea Bryzelius,
>   Hannah Bryzelius,
>   Mary Bryzelius,
>   Renatus Bryzelius,
> Rev. John and Joanetta Maria Ettwein,
>   Christel Ettwein,
> Nicholas and Mary Ann Garrison,
>   Benjamin Garrison,
>   Nicholas Garrison, Jr.,
> J. Valentine and Catherine Haidt,
> David and Regina Heckewelder,
>   Christian Heckewelder,
>   David Heckewelder,
>   John Heckewelder,
>   Mary Heckewelder,
> David Schmidt,
> David and Rosina Wahnert.

Single Men.

William Angel,	Andrew Hoeger,
Peter Brink,	Christian Jacobsen,
William Edmonds,	—— Jost,
Charles Frederick,	—— Leighton,
William Okely.	

Single Women.

Mary Evans,	—— Enrichen,
—— Wyke.	

On her ninth voyage, the *Irene* sailed from New York,
29 May, 1754; and from London, September 22, arriving
at her port November 16, having on board a colony of single
men in charge of Gottlieb Pezold.

Nicholas Anspach, farmer, Palatinate,
Matthew Bacher, shoemaker, Salzburg,
Lorenz Bagge, carpenter, Holstein,
Joseph Bulitschek, carpenter, Bohemia,
Jens Colkier, carpenter, Jutland,
Melchior Coumad, carpenter, Moravia,
Adam Cramer, tailor,
Detlof Delfs, shoemaker, Holstein,
Franz Christopher Diemer, baker,
Carl J. Dreyspring, tailor, Württemberg,
Gottfried Dust, potter, Silesia,
Jacob Ernst, baker, Switzerland,
Casper Fischer, miller, Hildburghausen,
August Henry Francke, Wetteravia,
Christian Freible,
Hans Nicholas Funk, farmer, Lobenstein,
Joseph Giers, miller, Moravia,
Matthias Gimmile, tailor,
John Henry Grunewald, farmer, Mecklenburg,
John Adam Hassfeldt, saddler, Ebersfeld,
Joseph Huepsch, shepherd, Moravia,
John Jag, Moravia,
Samuel John (Malay), Ceylon,
John Klein, saddler, Darmstadt,
Christopher Kloetz, shoemaker,
David Kunz, carpenter, Moravia,
John Henry Lenzner, book binder, Beyreuth,
Michael Linstroem, linenweaver,
Henry George Meisser, shoemaker,
John Matthew Miksch, gardener, Saxony,
Lorenz Nielsen, carpenter, Holstein,
Carl Ollendorf, tailor, Brandenburg,
Hans Petersen,
Philip Henry Ring, baker, Alsace,
Martin Rohleder, farmer, Moravia,
Samuel Saxon, clothier, England,
Martin Schenk, mason, Moravia,
George Schindler, carpenter, Moravia,

Peter Sproh, mason, Courland,
John George Stark, stocking-weaver,
Anton Steimer, mason, Prussia,
Christian Steimer, shoemaker, Prussia,
John Stettner, tailor, Anspach,
Edward Thorp, shoemaker, England,
Carl Weinecke, shoemaker,
Joseph Willy, clothier, England,
Jens Wittenberg, skinner, Norway,
John Wuertele, shoemaker, Württemberg,
Henry Zillman, tailor, Brandenburg,
Christian Frederick Post (Indian missionary).

In charge of Nicholas Garrison, Jr., as Master, the *Irene* sailed from New York February 4, 1755, and arrived from London, August 11, her tenth voyage, but brought over no colonists.

The *Irene*, Christian Jacobsen, Master, sailed for England, on her eleventh voyage, September 28, 1755, and was back in port again June 2, 1756, having brought over the following single men :

John B. Böninghausen,	Henry Ollringshaw,
Joachim Busse,	John M. Rippel,
James Hall,	John Roth,
Casper G. Hellerman,	Michael Ruch,
Elert Koortsen,	William Schmaling,
George E. Mentzinger,	George Seneff,
John Mueller.	Hans Jacob Schmidt.

The twelfth voyage of the *Irene* was made to London, July 1, 1756, and on December 12, she landed the following passengers at New York :

Peter Boehler,	Christian Bohle,
William Boehler,	Adolph Eckesparre,
Philip Christian Reiter.	

The thirteenth voyage of the *Irene*, to London, in March of 1757, is devoid of interest, and no colonists were brought over.

On November 20, 1757, the *Irene* sailed from New York on her fourteenth and last voyage. When ten days out she was captured by a French privateer, and proved a total loss to the Church. The news of her capture and wreck did not reach Bethlehem until May 19, 1758. Andrew Schoute, for five years one of her mates, who was returning to Europe in impaired health, prepared an account of his experiences, from which the following extracts are taken:

" On the 20th of November we cleared Sandy Hook. At noon on the 29th, we sighted a vessel to the north bearing down on us and soon after hoisting the English flag. Mistrusting the stranger, we showed no colors, but crowded on all sail in the hope of effecting our escape, whereupon the stranger ran up the French flag. It was now a trial of speed, in the course of which the *Irene* gave proof of her excellent sailing qualities; but at eleven o'clock at night our storm sails parted. The privateer now gained rapidly on us, and as she did so fired shot after shot. It being bright moonlight and no further hope of escape in our disabled condition, we backed our sails, and at midnight our ill-fated vessel was boarded—Lat. 36°, Long. 62°. Capt. Jacobsen and two of his crew were immediately transferred on board the privateer, which proved to be the *Margaret* from Louisburg, and the *Irene* given in charge of a prize crew who were ordered to take us into Louisburg. At daybreak we were ordered on deck, and stripped and plundered of all we had on our persons. The weather grew foul, and we found the prize crew inexperienced in seamanship, and occasionally they would call upon us to assist in navigating the vessel. . . . On the morning of January 12, 1758, the fog raising, we discovered an island close by the vessel, whereupon we put out to sea. In the afternoon the Frenchmen decided to make for the land again, when I went to the captain and pilot, and tried to dissuade them from so unseamanlike a course in foggy weather, and told them that they would certainly lose the vessel. As they would not listen to my protest, I prepared for the worst. At 2 p. m. breakers were reported; very soon we were among them, and struck a rock. The Frenchmen became so demoralized that I ordered the boat launched, into which we all got (twenty-two in number) and reached the shore in safety. On landing the French captain fell upon my neck, kissed and thanked me for saving the lives of all. We then entered the woods, made a fire, and on returning to the boat for provisions, found that it had drifted out to sea. The next morning the masts of the *Irene* only were seen above water. . . . On February 5, we reached Louisburg, and were taken before the Governor, who committed us to the common prison. At this time there were eight large men-of-war, four frigates, and transports laden with men and munitions of war, collected in the harbor, for the protection of the city against a demonstration it was known the English designed to make. On the 1st of June General Amherst's expedition hove in sight. . . .

"All the English prisoners in the city were ordered on board the men-of-war and confined below decks under guard. One week later the English effected a landing and four days thereafter succeeded in dislodging the French from their outworks. Cannonading was opened on the 14th simultaneously between five French vessels and the Island battery, and an English man-of-war and the Lighthouse battery. The French vessels were compelled to fall back on the 16th under cover of the fort. The ship on board of which I was, being in range, was riddled by three hundred shot. One night when I was asleep behind a barrel of flour in the hold, a ball came crashing through the hull and buried itself in the barrel! On the 16th the English opened a general cannonade against the city, which was sustained with unremitting fury for two days. Then they opened their mortars upon the fleet, pouring into the vessels a fiery hail, which soon wrapped three of them in flames. Compelled to abandon our burning ship (a 64) all hands took to the boats, but it was a desperate alternative, as the way of escape to the shore was commanded by the English batteries. On landing, we prisoners were immediately put in confinement. Thus another week passed, when on the 26th July, the cannonading ceased and news was brought to us that the garrison had capitulated.   The next day we were released."

The *Hope*, the fourth and last of the transport vessels of the Church, was built in 1760, at New Haven, Connecticut, "was 120 tons burthen, mounting four cannon, and navigated by thirteen seamen."   She was registered at the New York Custom House, and prohibited from taking out of the Province "any servant, debtor, or any person without a passport."

Securing a cargo for South Carolina, the *Hope* left her dock on her first voyage, Saturday, January 17, 1761, the day on which George III was proclaimed king in the Province.   Arriving at her destination, she sailed for England, February 20, under convoy.   Again under convoy, she arrived at New York, October 19, having on board the following passengers :

> Nathaniel and Anna Johanna Seidel,
> Frederick and Hedwig Elizabeth von Marshall,
> Paul and Anna Muenster.

Single Men.

> John Arbo, warden,
> John Angerman, tailor,
> John Valentine Beck, gun stock maker,
> John Brandmiller, baker,
> Christian Christiansen, shoemaker,
> Peter Danielson, hatter,
> Jeremiah Dencke, Chaplain,
> Ferdinand J. Dettmers,
> Ludwig C. Grunewald, carpenter,
> Philip J. Hoeger, tailor,
> Christian Hornig, shoemaker,
> Dominicus Krause, nail-smith,
> Niels Lund, locksmith,
> John M. Moehring, farmer,
> Niels Moos, farmer,
> Emanuel Nitschmann, student,
> John F. Oberlin, storekeeper,
> John H. Rauch, locksmith,
> August Schloesser, saddler,

John M. Schmidt, linenweaver,
David D. Schoenberg,
John E. Schoepfel, miller,
A. Paulus Thrane,
Matthias Tommerup, brazier,
Frederick Unger,
David Zeisberger.

Single Women.

Theodora Anders,	Elizabeth Kaunhauser,
Maria Beitel,	Mary M. Meyer,
Elizabeth Broksch,	Anna Nitschmann,
Dorothea Hammer,	Anna Seidel,

Esther Wapler.

Andrew Langaard (widower),	David Wahnert (widower),
Frederick Peter "	Juliana Benedicta von Gammern,

Anna Maria Philips.

During the ensuing two years, the *Hope* was engaged in the general freighting business, but on October 21, 1763, she landed at New York the following passengers, who reached Bethlehem November 4:

John Frommelt,	Dorothea Lefler,
Paul Tiersch,	Frederica Pietscher,
Justina Erd,	Elizabeth Seidlitz,
Susan von Gersdorf,	A. Salome Steinmann,
M. Barbara Horn,	Maria W. Werwing.

The first fire engine for Bethlehem, purchased in London, was brought over on this voyage, and is still preserved in that town. With the arrival of the *Hope* at New York, April 11, 1765, with the Rev. Frederick Smith and wife as passengers, her career as a transport vessel of the Church ends.

At a meeting held in Bethlehem, June 6, 1762, in which Bishop A. G. Spangenberg, who for almost twenty years was at the head of the American branch of the Moravian Church, announced his departure for Europe, he took occasion to review the Moravian immigration of the past twenty-six years, and stated that of the six hundred and more men and women, but one died—a remarkable instance of Divine protection.

"SERVANTS AND APPRENTICES BOUND AND AS-SIGNED BEFORE JAMES HAMILTON MAYOR OF PHILADELPHIA, 1745."

CONTRIBUTED BY GEORGE W. NEIBLE, CHESTER, PENNA.

October 2d. 1745.

(Passengers per snow George, Capt. Ambler.)

Charles Carrol, from Dublin, consideration £14 paid by John Carpenter of Gloucester township N. J. to Robert Wakely for his passage and in further consideration of Carpenter teaching him trade of a weaver—apprenticed for five years.

Robert Wakely assigns *Nicholas Smith*, from Dublin, to Nehamiah Baker of Chester Co., Pa., consideration £15. to serve four years from Sept. 22, 1745, and to have customary dues.

Bryan Dignan, from Dublin, consideration £15. paid by Edward Goff of Chester Co., Pa., to Robert Wakely for passage money—servant to said Goff for five years.

John Havey, from Dublin, consideration £15. paid by Joseph Phipps jun. of Chester Co. Pa., to Robert Wakely passage money to Penna., servant to said Phipps for term of five years Robert Wakely assigns *Robert Burleigh*, from Dublin, to Richard Smith of Salem N. J., consideration £14.10/, to serve four years and customary dues.

Robert Wakely assigns *Manus Marley*, from Dublin, to Robert Craig of Bucks Co. Pa., consideration £14.15/ to serve five years from Sept. 22, 1745, and customary dues.

William Adair, servant to William Campbell, of Chester Co. Pa., with consent of master goes as servant to William Clymer, of Philada., mariner, for two years. Consideration £8.15/ and customary dues.

Robert Wakely assigns *John Sullivan*, from Dublin, to

John Potts of Philada. consideration £15.10/ to serve four years from Sept. 22 1745, and customary dues.

Robert Wakely assigns *John Riely*, (from Dublin), to John Potts of Philada. Consideration £15.10/. to serve four years from Sept. 22 1745, with customary dues.

Robert Wakely assigns *Daniel Connell*, from Dublin, to John Potts of Philada. Consideration £15.10/ to serve four years from Sept 22 1745, and customary dues.

Robert Wakely assigns *Thomas Keaton*, from Dublin, to John Potts, of Philada. Conditions £15.10/ to serve four years from Sept. 22 1745, with customary dues.

Robert Wakely assigns *Constantine McGuire*, of Dublin, to George Taylor of Philada. Co. Consideration £15.10/ to serve four years from Sept. 22 last, with customary dues.

Robert Wakely assigns *Timothy Wright*, from Dublin to George Taylor of Philada County. Consideration £15.10/ to serve four years from Sept. 22 1745, with customary dues.

Robert Wakely assigns *Philip Egan*, from Dublin, to George Taylor of Philada County. Consideration £15.10/ to serve four years from Sept 22 1745, with customary dues.

Conyngham & Gardiner assign *John Steen*, from Londonderry, in the ship Woodstock, Geo Axton Com^d to Joseph England of Chester County—Consideration £12. to serve four years from 18 September last.

October 3rd.

Robert Dixon assigns *Mary Caffery* for the remainder of her time to Charles Moore of Phila. hatter, to serve five years from July 11, 1743. Consideration £12. and customary dues.

Samuel Powell, (son of Mary Powell) binds himself by consent of mother, apprentice to William Moode, shoemaker, for seven years and five months from this date, and is to have nine months schooling at writing and reading, and at the expiration of his time one complete suit of new apparel.

October 4th.

John Inglis assigns *Anthony Adams* (an East Indian from
Scotland in ship Anne Galley, Capt. Houston), to serve
Thomas Mullan six years from Sept. 20 last.   Consideration
£18. and customary dues.

Patrick Kirk (from Dublin, on snow George Capt. Ambler) in consideration £15. for passage, to Robert Wakely
and in further consideration of being taught trade of
butcher, binds himself an apprentice and servant to Edward
Ash, Philada. Co. to serve five years from date & to have
customary dues.

John Allen assigns *John Moor* (a servant from Ireland in
the brig^t Carolina, Capt John Allen) to serve Thomas
Paxton four years from Oct 3d inst.   Consideration
£18. 10/ and to have customary dues.

October 5th.

Edward Dowers assigns *Michael   Colley,* (a servant from
Ireland on the ship Bolton, Capt. Edward Dowers), to serve
Thomas Bailey and his assigns four years from Oct. 4 1745.
Consideration £16.—to have customary dues.

Robert Wakely assigns *Timothy Ryan,* (a servant from
Dublin) to serve John McCormick & his assigns four years
from Sept. 22 1745.   Consideration £14.10/, with customary
dues.

Edward Dowers assigns *John Welch,* (a servant from Ire-
land in Ship Bolton), to serve Anthony Turner, of Frederick
Co. Va., four years from Oct 4 1745—customary dues.
Consideration £16.

Edward Dowers assigns *John Brook,* (a servant from
Ireland in ship Bolton) to Alexander Crookshank, cordwainer, three years and a half from Oct 4th 1745, Consideration £20.—customary dues.

Edward Dowers assigns *Alexander Birch,* (a servant from
Ireland, on ship Bolton) to Abraham Farrington, Burlington Co. N. J., for four years from Oct 4th 1745.   Consideration £17.—customary dues.

Edward Dowers assigns *John Smith*, (a servant from Ireland on ship Bolton) to serve William Lawrence of Allenstown N. J. four years from Oct 4 1745. Consideration £17.—customary dues.

Edward Dowers assigns *Roger Maher?* (Servant from Ireland, on ship Bolton), to William Lawrence of Allenstown, N. J. for four years from Oct 4 1745. Consideration £17.—customary dues.

Edward Dowers assigns *James Harding*, (an Irish servant on ship Bolton) to William Lawrence of Allenstown N. J. for four years from Oct 4 1745. Consideration £17.,—customary dues.

Edward Dowers assigns *Edward Royall* (a servant from Ireland on ship Bolton), to William Garwood of Philada. for four years. Consideration £16. customary dues.

Robert Wakely— *William Murrough* (a servant from Ireland on snow George) to Ebenezer Brown, four years from Sept 22 last. Consideration £15.—customary dues.

October 7th.

James Thomson, late of New Brunswick, East Jersey, binds himself an apprentice to Jonathan Durell of Philada., potter, to learn the art and mystery of a Potter for five years from the 18th Sept. 1745; to have two quarters of year night schooling and at expiration of the said term to have two suits of apparel, one whereof to be new.

Nathaniel Ambler assigns *Francis McCann*, (servant from Ireland on snow George) to serve John Fullerton four years from Sept. 22d last. Consideration £19.—customary dues.

Jacob Casdrop and John Johnson, Overseers of the Poor of the Northern Liberties bind *Elizabeth Downey*, a poor child, of ten years of age, with her own consent and accord, to Charles Juisian of Philada Co., as an apprentice for eight years from this date—the said girl to be taught to read & write, and at expiration of the said time to have two suits of apparel, one of which is to be new.

John Erwin assigns *William Stewart* (a servant from Ireland, on snow George, Capt. Benj Buck,) to William Moode, for four years from Oct. 2. 1745. Consideration £22.—customary dues.

Edward Dowers assigns *Peter Dolan*, (a servant from Ireland, on ship Bolton) to John Kirkbride of Bucks Co. for four years from Oct 4 1745. Consideration £17.—customary dues.

Robert Wakely assigns *Mary Williamson*, (a servant from Ireland, snow George), to Anthony Newhouse, of Philada. Co., for four years from Sept. 22 1745, Consideration £13. customary dues.

Restore Lippincott assigns *John Kennedy* for remainder of his time, four years from Sept. 22, 1745 to Joseph Burr, of West Jersey. Consideration £16.—customary dues.

John Chase, late of Liverpool, England, in consideration of £10. paid Capt. Dowers for his passage binds himself a servant to Thomas Bartow, of Chester, for three years and a half from this date—to have customary dues.

October 8th.

John Reardon assigns *Margery Nicholson*, for the remainder of her time, five years from 22 June last to Reuben Swain of Cape May, West Jersey, consideration £14.10/.—customary dues.

John Erwin assigns *Bryan McCann* (a servant from Ireland) to Samuel Reynolds of Lancaster Co. for four years from Oct 2 1745.—customary dues.

John Gardner, from Ireland in brig Cleveland, Capt Wm Robinson, in consideration of £8. paid by John Faires of Philada, cordwainer, to said Robinson for his passage, binds himself a servant to said John Faires, for the term of eighteen months from this date.

Robert Wakely assigns *Luke Kelly* (a servant on snow George, from Ireland) to Robert Dunwiddie for four years from Sept 22, 1745, consideration £15.10/, customary dues.

"ACCOUNT OF SERVANTS BOUND AND ASSIGNED BEFORE JAMES HAMILTON, MAYOR OF PHILADELPHIA."

CONTRIBUTED BY GEORGE W. NEIBLE, CHESTER, PENNA.

October 9, 1745.

George OKill's assigned *Roger McDonnell,* (a servant from Ireland, in Brig⁺ Cliveland, Wm. Robinson, master), to William Miller, Chester Co., to serve three years from Oct. 5, 1745. Consideration £11.5., with customary dues.

John Inglis assigned *Agnes Mein,* (a servant from Scotland, on ship Anne Galley, Capt. Houston) to William Miller, Chester Co., to serve five years from Sept. 20, 1745 Consideration £15., to have customary dues.

Robert Wakely assigns *Thomas Martin,* (a servant from Ireland, on Snow George, Capt. Ambler) to Daniel Griffith, Chester Co. Consideration £16. to serve four years from Sept. 22, 1745, and customary dues.

Edward Dowers assigns *William Smith,* (a servant from Ireland. on ship Bolton, Capt. Edw. Dowers), to William Sandwith, of Philadelphia, to serve four years from Oct. 4, 1745. Consideration £17, and have customary dues.

Conyngham & Gardner assigns *Catherine McGinnis* (a servant from Ireland, on the Snow John, Capt. Thos. Marshall), to John Bell, Chester Co., for three years and a half from Sept. 3, 1745. Consideration £12, with customary dues.

Edward Dowers assigns *Bryan O'Hara,* (a servant from Ireland, on ship Bolton, himself master), to Robert Christy, of Phila., to serve four years from Oct. 4, 1745. Consideration £18, with customary dues.

James Simple, late of the County of Tyrone, Ireland, in

consideration of his passage from Ireland to Pennsylvania, indents himself voluntarily to Edward Dowers, of Phila., mariner, as a servant and appointed for nine years from Oct. 4, 1745; to have two suits of apparel, one to be new at the end of the term.

Edward Dowers assigns *Thomas Hetherton*, (a servant from Ireland, on ship Bolton, himself master), to Samuel Ainsworth, of Lancaster Co., for four years from Oct. 4, 1745. Consideration £16, with customary dues.

John Erwin assigns *William Holdercroft*, (a servant from Ireland, on Snow George, Capt. Benj. Burk), to Josiah Abbetson, Gloucester Co., W. Jersey, for four years, from Oct. 2, 1745. Consideration £16, with customary dues.

Edward Dowers assigns *James Simple*, (a servant from Ireland, on ship Bolton), to Isaac Norris, Esq., Phila. Co., for nine years from Oct. 4, 1745. Consideration £10, to have two suits of apparel at end of term, one to be new.

John Murphy, late of Killdair, Ireland, in consideration of £16. paid by Daniel Heister, of Phila. Co., to Edward Dowers, for his passage from Ireland, and in further consideration of being taught the trade of a Tanner and Currier, binds himself a servant for five years, from Oct. 4, 1745. To have two suits of apparel, one to be new.

October 11.

Edward Dowers assigns *Dominick Meath*, (a servant from Ireland on ship Bolton), to Theophilus Simontown, of Lancaster Co., for four years, from Oct. 4, 1745. Consideration £15. 15, with customary dues.

William Gardner, late of Antrim Ireland, in consideration of £11.9. paid William Robinson for his passage to Penna., by Robert Shields, of Hunterdon Co., West Jersey, indents himself a servant of said Shields, for two years, eight mo. and two weeks. At end of term one new suit of apparel.

Robert Wakely assigns *Thomas Pritchit*, (a servant from Ireland, on Snow George) to John Thomas, of Phila. Co., for four years, from Sept. 22, 1745. Consideration £13.10 with customary dues.

Edward Dowers assigns *John Brien*, (a servant from Ireland on ship Bolton), to Henry Brooks, Salem Co., West Jersey, for four years, from Oct. 4, 1745. Consideration £17., customary dues.

October 12.

Edward Dowers assigns *Latin Morgan*, (a servant from Ireland, on ship Bolton), to David Spear, Bucks Co., to serve four years, from Oct. 4, 1745. Consideration £16., with customary dues.

Robert Wakely assigns *John Conner*, (a servant from Ireland, on Snow George) to John Ross, of Lancaster Co., to serve four years, from Sept. 22, 1745. Consideration £14.10, with customary dues.

Robert Wakely assigns *John Mahan*, (a servant from Ireland, on Snow George) to John Ross, of Lancaster Co., to serve four years, from Sept. 22, 1745. Consideration £14.10, with customary dues.

Robert Wakely assigns *Patrick Tunbridge*, (a servant from Ireland, on Snow George) to John Ross, of Lancaster Co., to serve four years, from Sept. 22, 1745. Consideration £16, with customary dues.

Robert Black, (son of Elizabeth Black, widow) an infant of seven years or thereabouts, by and with the consent of his mother, (who was likewise present and expressed her consent) in consideration of his being educated and maintained, and his being taught to read and write, binds himself a servant to Andrew Hodge, of Philadelphia Co., baker, for thirteen years and five months from this date, and at expiration of term to have one suit of new apparel besides his old ones.

Matthew Gleave assigns *John Marlay*, (a servant from Ireland, on the Snow George), to serve four years, from Sept. 22. Consideration £20, with customary dues.

Thomas Page, late of Dublin, in consideration of £16. paid by John Jones, of Whitemarsh, for his passage from

Ireland and of his being taught the trade of a cooper, indents himself for six years, eleven months and twenty-two days, from this date, and at expiration of time to have two suits of apparel, one of which is to be new and forty shillings in money.

Robert Wakely assigns *Patrick White*, (a servant from Ireland, on the snow George), to Silas Pawin, of Philada, for four years, from Sept. 22, 1745. Consideration £15, with customary dues.

John Erwin assigns *Daniel Fearon*, (a servant from Ireland, on snow George), to James Downey, of Prince George Co., Md., for four years, from Oct. 2, 1745. Consideration £16.10, customary dues.

Robert Wakely assigns *Bryan Riely*, (a servant from Ireland, on Snow George), to George Walker, of Chester Co., for five years. Consideration £16, customary dues.

John Erwin assigns *Edward McDonnell*, (a servant from Ireland, on Snow George), to John Ross, of Lancaster Co., to serve nine years from Oct. 2, 1745. Consideration £16, to have customary dues.

John Erwin assigns *Hector McLene*, (a servant from Ireland, on snow George), to John Ross of Lancaster Co., for four years, from Oct. 2. 1745. Consideration £18, customary dues.

October 14.

John Erwin assigns *Patrick Duffy*, (a servant from Ireland, on Snow George), to John Allison, of Lancaster, for four years, from Oct. 2 1745. Consideration £17.10., customary dues.

Robert Wakely assigns *James Little*, (a servant from Ireland, on Snow George), to James Allison, of Lancaster Co., for four years from Sept. 22, 1745. Consideration £14, usual dues.

Conyngham & Gardner assigns *Barnard Kerr*, (a servant from Ireland, on ship Woodstock) to John Katteringer, for four years from Sept. 18 1745. Consideration £18.— customary dues.

James Mahan, from Ireland, in ship Bolton, in consideration of £16. paid for his passage, indents himself to Ezekiel Forman of East Jersey, for three years eleven months & twenty days,—two suits of apparel, one to be new, and forty shillings proclamation money.

Robert Wakely assigns *Patrick Bryan* (a servant from Ireland on Snow George) to Thomas McKee of Lancaster Co., to serve five years, from Sept. 22nd 1745. Consideration £15., customary dues.

Robert Wakely assigns *Michael Redmond* (a servant from Ireland on snow George), to Thomas McKee of Lancaster Co., to serve four years, from Sept. 22d, 1745. Consideration £15., customary dues.

Edward Dowes assigns *James Dougharty* (a servant from Ireland on Ship Bolton) to David Lawrence of Chester Co., to serve four years from Oct. 4th, 1745. Consideration £16. Customary dues.

William Robinson assigns *Samuel Davison* (a servant from Ireland on Brg^t Cleveland) to Samuel Rowland of Sussex Co., to serve five years from Oct. 5th 1745. Consideration £16. Customary dues.

John Gill (late servant to Morris Morris of Phila., brewer; in consideration of £2 paid by Dr. Cadwalader Evans to said Morris for remainder of his time) indents himself to Dr. Evans for two years, one month and fourteen days from this date, to have one new suit of apparel.

October 15th.

Teddy O'lanshalin (late of the Kingdom of Ireland). In consideration of £14 paid by Robert Worrel of Phila. to James Moor for his passage and in further consideration of his being taught the trade of a shoemaker indents himself a servant to the said Robert Worrel for four years from this date, to have customary dues.

John Allen assigns *Hugh Moore* (a servant from Ireland in the Brig^t Carolina) to John Johnson of Phila. Tallow-chandler to serve four years from Oct. 3rd 1745. Consideration £18 10.—to have customary dues.

John Allen assigns *Richard Johnston* (a servant from
Ireland in the Brig^t Carolina) to Hugh Hodge of Phila.
Tobacconist to serve seven years from Oct. 3rd 1745.   Con-
sideration £12—to have customary dues.

John Inglis assigns *Hugh McDonald* (a servant from Scotland in the ship Anne Galley) to Philip White of Bucks Co.,
to serve six years from Sept. 20 1745.   Consideration £18
—to have customary dues.

John Inglis assigns *William Cock* (a servant from Scotland
in the ship Anne Galley) to William Davis of Bucks Co., to
serve four years from Sept. 20th 1745. consideration £18—
to have customary dues.

Elizabeth Shaw (late of the Kingdom of Ireland), in consideration of ten pounds, eleven shillings and nine pence
paid by Baptist Clark of Lancaster Co. to John Erwin for
her passage, indents herself a servant to Baptist Clark for
three years and three months from this date to have
customary dues.

Charles West (late of the Kingdom of Ireland), in consideration of ten pounds, ten shillings paid by Mr. McMeen of
Lancaster Co. to John Erwin for his passage, indents himself a servant to William McMeen for three years, eleven
months and nineteen days from this date.   Customary dues.

Mary Hazleton (late of the Kingdom of Ireland) in consideration of ten pounds ten shillings paid by William
McMeen of Lancaster Co. to John Erwin for his passage
indents himself a servant to William McMeen for three
years eleven months and nineteen days from this date; to
have customary dues.

Archibald Armstrong (late of the Kingdom of Ireland) in
consideration of ten pounds ten shillings paid by William
McMeen of Lancaster Co., to John Erwin, for his passage,
indents himself a servant to William McMeen for three
years and a half from this date; to have customary dues.

Jacob Heashey, jun., in consideration of twelve pounds
paid by Lawrence Good of Bucks Co., to John Markill, for
the remainder of his time, by and with the consent and

approbation of his father Jacob Heashey who was present
& expressed his consent, indents himself as servant to
Lawrence Good for nine years and three months from this
date, to have at the expiration of his time one complete
suit of new apparel and one cow.

October 16th.

John Inglis assigns *Robert Man* (a servant from Scotland
in the ship Anne Galley) to Mahlon Kirkbride to serve four
years from Sept. 20th 1745; consideration £14. to have
customary dues.

James Gardner, late of Lancaster Co. in consideration ot
£22. paid by John Howell of Phila., tanner, for his use and
at his request, indents himself a servant to John Howell for
three years from this date; to have one new suit of
apparel.

Robert Wakely assigns *Daniel M'cauley* (a servant from
Ireland in the Snow George) to William Branson of Phila.
to serve four years from Sept. 22nd 1745; consideration
£15:10s; to have customary dues.

Robert Wakely assigns *William Cosgrave* (a servant
from Ireland in the Snow George) to William Branson to
serve four years from Sept. 22nd 1745; consideration
£15:10/—to have customary dues.

Robert Wakely assigns *John Grenan* (a servant from
Ireland in the snow George) to William Branson of Phila.,
to serve four years from Sept. 22nd 1745 :—consideration
£15:10/. to have the customary dues.

Robert Wakely assigns *Dennis Bryan* (a servant from
Ireland in the snow George) to William Branson of Phila.
to serve four years from Sept. 22nd 1745;—consideration
£15:10/ and to have the customary dues.

Andrew Frank, late of Lancaster Co. In consideration
of £12. paid for his use and at his request, by Henry
Bostler of Lancaster, indents himself a servant to Henry
Bostler for two years from this date;—without freedom
dues.

Hendrick Decker, in consideration of 8 pistoles paid by

Joseph Pennock of Chester Co., for his passage from
Holland, indents himself a servant to Joseph Pennock for
eight years from this date.   To have the customary dues.

Mary Jones (an infant of one year) in consideration of
her maintenance and education with consent and approbation of her mother, Jane Jones, binds herself a servant to
John Warmes and Mary his wife, for seventeen years from
this date ; is to learn to read and have the customary dues.

October 17th.

Peter Knepley in consideration of thirteen pounds, six
shillings and six pence, paid by Caspar Wistar of Phila., to
Capt. John Brecune for his passage from England, indents
himself a servant to said Wistar for six years from this
date.   To have customary dues.

Jacob Becktell, in consideration of thirteen pounds, eight
shillings, paid by Caspar Wistar of Phila., to Capt. John
Brecune for his passage from England, indents himself a
servant to Caspar Wistar for four years from this date, to
have customary dues.

Elisha Boss, assigns *Grizzil McCala* for the remainder of
her time, five years from last June 22nd, to William Wood
of Phila. for the consideration of £10. the said servant to
have customary dues.

John Erwin assigns *Patrick Monaghan* (a servant from
Ireland on the snow George) to Andrew Buchanan of Lancaster Co. for four years from Oct. 2nd. 1745.   Consideration £27:—to have customary dues.

October 18th.

Samuel Howell assigns *George Gibson* to John Head Jr.,
for the remainder of his time for one year from last July
15th.   Consideration £12. 12. 6.

James McAlice assigns *John Roe* to Dr. Thomas Graeme
for the remainder of his time four years from last April
28th.   Consideration £18.

Anne Paterson, in consideration of £10.— paid by John
Hopkins of Phila. for her passage from Ireland, to Samuel

McCall Jr. indents herself a servant to John Hopkins for five years from this date; to have customary dues.

John Freeman, by the consent and approbation of his mother Anne Marie Freeman, testified by her signing his Indenture, indents himself as apprentice to John Moses Conty for eight years from this date, is to be taught to read and write the German language, and to have five pounds at the expiration of his time instead of freedom dues, and tools and implements befitting a journeyman shoemaker.

Henry Miller assigns *John Michael* to Thomas Bond of Phila., for the remainder of his time fourteen years from Nov. 19th 1741. Consideration £16— to have the customary dues.

Arthur Burrows assigns *Agnes Leagen* (a servant from Ireland) to William Murdoch of Phila., taylor—to serve five years from June 17th, 1745. Consideration £13:— to have the customary dues.

William Hamilton assigns *John Gillaspy* (a servant from Ireland) to James Baird, of Orange Co., Virginia, for three years and a half from Sept. 1st, 1745. Consideration £11.10, to have customary dues.

October 19th.

Thomas Williamson, in consideration of £19, paid by Robert Fleming of Phila. to Capt. John Allen for his passage from Ireland, and his being taught the art of a barber and peruke maker, indents himself a servant to Robert Fleming for four years, eleven months and seventeen days from this date. Customary dues.

Jacob Casdrop and John Johnson, overseers of the poor for the Northern Liberties bind *Deborah Dobson,* a poor child (2 yrs and 9 months) to Frederick Gyger to serve him fifteen years and three months from this date, the said child to be taught to read and write the English language, and to knit, sew and spin, and at the end of her time to have one new suit of apparel besides her old ones.

Samuel Mumma assigns *Anne Strawbridge* to Benjamin Mason of Phila. Co., for the remainder of her time three

years from August 4th, 1745. Consideration £9. 10;—
to have customary dues.

October 21st.

William Robinson assigns *Robert McCrery* (a servant from
Ireland in the Brig Cleveland) to Thomas Broome of Phila.
for seven years from Oct 5th, 1745. Consideration £16. 10;
to have customary dues.

Robert Wakely assigns *Saunders Campbell* (a servant from
Ireland in the snow George) to Samuel Birchfield for seven
years from Sept. 22d, 1745. Consideration £15:— to have
the customary dues.

October 22nd.

Robert Wakely assigns *Paul Phillips* (a servant Ireland
in the snow George) to Anthony Morris Jr. for four years
from Sept. 22nd, 1745. Consideration £15., to have customary dues.

John Collins, of Phila., laborer, in consideration of £10.4
by him due and owing to Daniel Boyle of Phila., County
yeoman, indents himself a servant to Daniel Boyle for one
year and a half from this date.

Abram Mason, late of Kent County, on Delaware, indents
himself an apprentice to Joseph Jones of Phila., for six
years, three months and twenty-one days, from October
21st, 1745, to have two winters schooling at a boarding
school to learn to write and cypher, one of the said winter
schooling to be paid for by Joseph Jones, the other by
Joseph Mason, brother to Abram, to be taught the art or
mystery of a joiner or cabinet maker and at the expiration
of the said time to have two suits of apparel, one of which
is to be new.

Robert Wakely assigns *Thomas McGuire*, (a servant from
Ireland in the snow George) to William Caughdry for four
years from Sept. 22nd, 1745. Consideration £16; customary
dues.

'ACCOUNT OF SERVANTS BOUND AND ASSIGNED BEFORE JAMES HAMILTON, MAYOR OF PHILADELPHIA."

CONTRIBUTED BY GEORGE W. NEIBLE, CHESTER, PENNA.

October 23rd.

James Cloyd assigns *John Conelin* (a servant from Ireland in the Snow Happy Return) to William Murdock for four years from Oct 12th 1745. Consideration £16. customary dues.

Isaac Hutchinson assigns *Richard Welch* (a servant from Ireland in the Snow Happy Return) to Nathaniel Scarlet of Chester Co., for six years and a half from Oct 12th 1745. Consideration £14. customary dues.

Michael Wooldridge, in consideration of fifteen pounds paid by James Payne of Phila. Cooper, to Robert Wakely for his passage from Ireland, and in further consideration of being taught the art or mystery of a cooper, indents himself a servant to James Payne for seven years and five months from this date, to have two suits of apparel at the expiration of his time, one of which new.

James Cloyd assigns *John Stuart* (a servant from Ireland in the Snow Happy Return) to Robert Thompson of Phila. County for four years from Oct. 12th 1745. Consideration £15: customary dues.

Elizabeth Hoy assignes *Mary Parker* to William Morris of the County of Chester for the remainder of her time two years and a half from Nov. 29th 1745—Consideration £8.

Edward Dowers assignes *William Brian* (a servant from Ireland in the ship Bolton) to Stephen Onion of Maryland for four years from Oct. 4th 1745—Consideration £16 :— customary dues.

Edward Dowers assignes *George Quinland* (a servant from Ireland in the ship Bolton) to Stephen Onion of Maryland for four years from Oct. 4th 1745, consideration £16 :—to have customary dues.

Edward Dowers assignes *Thomas Landricking* (a servant from Ireland in the ship Bolton) to Stephen Onion of Maryland for four years from Oct. 4th 1745, consideration £16 : —customary dues.

Edward Dowers assignes *Patrick Morgan* (a servant from Ireland in the ship Bolton) to Stephen Onion of Maryland for four years from Oct. 4th 1745—Consideration £16 :—to have customary dues.

Edward Dowers assignes *Christopher Lynch* (a servant from Ireland in the ship Bolton) to Stephen Onion of Maryland for four years from Oct 4th 1745. Consideration £15, customary dues.

Edward Dowers assigns *Moses Campbell* (a servant from Ireland in the ship Bolton) to Stephen Onion of Maryland for four years from Oct. 4th 1745. Consideration £16 : customary dues.

Edward Dowers assigns *Jonathan McNomara*, (a servant from Ireland in the ship Bolton) to Stephen Onion of Maryland for four years from Oct. 4th 1745. Consideration £16. —customary dues.

Edward Dowers assigns *William Kenny* (a servant from Ireland in the ship Bolton) to Stephen Onion of Maryland for four years from Oct 4th 1745. Consideration £16 : customary dues.

Edward Dowers assigns *Bryan Carty* (a servant from Ireland in the ship Bolton) to Stephen Onion of Maryland for four years from Oct. 4th 1745. Consideration £16. customary dues.

October 24th.

Margaret Bullock by consent of her grandfather Nathan Watson indents herself a servant to Obadiah Eldridge of Phila. and his wife, for eight years and a half from Aug. 19th. 1745, to be taught reading writing and sewing and at the expiration of her time to have two suits of apparel, one of which to be new.

James Mitchell assigns *Hugh Gallougher* (a servant from Ireland in the snow Happy Return) to John Gillcrest of Lancaster County for four years from Oct. 12th 1745—Consideration £15—to have customary dues.

James Mitchell assigns *John McKenny* (a servant from Ireland in the snow Happy Return) to John Neal of Lancaster Co., for five years from Oct. 12th 1745. Consideration £15. customary dues.

Patrick Coll assigns *John Connaghan* (a servant from Ireland in the snow Happy Return) to James Gillcrest of Lancaster Co., for five years from Oct. 12th 1745. Consideration £15, customary dues.

William Robinson assigns *John Willson* (a servant from Ireland in the Brigg⁺ Cleveland) to Francis Alexander of Chester County, for eight years from Oct. 5th 1745. Consideration £12.10/. customary dues.

William Robinson assigns *John Woodside* (a servant from Ireland in the brigg⁺ Cleveland) to Mathew Robinson of Chester County for five years from Oct. 5th 1745. Consideration £13, customary dues.

Grace Obryan of her own free will and accord and by the consent of her father Christopher Obryan, binds herself a servant to Alexander Edwards of Phila. county for four years and seven months from this date, to be taught to read and write, and at the expiration of the said time to have one cow and calf and two suits of apparel, one of which shall be new.

Isaac Hutchinson assigns *Allen McDugal* (a servant from Ireland in the snow Happy Return) to Samuel Scott of Lancaster County for three years from Oct. 12th 1745. Consideration £14—Customary dues.

John Karr assigns *John Morrin* (a servant from Ireland in the snow Happy Return) to Josiah Scott of Lancaster county for four years from Oct. 12th 1745. Consideration £15— Customary dues.

October 25th.

William Robinson assigns *John Stewart* (a servant from Ireland in the Brigg* Cleveland) to Bristow Browne, mariner, to serve seven years from Oct. 5th 1745. Consideration £10., customary dues.

Robert Wakely assigns *Anne Doran* (a servant from Ireland in the snow George) to John Reardon, of Phila., for four years from September 22nd 1745. Consideration £10. customary dues.

Edward Cathrall assigns *Adam Stoles* his servant to Hugh Roberts of Phila. for the remainder of his time for thirteen years from Feb. 12th 1738. Consideration £20: customary dues.

October 26th.

Robert Wakely assigns *William McGlinn* (a servant from Ireland in the snow George) to Francis O'neal of Chester Co, for four years from Sept. 22nd 1745. Consideration £16: to have customary dues.

John Inglis assigns *John Drummond* (a servant from Scotland in the ship Anne Gally) to Jonathan Robeson for six years from Sept. 20th 1745. Consideration £18:, customary dues.

October 30th.

George Okill assigns *Magraret Hackabuck* to Thomas Lacey, of New Jersey, for the remainder of her time eight years from Nov. 3rd 1743. Consideration £14 customary dues.

George Okill assigns *Mary Magrogan* (a servant from Ireland in the Brigg* Cleveland) to Abigail Pedroe of Phila. for seven years from Oct. 5th 1745. Consideration £11:5/. customary dues.

Abigail Petro assigns *Mary Murray* to William White of Kent Co. for the remainder of her time, four years from April 10th 1745. Consideration £13:, customary dues.

Thomas Breach of Newton, West Jersey, indents himself an apprentice to Ebenezer Zanes of Phila. for six years and eleven months from this date, is to be taught the trade of a house carpenter, to have six months evening schooling, and at the expiration of his time to have two suits of apparel, one whereof shall be new.

Oct. 31st.

Alexander Farquhar of Kent Co. in Delaware by the consent and approbation of his father-in-law James Gonele, binds himself an apprentice to William Russell of Phila., house carpenter, for five years and nine months from this date, to be taught the trade of a house-carpenter, and to be found in meat, drink, washing and lodging, but not in apparel, neither is he to have any freedom dues.

John Mooney in consideration of fourteen pounds paid by George Kelly to Mathias Ferrale for his passage from Ireland indents himself a servant to George Kelly for five years from this date, to be taught the trade of a blacksmith, and at the expiration of said term to have one new suit of apparel besides his old ones.

November 1st.

Robert Bulcock Jr. of Barbados by the consent and approbation of his father who was present, indents himself an apprentice to Thomas Penrose of Phila. shipwright for seven years from Oct. 30th 1745—to be taught the trade of shipwright in every branch; is to be at liberty to go to an evening school every winter at his fathers expense, and to be found in apparel at the expense of his father.

November 5th.

John Carroll assigns *James Miller* (a servant from Ireland in the ship Katharine) to Thomas Trueman of Phila. for five years and a half from Oct. 31st 1745. Consideration £15—to have customary dues.

James Foster assigns *Matthew McCalley* (a servant from Ireland in the ship Katharine) to Edmund Burk of Phila. for three years from Oct. 31st 1745. Consideration £14;—to have customary dues.

John Cook from Ireland in the ship Katharine in consideration of ten pounds for his passage paid by Thomas

Herbert of Phila. indents himself a servant to said Herbert for five years from hence, customary dues.

November 6th.

Joseph Eaton by consent and approbation of his father John Eaton, indents himself an apprentice to Samuel Cheesman of Phila., cordwainer for five years and two months from this date, is to be taught the trade of a shoemaker and at the expiration of his time to have two suits of apparel, one of which to be new.

Stephen Maddin in consideration of fifteen pounds paid by Nathaniel Eavenson of Chester Co—to Robert Wakely for his passage from Ireland indents himself a servant to said Nathaniel for six years, ten months and sixteen days from this date, customary dues.

Thomas Locky assigns *Bryan McGinley* (a servant from Ireland in the ship Katharine) to John Lewis of Phila. Co., for four years from Oct. 31st 1745.   Consideration £15:5/— customary dues.

John Arnold, in consideration of £12 to him paid by James Ward of Gloucester Co. in New Jersey binds himself a servant to the said James Ward for three years from this date—customary dues, all but the freedom dues.

Francis Caughlan in consideration of £9 paid by Alex. Huekinbottom to Joshua Morris for the remainder of his time and in further consideration of being taught the trade of bricklayer, indents himself a servant to the said Huekinbottom for four years from this date; customary dues.

November 7th.

Jacob Cooper assigns *Dorothy Calfinkin* to Isaac Browne of Phila. for the remainder of her time nine years from Dec. 20th 1744—Consideration £8.8.6., customary dues.

November 8th.

Joseph Smith assigns *Laughlin O'Stevin* (a servant from Ireland in the ship Katharine) to Alexander Miller of Lancaster Co., for four years from Oct. 31st 1745.   Consideration £14—customary dues.

John Moore assigns *Thomas White* a servant, to Barnabas Roads of Phila. Co. for the remainder of his time seven years from August 27th 1741. Consideration £16—customary dues.

William Herbert assigns *John Herbert* his apprentice to John Stamper of Phila. for the remainder of his time nineteen years from March 24th 1740. Consideration 5/—customary dues.

Sarah Dearman with the consent of Mary Herbert, her mistress, hath put herself a servant to William Bingham of Phila. and Mary his wife, for four years from Nov. 1st instant—customary dues.

James Foster assigns *Ezekiel Bullock* (a servant from Ireland in the ship Katharine) to Andrew Stephen of Lancaster Co. for five years from Oct. 31st 1745. Consideration £10:7.6. customary dues.

November 9th.

Daniel Jappie assigns *Darby Collings* (a servant from Ireland in the snow City of Cork) to John Riveyans of Lancaster Co., for four years from Nov. 8th 1745. Consideration £16—Customary dues.

Daniel Jappie assigns *Dennis Horgan* (a servant from Ireland in the snow City of Cork) to Andrew Miller of Lancaster Co., for four years from Nov. 8th 1745. Consideration £15. Customary dues.

Daniel Jappie assigns *Catherine Irley* (a servant from Ireland in the snow City of Cork) to William Nicholson of Phila. for four years from Nov. 8th, 1745 Consideration £14: Customary dues.

Daniel Jappie assigns *John Dunn* (a servant from Ireland in the snow City of Cork) to George Kelly of Phila. for four years from Nov. 8th 1745. Consideration £22: customary dues.

John Inglis assigns *Neil Brown* (a servant from Scotland in the ship Anne Galley) to George Houston for six years from Sept. 24th 1745. Consideration—customary dues.

James Templeton assigns *Andrew Christy* (a servant from
Ireland in the Brigg¹ Couli Kan) to Thomas Harris of
Lancaster Co. for five years from Nov. 1st., 1745   Consideration £22 : customary dues.

November 11th.

Clement Russell assigns *John Doud* his servant to Patrick
Devor of Phila. marriner, for the remainder of his time for
four years from June 15th., 1745. Consideration £16 : customary dues.

Joseph Smith assigns *Arte McClaskey* (a servant from
Ireland in the ship Catharine) to Isaac Jennings of Gloucester Co. for four years from Oct. 31st, 1745. Consideration £13:10/. Custom ry dues.

Daniel Reardon of Lancaster Co., in consideration of being
instructed in the trade of a coppersmith puts himself
apprentice to William Love of Phila. for one year from this
date, to have one new cloth waistcoat, two new checque
shirts and one new pair shoes, at the end of his time.

Daniel Jappie assigns *Teague Hanan* (a servant from
Ireland in the snow City of Cork) to John Guthry for four
years from Nov. 8th., 1745. Consideration £16 : customary dues.

Daniel Jappie assigns *Timothy Bryan* (a servant from
Ireland in the snow City of Cork) to Joseph Walter of
Chester Co., for four years from Nov. 8th., 1745. Consideration £16 : customary dues.

John Dwyer, late of Ireland, in Consideration of £20 :
paid by Andrew Farrell of Phila. to Cap. Daniel Jappie for
his passage from Ireland indents himself a servant to the
said Andrew Farrell for three years, eleven months, and
twenty four days from this date—at the end of his time to
have one new suit of apparel besides his old ones and £5 :
currant money.

Daniel Pilliting, Jr. by consent of his father Daniel
Pilliting (who signs his indenture) puts himself apprentice
to Hugh Hodge of Phila. tobacconist, for fourteen years and

nine months from this date, to have three quarters of a year day schooling to learn to read and write, and at the expiration of the said term to have two suits of apparel one of which is to be new and to be taught the trade of a Tobacconist in all its branches.

Daniel Jappie assigns *Daniel Hurley* (a servant from Ireland in the snow City of Cork) to Samuel Burrough, of West Jersey, for four years from Nov. 8th, 1745. Consideration £16 : customary dues.

Catharine Abel in consideration of £12 : paid by Christian Crasshold, for her passage from London, indents herself a servant to said Christian for three years and a half from this date. Customary dues.

Abraham Collings assigns *Thomas Linon* (a servant from Ireland in the ship Bolton) to Edward Collings of Phila. for four years from Oct. 4th, 1745. Consideration £12 : customary dues.

Nov. 12th.

John Murrough, in consideration of £15 : paid by Alex. Armstrong of Lancaster County to Elizabeth Ken for his time of his own free will and accord indents himself a servant to said Alexander for four years and a half from this date at the end of his time to have two complete suits of apparel one of which is to be new.

Conrad Abel in consideration of £6 : paid by Jacob Newman to Casper Wistar for his passage from London, indents himself a servant to the said Jacob Newman for eight years from this date. To have the customary dues.

Nov. 13th.

James Templeton assigns *John Kernell* (a servant from Ireland in the Brig⁴ Couli Kan) to George Curry of Chester County for four years from Nov. 1st, 1745. To have customary dues, consideration £16:10

James Templeton assigns *William Anderson* (a servant from Ireland in the Brig⁴ Couli Kan) to Mary Grimes of

Chester County for four years from Nov 1st, 1745. Consideration £15.10/ customary dues.

John Stinson assigns *Anne Steven* his servant to James Gault, of Lancaster County, for the remainder of her time, for three years, from April 30th 1745 Consideration £11:10/. Customary dues.

Nov. 14th.

George James Ex^r of Joseph James assigns *Jacob Chrisstler* late apprentice to said Joseph James deceased, to Christian Crosshold, of Phila., for the remainder of his time eleven years and ten days from Dec. 2nd, 1741, to have schooling to learn him to read and write English, and at the end of his time to have two suits of apparel, of which one is to be of new broadcloth, also a taylors goose and sheers and twenty shillings in money. Consideration £10:—

Walter Jones assigns *Arthur Mclaske* (a servant from Ireland in Ship Katherine) to William Rush of Chester County, for four years from May 11th, 1745. Consideration £13:10/ to have customary dues.

Davies Bendall assigns *Jacob Simson* (a servant from Ireland in the Snow Martha) to Robert Bulcock of the Island of Barbadoes for three years and a half from Sept. 14th, 1745. Consideration £16: customary dues.

James Templeton assigns *John Morrison* (a servant from Ireland in the Brig^t Couli Kan) to Henry Sloan of East Jersey for five years from Nov. 1st 1745. Consideration £16: customary dues.

Philip Hime, by consent of his mother Mary Elizabeth Hime, who was present, In consideration of £13:12.6 paid by John Gebherd, for his passage from Holland to Benjamin Shoemaker, indents himself, a servant to John Gebherd for twelve years from this date to be taught to read and write the English and German languages and to have the customary dues.

Daniel Jappie assigns *Dennis Kitney* (a servant from Ireland in the Snow City of Cork) to Joseph Seal of Chester

County for four years from Nov. 5th 1745. Consideration £14:10/ customary dues.

Nov. 16th.

Daniel Boyle assigns *Mary Dirrham* his servant to Daniel Corbett of Chester County for the remainder of her time, four years from Sept. 18th, 1744. Consideration £10 customary dues.

Nov. 18th.

George James Ex^r of Joseph James deceased, assigns Johannes Gebele, late apprentice to the said Joseph to David Tishell of Phila. for three years from Dec. 12th, 1744. Consideration £12: customary dues.

William Dean indents himself a servant to John McMinn of Chester County for two years and eleven months from Nov. 11th, 1745. Consideration £16: paid to Abram Willson—Customary dues.

William Andrew in consideration of £18: paid by John Kerr to Capt. Huston for his passage from Scotland, indents himself a servant to said John Kerr for five years and eleven months from this date, is to be taught the Art or Mystery of a plasterer and to have the customary dues at the end of his time.

Nov. 20th.

James Templeton assigns *James Cunningham* (a servant from Ireland in the Brig^t, Couli Kan) to William Fullerton of Lancaster County for four years from Nov. 1st 1745. Consideration £16: customary dues.

Margaret Piling in consideration of £8: paid by Francis Creek of Lancaster County to George Rood for her maintenance and education, of her own free will and accord, indents herself a servant to Francis Creek for three years and a half from this date, at the expiration of her time to have one good yearling heifer and one new suit of good full'd stuff.

Caleb Emlen assigns *John Hill*, his apprentice, to Joseph Armit of Phila. joyner for the remainder of his time seven

years and fifty eight days from June 4th 1741:—to be taught
the trade of a joyner and to have customary dues.   Consideration £12.

Nov. 21st.

Hugh Hall son of William Hall of Phila., taylor, by the
consent and approbation of his father, indents himself an
apprentice to John Kateringer of said City, taylor, to serve
seven years from this date, to have two winters schooling at
an evening school, to read and write, and at the end of his
time to have customary dues.

Robert Wakely assigns *Bryon Campbell* (a servant from Ireland in the Snow George) to John Pass of Phila. for four
years from Sept. 22nd 1745.   Consideration £15 : customary dues.

Daniel Jones son of Mary Jones, by consent of his mother,
indents himself apprentice to Richard Allen of Phila., brass
founder, for six years from Nov. 20th 1745, to be taught
the trade of a brass founder and at the expiration of his
apprenticeship in case his mother should die before that
time, to have a new suit of clothes.

Daniel Jappie assigns *Owen Quigley* (a servant from Ireland
in the Snow City of Cork) to William Browne of Lancaster
County for four years from Nov. 5th, 1745 : consideration
£14 : customary dues.

Daniel Jappie assigns *Timothy Linchey* (a servant from Ireland in the Snow City of Cork) to Thomas Dewell, of Salem County, in West Jersey, for four years from Nov. 5th,
1745.   Consideration £14 : customary dues.

Daniel Jappie assigns *James Bryan*, (a servant from Ireland, in the Snow City of Cork), to Aaron Mendenhall of
Chester County for four years from Nov. 5th 1745.   Consideration £5 : customary dues.

Nov. 22nd.

James Templeton assigns *Robert Barnett* (a servant from
Ireland in the Brig' Couli Kan) to John Price of Lancaster

County for six years from Nov. 1st 1745.   Consideration
£17 : customary dues.

Walter Jones assigns *Cormick O'brien* (a servant from
Ireland in the ship Katherine) to Samuel McCree of Chester County for five years from Oct. 31st 1745.   Consideration £14: customary dues.

Nov. 23rd.

Christopher Gyger of Phila country labourer indents himself a servant to Reuben Forster of Phila wheelwright for
two years, two months and eleven days from this date; is to
be taught the Art or Mystery of a wheelwright in all its
branches and to be found in meat, drink, washing and
lodging.

Daniel Jappie assigns *Anne St. John* (a servant from Ireland in the snow City of Cork) to Gilbert Deacon of Phila.
for four years from Nov. 5th, 1745.   Consideration £14;
Customary dues.

Thomas Griffith assigns *Daniel Beatty*, his servant for the
remainder of his time, five years from Nov. 1st 1744, to
Thomas Kenton Jr. of Phila. County.   Consideration £17:
customary dues.

John Dight son of Abram Dight of Chester County with
the consent of his father indents himself an apprentice to
Benjamin Loxley, of Phila., house carpenter for five years
and nine months from this date, to have one quarters evening schooling at reading and writing and at the end of his
time the customary dues.

James Templeton assigns *John McDonald* (a servant from
Ireland in the Briggt. Couli Kan) to John Painter of Chester County for five years from Nov. 1st, 1745.   Consideration £14:10/ customary dues.

James Berry late of Ireland indents himself of his own
free will and accord an apprentice to William Hamilton of
Lancaster County for five years from this date, to be taught
the trade of a blacksmith and at the end of his time to have
one complete suit of new apparel and three pounds in
money.

Nov. 25th.

Jacob Grubb, son of Peter Grubb, late of Phila., indents himself an apprentice to Daniel Billger of Phila., Cooper, for five years from this date, is to have six months schooling to learn to read and write the German language and at the expiration of his time, is to have given to him five hundred cedar hoop poles, fifty cedar blocks, two drawing knives, one compass, one joyner, one axe, and one saw, and one suit of new apparel besides his old ones.

Edward Evans assigns *William Maylan*, his apprentice, to Thomas Overing of Phila. cordwainer, for the remainder of his time five years and three months from Nov. 1st 1741. Consideration £10 : to have customary dues and it is agreed between the said Thomas Overing and William Maylon that in case William Maylon does his six pairs of leather shoes a week (unless prevented by sickness), that the said master shall pay for two quarters schooling for the said apprentice at a evening school to learn to read and write.

Nov. 26th.

James Templeton assigns *James Low* (a servant from Ireland in the Briggt. Couli Kan) to Thomas Ivans, of West Jersey, for five years from Nov. 1st 1745. Consideration £15.10/. Customary dues.

James Templeton assigns *Charles Stewart*, (a servant from Ireland in the Brig'. Couli Kan) to Joseph Reeve of Cohansie for five years from Nov. 1st 1745. Consideration £16: 10/. Customary dues.

James Templeton assigns *Alexander Forrentine*, (a servant from Ireland in the Brig'. Couli Kan) to Neal McClaskey of Chester County for four years from Nov. 1st 1745. Consideration £18 : customary dues.

Daniel Jappie assigns *George Hill* (a servant from Ireland in the snow City of Cork) to Joseph Chainpress of Salem County, for four years from Nov. 5th 1745. Consideration £14 : customary dues.

Daniel Jappie assigns *Solomon Walsh* (a servant from Ireland in the snow City of Cork) to John Elwell of Salem

County, for four years from Nov. 5th 1745. Consideration
£14 : Customary dues.

Nov. 27th.

James Templeton assigns *William Willson* (a servant from
Ireland in the Brig'. Couli Kan) to Joseph Mackleduff of
Chester County for four years from Nov. 1st, 1745. Con-
sideration £14 : customary dues.

Nov. 28th.

Andrew Paterson with the consent of his mother Sarah
Paterson, widow, indents himself an apprentice to William
Sutor of the Northern Liberties, turner, for six years from
this date, is to be taught the trade of a turner and to be
taught to read, write and cypher, as far as the rule of three
and at the end of his time to have customary dues.

Nov. 29th.

James Templeton assigns *Samuel Forrentine* (a servant
from Ireland in the Brig'. Couli Kan) to John Dicky of
Chester County, for four years from Nov. 1st 1745. Consideration £18 : customary dues.

Nov. 30th.

Michael Bikker assigns *Philip Boogle* his servant to William Hinton of Phila. for the remainder of his time six
years from Jan. 15th, 1744-5 : consideration £15:14/ customary dues.

Dec. 2nd.

Daniel Jappie assigns *Daniel Kelly* (a servant from Ireland
in the snow City of Cork) to John Barnes, of Trenton, for
four years from Nov. 5th, 1745. Consideration £15 : Customary dues.

Daniel Jappie assigns *Barnaby Grimes* (a servant from
Ireland in the snow City of Cork) to Kendall Cole of West
Jersey for four years from Nov. 5th, 1745. Consideration
£15 : customary dues.

Daniel Jappie assigns *William Trow* (a servant from Ireland in the snow City of Cork) to Benjamin Cooper of

West Jersey for four years from Nov. 5th, 1745. Consideration £17: customary dues.

Daniel Jappie assigns *John Jones* (a servant from Ireland, in the snow City of Cork) to Robert White of Bucks County for four years from Nov. 5th, 1745. Consideration £15: customary dues.

Daniel Jappie assigns *Thomas Connor* (a servant from Ireland in the snow City of Cork) to Robert Hunt, of Burlington, for four years from Nov. 5th, 1745. Consideration £16: customary dues.

Dec. 4th.

Samuel Boon son of Elizabeth Sims of Phila. with the consent of his mother, binds himself apprentice to John White of Germantown, house-carpenter, for seven years and ten months from this date, to learn his trade, and to be taught to read and write, and at the end of his time to have one new suit, besides his old one.

William Dickeson, Jr., son of William Dickeson of Salem, with the consent of his said father binds himself apprentice to Ebenezer Zane of Phila. house-carpenter, for six years and six months from Nov. 15th, 1745, to be taught the trade of a house-carpenter and at the end of his time to have one new suit beside his old one.

Dec. 7th.

Garret Fiscus, of Phila., taylor, in consideration of twenty-one pounds paid by Conrad Reif, of Phila., to Benjamin Shoemaker for his and his wife's passage from Holland indents himself a servant to Conrad Reif, for four years from this date. Customary dues.

William Silliker son of William Silliker deceased, by consent of his Uncle Benj. Leigh, binds himself apprentice to Benj. Ellis of Chester County, cooper, for nine years and seven months from this date to have six months schooling at reading and writing, to be taught the trade of a cooper and husbandman—customary dues.

Dec. 9th.

James McDonald, of Phila., mariner, indents himself a servant to Joseph Gaven of Phila., cordwainer, for five years from this date, to be taught the trade of a shoemaker to have one whole years schooling at an evening school, and at the end of his time to have one new suit of broad cloth besides his old ones.

Dec. 10th.

William Ellicot, of Phila., indents himself an apprentice to Richard Swan of Phila., hatter, for three years one month and twelve days, from this date, to be taught the trade of a hatter, and at the end of his time to have one new suit of cloath, besides his old ones.

Richard Knowles, by consent of his mother Rebecca Clayton indents himself an apprentice to Richard Swan of Phila., hatter, for two years and one month from this date, to be taught the trade of a hatter, and reading, writing and cyphering as far as the rule of multiplication, and at the end of his time to have one new suit of apparel besides his old ones.

Dec. 11th.

George James executor of Joseph James, deceased, assigns *John Smith*, late apprentice to the said Joseph James to John Katteringer of Phila., taylor, for the remainder of his time ten years from April 25th, 1743 to be taught the trade of a taylor and to read, write and cipher as far as the rule of three, and at the end of his time to have two suits of apparel one of which to be new, and also a taylor's goose and shears to be given by his master. Consideration 5/7.

George Pyall assigns *John Smith*, his servant, to John Warner of Phila. County for the remainder of his time four years from May 19th, 1744. Consideration £12:— customary dues.

Dec. 12th.

Jonathan Hanson by consent of his mother Esther Hanson, binds himself apprentice to Francis Holton, of

Phila. County, shipwright, for five years from Nov. 29th,
1745; to be taught the trade of a shipwright and to be found
in shoes by his master, but no freedom dues.

George Doblewart, with consent of his uncle Jacob Maux,
indents himself a servant to John Gibhart of Phila., turner,
for twelve years from this date to be taught the trade of a
turner and to read and write in the German language and
at the expiration of his term to have one new suit of apparel
besides his old ones.   Consideration £10:15/, paid Jacob
Maux.

Elizabeth Keplery, in consideration of five pounds paid to
Jacob Maux, by Peter Hindworker of Phila., with consent
of Jacob Maux, indents herself a servant to Peter Hindworker for ten years from this date, to have customary dues.

Joseph Clayton with consent of his mother Esther Harris
of Chester County, indents himself an apprentice to Joseph
Govett of Phila., taylor, and Esther his wife, for four years
and ten months from this date to be taught the trade of a
taylor, to have two quarters schooling at an evening school
and at the end of his time to have one new suit of apparel
besides his old ones.

Dec. 14th.

Daniel Jappie assigns *Lawrence Mahoney* (a servant from
Ireland in the snow City of Cork) to Ephraim Daten, of
West Jersey, for four years from Nov. 5th 1745.   Consider-
ation £14: customary dues.

Dec. 16th.

Hugh Carberry of his own free will and accord and in
consideration of £13: paid by Thomas Noorington to Anthony Whitely for his passage from Ireland, indents himself a servant to Noorington for six years from May 11th
1745, to be taught the trade of a loaf bread baker, and
have customary dues.

Dec. 19th.

William Cuzzins assigns *Maria Furnery* his servant to
Mathias Young, of the Borough of Lancaster, for the

remainder of her time five years from Feb. 14th 1744/5 Consideration £16 : customary dues.

Abraham Wood, late of Burlington with the consent of his mother Ursula Rose indents himself apprentice to Jacob Lewis of Phila. house carpenter for five years seven months and a half, to be taught the trade of a house-carpenter, to have six months schooling at an evening school at reading and writing and at the end of his time to have one complete suit of new apparel besides his old ones.

Dec. 23rd.

Daniel Jappie assigns *Michael Hogan* (a servant from Ireland in the snow City of Cork) to John Paul, of Phila. County, for four years from Nov. 5th 1745. Consideration £14 : customary dues.

Daniel Jappie assigns *John Byrn* (a servant from Ireland in the snow City of Cork) to Joshua Jones of Phila. County for four years from Nov. 5th 1745. Consideration £14 : customary dues.

Dec. 24th.

Daniel Jappie assigns *Joan Sullivan* (a servant from Ireland in the snow City of Cork) to William Craig of Bucks County for four years from Nov. 5th 1745. Consideration £12 : customary dues.

Dec. 27th.

George Moore late of Ireland but now of Penna., indents himself an apprentice to Samuel Howell of Phila., hatter for one year from this date, to be taught the trade of a hatter, is to be allowed by his master during his apprenticeship three new shirts, three new pair of stockings, and three new pair of shoes, as the same shall become necessary for him, to work one month in wool if required by his master.

Dec. 30th.

Antonio Vosia, (a free negro man from Jamaica) indents himself an apprentice to Peter Allrick, of Phila. baker, for five years from this date to be taught the trade of a biscuit baker, customary dues.

Honour Edwards, of her own free will and accord in consideration of seven pounds ten shillings paid by John Clemson to Samuel King, for the remainder of her time, indents herself a servant to John Clemson for two years and three months from this date, to have cloathes during her service, but no freedom dues.

John Bell assigns *Catherine McGinnis*, his servant, to Conyngham and Gardner, for the remainder of her time, three years and a half from Sept. 3d 1745. Consideration £12:10/ customary dues.

Judith Williams of Phila., spinster, indents herself servant to John Bell of Chester County for two years from this date, to be found in meat, drink, washing, lodging and apparel, but no freedom dues. Consideration £4.17.8.

"ACCOUNT OF SERVANTS BOUND AND ASSIGNED BEFORE JAMES HAMILTON, MAYOR OF PHILADELPHIA."

(CONTRIBUTED BY GEORGE W. NEIBLE, CHESTER, PENNA.)

Jan. 2nd. 1746.

Patrick McClanehan late of Lancaster County in consideration of £12: paid for his use and at his request by James Dougharty of Phila. County, weaver, indents himself a servant to said James for three years from this date, to be found in meat, drink, washing, lodging, and apparel during said term, but not to have any freedom dues.

John Erwin assigns *Bryon McDermot* (a servant from Ireland in the snow George) to William Nicholson of Phila., Innholder, for five years from Oct. 2nd 1745. Consideration £18: customary dues.

Honour Sullivan in consideration of her passage from Ireland paid by John Erwin of Phila., merchant, indents herself servant to the said John, for fifteen months and fifteen days from this date. Customary dues and new suit of clothes.

Jany. 3rd.

James Rossam, of Gloucester County, in consideration of £15: paid and to be paid to him by Samuel Jones of Phila. County indents himself a servant to said Jones for two years from this date, to be found in meat, drink, lodging and washing, but no freedom dues, and at the end of the term to have a cow of the value of three pounds, ten shillings.

Jany. 10th.

Robert Thompson, of Phila., sailmaker, in consideration of £15: paid for his use and at his request by Abram Mason

of Said City, sailmaker, binds himself a servant to Said
Mason for one year, eleven months, and twenty days; to
have one new suit.

John Troy assigns *Richard Berry* his servant, to William
Rush of Phila., blacksmith, for the remainder of his time,
for four years from April 10th 1745.   Consideration £19 :
Customary dues.

Jany. 11th

Silas Parvin assigns *Patrick White* his servant to Jeremiah
Parvin, of West Jersey, for the remainder of his time from
Sept. 22nd 1745.   Consideration £15 : Customary dues.

Daniel Jappie assigns *James Reiley* (a servant from Ireland in the snow City of Cork) to Quintin Moore, of Chester
County, for four years from Nov. 5th 1745.   Consideration
£11 :—Customary dues.

Jany. 16th.

Joseph Griffin with consent of his mother Jane Griffin,
widow, indents himself apprentice to Ebenezer Jones of
Phila., housecarpenter, for seven years from Dec. 20th 1745 :
to have one quarters schooling at the expence of his mother,
to be taught the trade of a carpenter, to be found in cloathes
&c. and to have customary dues.

John White of Phila., laborer, in consideration of £9:10/.
paid for his use and at his request by Robert Wood of
Phila., mariner, indents himself a servant to the said Robert
for three years from this date, customary dues.

Jany. 18th.

Elizabeth Barnes in consideration of £15 : paid by Denis
Flood at her request, indents herself to David Knox for five
years from this date.   Customary dues.

Morgan McMahon in consideration of £8 : paid to Daniel
Jappie for his passage from Ireland indents himself servant
to William Blanchfield for two years and nine months from
this date, customary dues.

Jany. 20th.

William Nicholson assigns *Catherine Orley* his servant to Moses Hayman of Phila. County, for the remainder of her time, four years from Nov. 8th 1745. Consideration £14: Customary dues.

Mathias Krabb with consent of his father Simon Krabb, binds himself apprentice to Jacob Videry of Phila. potter, for twelve years from this date, to be taught the trade of a potter, and read and write the German language: customary dues.

Mary Reckiner, in consideration of sundry sums of money expended on her account by Mary Johnson, of Wiccacoo, indents herself a servant to the said Mary Johnson for three years from this date. Customary dues.

Thomas Elliot Hutchins assigns *Samuel Bowden*, his servant, to Robert Jewell of Phila., ropemaker, for the remainder of his time three years and a half from May 30th 1745. Consideration £10:

Jany. 21st.

Robert Wakely assigns *Philip Dingwell* (a servant from Ireland in the snow George) to Stephen Anthony of Phila., leather-dresser, for four years from Sept. 22nd 1745. Consideration £16: Customary dues.

Jany. 22nd.

Jacob Casdrop and John Johnson, overseers of the poor of the Northern Liberties, bind *John Dawson*, son of John and Annie Dawson, an apprentice to George Pallmer of Phila. County, farmer, for thirteen years, eleven months from this date, to be taught husbandry and to read and write and at the end of his time to have customary dues.

Jany. 24th.

Annie McGuire in consideration of £9.10/ paid by Mary Boardman, widow, to John Postlethwait for the remainder of her time (the indenture to Postlethwait being lost or mislaid) binds herself servant to Mary Boardman for three years, three months and twenty one days from this date. Customary dues.

Jany. 27th.

James Templeton assigns *Edward McKage* (a servant from Ireland in the Brigh^t. Couli Kan) to Robert Wall of the Northern Liberties for four years from Nov. 1st 1745. Consideration £16:10/. Customary dues.

Jany. 29th.

John Troy Jr. with consent of his father John Troy of Phila., marriner, (who signs his indenture) binds himself apprentice to John Jackson of Chester County, blacksmith, for nineteen years from this date, to be taught the trade of a blacksmith and to read, write and cipher, and at the end of his time to have one complete suit of new apparel besides his old ones.

Jany. 30th.

Barbara Gordon in consideration of five shillings paid William Dames for the remainder of her time by John Frederick of Phila., flatman, indents herself a servant to the said John for one year and eleven months from this date, to find the said servant in apparel and give her freedom dues and to indemnify the said William Dames of all cost and charge for or concerning the said Barbara and her child during the term of the indenture.

Jany. 31st.

John Johnston assigns *Hugh Moore* his servant to John Paxton, of Lancaster County, for the remainder of his time four years from Oct. 3rd, 1745. Consideration £18 : customary dues.

Feby, 1st.

Mary Johnson assigns *Mary Rachinor*, her servant, to John Beaumont of Bucks County, for the remainder of her time three years from Jan. 20th 1745. Consideration £9. Customary dues.

Feby. 4th.

Mary Gollohan in consideration of £12:10/ paid Robert Drakely for her passage from Ireland by Dennis Flood of Phila., taylor, indents herself a servant to said Dennis for three years, ten months and one week from this day; customary dues.

Mary Strong by consent of her mother Mary Lamb, signified by a writing under hand, indents herself a servant to John Freston and Annie his wife, for six years and a half from this date, to be taught to read and to sew plain work; customary dues.

Margaret Greenless by consent of her mother Mary Chancellor (who signs her indenture) indents herself a servant to James Reuecdot, of Phila., shopkeeper, for ten years and eleven months from this date, to be taught to read and sew plain work, and to have customary dues.

Feby. 6th.

Jonathan Mifflin, Atwood Shute, and White Massey, overseers of the poor of Phila., bind *Alexander Peddy* an orphan, to Isaac Warren of Phila., blacksmith, for fourteen years from this date to teach him the trade of a blacksmith and to read and write, and at the expiration of his time to give him customary dues.

Jonathon Mifflin, Atwood Shute and White Massey, overseers of the poor of Phila., bind *William Peddy* an orphan, to Richard Blackhouse of Phila., blacksmith, for sixteen years from this date to teach him to read and write and at the end of his time to give him the customary dues.

Darby Daly in consideration of £11:10/ paid Isacher Prise by William Arbour of Phila., for the remainder of his time, indents himself servant to William Arbour for two years and five months from this date; customary dues.

Feby. 8th.

Anthony Newhouse assigns *Mary Williamson* his servant to Abram Shelly of Phila., for the remainder of her time, four years from Sept. 22nd 1745.   Consideration £10 : customary dues.

Feby. 10th.

William Finlay assigns *Robert Reside* his servant to William Plumsted of Phila., Merchant, for the remainder of his time six years from August 1st 1741.   Consideration £12 : Customary dues.

Feby. 13th.

James Poor, late of Trenton in consideration of £17 : paid by David Budd of Burlington County, farmer, to Alexander Maine for his use and at his request indents himself a servant to David Budd for four years from this date and, at the expiration of the said term, to have the customary dues.

Feby. 17th.

William Hamilton late of Virginia, but now in Phila., indents himself an apprentice to James Payne of Wiccocoe in Phila. County for four years from this date; is to be taught the trade of a cooper, to have one quarters evening schooling, to learn to write, and at the end of his time to have customary dues.

George Grim, son of Phetha Grim, by consent of his father, indents himself servant to Benjamin Shoemaker Esq., for five years and seven months from this date.   Consideration £20 : due to Shoemaker for passage of Phetha and his family.

Feby. 18th.

Charles Moore assigns *John Rogherty* his servant to Hugh Patrick of Lancaster County for the remainder of his time three years from May 28th 1745.   Consideration £12, customary dues.

John Prawll, of Phila., yeoman, in consideration £12 : paid for his use and at his request by Dr. Richard Farmer, of Phila., indents himself servant to Richard Farmer, for two years from this date; customary dues.

Feby. 19th.

Jacob Sillker son of Sarah Sillker who signs his indenture by consent of his mother, indents himself servant to Joseph Johnson of Wiccacoe in Phila. County for seventeen years and two months from this date, to be taught to read and write the English language, and at the end of his time to have customary dues, and one horse of five pounds value.

Feby. 20th.

Jacob Willkins, son of John Willkins, deceased, with consent of his mother who was present, binds himself an apprentice to Richard Blackhouse of Phila., blacksmith, for ten years six months and sixteen days, to be taught the trade of a blacksmith, and to read, write and cipher as far as the rule of three, customary dues.

Owen Cunningham late of the Province of New York, in consideration of six pounds paid by Anthony Whitely of Phila. for his use and at his request binds himself servant to Anthony Whitely for two years from this date, to be found in meat, drink, washing, lodging and apparel, but not to have any freedom dues.

David Patterson in consideration of seven pounds, ten shillings paid by William McCrea of Phila. to Cunningham & Gardner for his passage from Ireland, indents himself a servant to William McCrea for five months and twenty days from this date to be found in meat, drink, washing & lodging, but not to have apparel or freedom dues.

Feby. 21st.

John Stoop assigns *Andrew Charles* his servant to Daniel McClean of Bucks County for the remainder of his time one year and nine months from August 6th 1745.

Feby. 25th.

Thomas Hush binds himself a servant to Jacob Cooper of Phila., shopkeeper, for two years from this date. Consideration £12: paid for his use and at his request, to be found in apparel during his servitude, but not to have freedom dues.

Feby. 27th.

Richard Harthey, son of Henry Harthey, by consent of his father, indents himself an apprentice to John Palliner of Phila., bricklayer, for four years and eleven months from this date, to have one quarters schooling at an evening school every winter at his fathers' expense, to be taught the trade of a bricklayer customary dues.

William Fordham of Phila., joiner, indents himself apprentice to John Ashton of Phila, house-carpenter, for two years, eleven months and twenty-five days from this date, to be taught the trade of a house-carpenter, and at the end of his time to be paid £10: in manner following, £5: in new apparel; 50 shillings in money and fifty shillings in carpenter tools.

Feby. 28th.

Robert Wakley assigns *Daniel McDaniel* (a servant from Ireland in the snow George) to John Troy of Phila. mariner for five years from Sept. 22nd 1745. Consideration £16: customary dues.

Griffith Evans Jr., with consent of his father Griffith Evans, binds himself apprentice to John Biddle of Phila., cordwainer, for four years and a quarter from this date, to be taught the trade of a shoemaker, to have two quarters at writing and ciphering at an evening school in the first part of his time, and to be found in shoes and aprons during his time.

March 4th.

Thomas Charlton assigns *Mary Robinson* his servant to Joseph Boore of Phila. County for the remainder of her time, five years from June 22nd 1745. Consideration £10: customary dues.

March 5th.

Charles Willson in consideration of £12: paid for his use and at his request by John Chaes of Chester County indents himself a servant to John Chaes for three years from this date, to be found in apparel but no freedom dues.

Elizabeth Burkhard assigns *Martin Hendrick,* her servant to Jacob Poor of Phila. shoemaker, for the remainder of his time seven years from Dec. 12th 1741. Consideration £14: Customary dues.

Feby. 28th.

Reigner Tyson assigns *Roger Cane,* his servant to Isaac Roberts of Phila. bricklayer for the remainder of his time for three years and eleven months from July 10th 1745. Consideration £16:10/ Customary dues.

March 1st.

John Winsor assigns *Mary Catharine Hersh* his servant to William Hughs of Phila. County for the remainder of her time, eight years from March 13th 1745. Consideration £9: Customary dues.

Anthony Magner son of Barbara Magner indents himself apprentice to Robert Barnard of Phila. County his executor for 18 years and 8 months from Feb. 22nd 1745, to be taught husbandry and to read and write, and to have customary dues. (by consent of his mother.)

Samuel Smith, son of Elizabeth Smith, indents himself apprentice to Benj. Peters of Phila. cordwainer (for five years and ten months) to be taught the trade of a shoemaker and to read, write, and cipher as far as rule three, to be found in apparel and to have customary dues.

March 8th.

John Postlethwaite assigns *John Barret* his servant to Maurice and Edmund Nihil for the remainder of his time three years and seven months from Feb. 2nd 1745. Consideration £16: Customary dues.

March 11th.

Jacob Harman of Phila., labourer, indents himself an apprentice to Joseph Derr of Phila. cordwainer for three years from this date to be taught the trade of a shoemaker to be found in apparel and to be allowed two weeks in every harvest to work for himself.

James Kelly of Maryland indents himself apprentice to William Moore of Phila. cordwainer for two years and nine months from this date to be taught the trade of a shoemaker, but not to have cloathes or freedom dues.

Benjamin Hooper, with consent of his mother Sarah Hooper indents himself apprentice to William Moore for seven years, one month and seventeen days from March 3rd 1745, to be taught the trade of a cordwainer, and to have eight quarters evening schooling, four of which to be at the expense of said Sarah, customary dues.

William Rush Ex. of Thomas Rush assigns *Cornelius Vanostin* late apprentice to said Thomas, to Joseph Rush of Phila. house-carpenter for the remainder of his time four years and a half from Jan. 14th 1745.   Consideration £14:

Thomas Lawrence Ex. assigns *John Wheeler* his servant to Robert Hugh of Phila. county bricklayer, for the remainder of his time four years from Jan. 18th 1744.   Consideration £20 :—

Ephraim Shirrald, son of George Shirrald of Gloucester county with consent of his father indents himself apprentice to Peter Stilley of Phila; house carpenter, for nine years, eleven months and two days, to be taught the trade of a carpenter, to have six months day schooling, and three months night schooling every winter during his service, customary dues.

March 13th.

Thomas Fairbrothers in consideration of £8.18.1. paid for his use and at his request by John Phillips of Phila. carpenter, indents himself a servant to said John his Exc. for two years from this date, to be found in apparel &c, and at the end of his time to have one new suit of clothes of the value of £6:, or the like value in carpenters tools, as he shall choose.

March 14th.

Johnathan Mifflin, Attwood Shute & White Massey, overseers of the poor, &c, bind *Thomas Richardson*, an orphan, apprentice to Thomas Harris of Lancaster county for eleven years and nine months from this date to be taught to read and write, and the trade of a millwright, to have customary dues.

Robert Wakely assigns *Timothy Castleton* a (servant from Ireland in the snow George) to John Scoggin of Phila. bricklayer, for four years from Sept. 22nd 1745. Consideration £15: customary dues.

March 15th.

John Dond of Phila, labourer, indents himself apprentice to Clement Russell of Phila. for four years and three months from this date to be taught the trade of a plasterer, customary dues.

Edmund Butler in consideration £12: paid to William Branson for the remainder of his time by John Micon of Virginia indents himself servant to said John for one year and eight months from this date, to have the freedom dues as is the custom of Virginia.

March 17th.

Hugh Boyd in consideration £15: paid to his Master John Wiley for his use and at his request by William Anderson of Phila. Mariner, indents himself servant to William Anderson his exc. for three years from this date, customary dues.

March 18th.

John Wilson by consent of his father Patrick Wilson indents himself apprentice to Jonathan Durell of Phila. potter, for six years and four months from March 12th 1745, to be taught the trade of a potter, to have four quarters schooling in winter evenings, two of the first and of the last years of the term afixed, customary dues.

George Arnold in consideration ten pistoles paid for his passage from Holland indents himself servant to George Passasky of Phila. for two years from this date at the end of his time to have one pistole and a new coat, waistcoat and pair of breeches.

John Conlin in consideration of £20: paid to William Murdock for his time of servitude by John Storey of Bucks, Taylor, indents himself servant to said Storey for four years from this date, customary dues.

Jacob Casdrop and John Johnson overseers of the poor of the Northern Liberties &c, bind *Mary Hutchins*, an orphan, apprentice to Thomas Williams of Phila. boat builder for five years and three months, next ensuing, to be taught to read and write, and sew plain work, and besides freedom dues, to have one new pair of stays and one new quilted petticoat.

March 19th.

Thomas Price son of David Price with consent of his uncles Evan Evan & James Freedman, binds himself apprentice to Arthur Burrows of Phila. Mariner, for six years from this date, to be taught the mystery of a mariner and to have customary dues.

"ACCOUNT OF SERVANTS BOUND AND ASSIGNED BEFORE JAMES HAMILTON, MAYOR OF PHILADELPHIA."

(CONTRIBUTED BY GEORGE W. NEIBLE, CHESTER, PENNA.)

April 5th 1746.

William Nixon assigns *Elizabeth Conner*, his servant, to Charles Stow Jr. of Phila. for the remainder of her time for ten years from Nov. 1st 1741. Consideration £10: to have customary dues.

Ellinor Plunket in consideration of £3 : 10/. paid for her use and at her request by Francis O'Neal of Chester County, indents herself servant to Francis O'Neal for two years from this date.

April 9th.

Edward Wells assigns *Hugh Cairy* his servant for the remainder of his time to Pyramus Green and Peter Bard for seven years from May 20th 1745. Consideration £16— customary dues.

April 10th.

Deborah Hudson by consent of William Hudson, Samuel Emlen and William Moods indents herself apprentice to Anne Rakestraw, mantua maker, for two years from this date to be taught the trade of a mantua maker and to have one quarters schooling to learn to write, at the expense of the said apprentice.

April 11th.

Baltzer Elslegel with consent of his late master John Jacob Fleck indents himself apprentice to Adam Lister of Phila. mariner, for five years and two months from April 9th 1746 to be taught to read and write and the art of navigation.

April 12th.

Alexander Lang assigns *Thomas Armstrong* (a servant
from Ireland in the Brigt. Couli Kan) to Joseph Barton of
Chester County for four years from Nov. 1st 1745.   Consideration £18: customary dues.

April 14th.

John Maclay indents himself apprentice to Hugh Lindsay
of Phila. carpenter, for five years from Sept. 22nd 1745, to be
taught the trade of a house carpenter and writing and arith-
metic as far as the common rules and to have customary dues.

John Jones late servant of Robert White of Bucks County
consideration £13. 10/— paid said White by Edward Wells of
Phila, indents himself servant to Edward Wells for four years
and six months from this date, customary dues.

Patrick Dennis by consent of his brother Richard Dennis
shipwright indents himself apprentice to John Goodwin of
Phila. house carpenter for seven years from March 17th
1745, to be taught the trade of a house carpenter and to be
found in apparel during said term, all but the first two
years; customary dues.

William Taylor assigns *Elizabeth Siblin* his servant to
Nathaniel Petit of Huntedon County New Jersey for the
remainder of her time for ten years from March 22nd 1741.
Consideration £10: customary dues.

Mary Denny daughter of William Denny by consent of
her father indents herself apprentice to Ralph Collins of
Phila. flatman, for eleven years from this date to be taught
to read and write and housewifey; customary dues.

April 15th.

Patrick Baker with consent of his Master Robert Lee of
Lancaster indents himself servant to David Carge of Phila.
innholder for three years from this date consideration £15:
paid said Lee at his request, customary dues.

April 18th.

William Rankin assigns *Thomas Welsh* (a servant from
Ireland in the snow Dublin's Prize) to Joseph Ellis for four

years from April 17th 1746. Consideration £19 :—to have
customary dues, this done before Sam. Hasell Esq.

April 19th.

William Rankin assigns *John Corporall* (a servant from
Ireland in the snow Dublin's Prize) to John Stamper of
Phila. merchant, for four years from April 17th 1746.
Consideration £25: customary dues.

William Rankin assigns *Andrew Clifford* (a servant from
Ireland in the snow Dublin's Prize) to Samuel Hasting of
Phila. shipwright, for four years from April 17th 1746.
Consideration £25: customary dues.

William Rankin assigns *Patrick Kelly* (a servant from
Ireland in the snow Dublin's Prize) to Joseph Gibbons of
Chester County for four years from April 17th 1746. Con-
sideration £19. Customary dues.

April 21st.

William Rankin assigns *Dennis Brady* (a servant from
Ireland in the snow Dublin's Prize) to Jacob Vernon of
Chester County for four years from April 17th 1746. Con-
sideration £19 : customary dues.

Samuel Robinson assigns *Isabelle Miller* his servant to
John Stenson of Phila. lawyer, for the remainder of her
time four years from July 17th 1743. Consideration £4:
customary dues.

William Rankin assigns *William Regan* (a servant from
Ireland in the snow Dublin's Prize) to William Whiteside
of New Castle County yeoman for four years from April
17th 1746. Consideration £19: to have customary dues.

April 22nd.

William Rankin assigns *Edward King* (a servant from
Ireland in the snow Dublin's Prize) to Emanuel Grubb of
New Castle County yeoman for four years from April 17th
1746. Consideration £19: customary dues.

Ruth Tustin with consent of her parents Thomas & Anne
Tustin indents herself servant to Mary Dowell wife of William Dowell for four years, to have one quarters schooling

at reading, another at writing and a third at sewing, and
one new suit of clothing.

April 21st.

William Rankin assigns *James Hunter* (a servant from
Ireland in the snow Dublin's Prize) to Daniel Cooper for
four years from April 17th 1746; Consideration £19:
customary dues, assigned before Thomas Lawrence Esq.

William Rankin assigns *Patrick Fanan* (a servant from
Ireland in the snow Dublin's Prize) to Reiner Tyson Jr. for
four years from April 17th 1746. Consideration £19:
customary dues before Thomas Lawrence Esq.

William Rankin assigns *John Donnell* (a servant from
Ireland in the snow Dublin's Prize) to John Roberts
for four years from April 17th 1746. Consideration
£19: customary dues, assigned before Thomas Lawrence
Esq.

William Rankin assigns *James Morton* (a servant from
Ireland in the snow Dublin's Prize) to Reinier Tyson for
four years from April 17th 1746. Consideration £19:
customary dues; assigned before Thomas Lawrence Esq.

April 22nd.

William Rankin assigns *Edward Meehan* (a servant from
Ireland in the snow Dublin's Prize) to Thomas Morris of
Phila. county for four years from April 17th 1746. Con-
sideration £18: 10/—customary dues.

April 23rd.

William Rankin assigns *Bartholemew Myles* (a servant
from Ireland in the snow Dublin's Prize) to Henry Cooper
of Burlington County for four years from April 17th 1746.
Consideration £18: customary dues.

Willam Rankin assigns *Demetrius Rogers* (a servant from
Ireland in the snow of Dublin's Prize) to John Monroe of
Burlington County for four years from April 17th 1746.
Consideration £18: customary dues.

Willian Rankin assigns *Martin Lee* (a servant from Ireland in the snow Dublin's Prize) to Nathaniel Pennock of

Chester county for four years from April 17th 1746. Consideration £19 : customary dues.

William Rankin assigns *John Carve* (a servant from Ireland in the snow Dublin's Prize) to Thomas Robinson of Phila. Merchant, for four years from April 17th 1746. Consideration £19 : customary dues.

Catherine Englehart by consent of her father Andrew Englehart, indents herself servant to Michael Imble of Lancaster County for six years from this date. Consideration £11 : 10/ paid to her said father by said Imble and at the end of her time is to have given her by her master, one cow of the value of fifty shillings, and one new suit of apparel besides her old ones.

William Rankin assigns *Mathew Gorman* a servant from Ireland in the snow Dublin's Prize) to Patrick McCornish of Phila. plasterer for four years from April 17th 1746. Consideration £24 : customary dues.

April 24th.

William Rankin assigns *William Fagan* (a servant from Ireland in the snow Dublin's Prize) to William Coulton for four years from April 17th 1746. Consideration £18; to have customary dues.

April 25th.

William Rankin assigns *Jacob Carroll* (a servant from Ireland in the snow Dublin's Prize) to Jacob Lippincot for four years from April 17th 1746. Consideration £17 : Customary dues.

John Clemson assigns *Honour Edwards* his servant to Nathan Levy of Phila. merchant, for the remainder of her time two years and three months from Dec. 30th 1745. Consideration £7 : 12 : 6—

April 26th.

William Rankin assigns *Walter Mealy* (a servant from Ireland in the snow Dublin's Prize) to John Morgan of Lancaster County for four years from April 17th 1746. Consideration £18 : Customary dues.

William Rankin assigns *William Dobson* (a servant from Ireland in the snow Dublin's Prize) to John Morgan of Lancaster county for four years from April 17th 1746. Consideration £18: Customary dues.

Phillis Harwood in consideration of £2 : 3 : 8 : paid Joseph Scull and sundry other small sums of money paid for her use and at her request by Allmer Grevile, indents herself a servant to said Grevile for four years from this date, customary dues.

William Musgrove Jr. by consent of his father Wm. Musgrove, indents himself a servant to Aylmer Grevile of Phila. for five years from this date; is to be taught to read, write, and cypher, and at the end of his time, is to have five pounds in money and a new suit of clothes.

William Rankin assigns *Robert Murphy* (a servant from Ireland in the snow Dublin's Prize) to Joseph Conyers of Phila., Mariner from April 17th 1746.   Consideration £17: 10—customary dues.

William Rankin assigns *Sarah White* (a servant from Ireland in the snow Dublin's Prize) to James Shannon of Phila. County for four years from April 17th 1746. Consideration £12: to have customary dues.

William Rankin assigns *Margery Roddy* (a servant from Ireland in the snow Dublin's Prize) to Samuel Osbourn of the county of Chester for four years from April 17th 1746. Consideration £12: customary dues.

Jacob Lewis assigns *Mary Norley* his servant to Robert Powel of the county of Chester for the remainder of her time, for eleven years and six months from October 7th 1736.   Consideration 5/-

April 28th.

William Rankin by James Pemberton assigns *John Mulvay* (a servant from Ireland in the snow Dublin's Prize) to William Conch of Phila County yeoman, for four years from April 17th 1746.   Consideration £18: customary dues.

Nathan Levy assigns *Honour Edwards* his servant to

Simon Girtie of Lancaster County yeoman, for two years and three months from Dec. 30th 1745. Consideration 5/-

April 29th.

Margaret Phillips in consideration of £6 : 11 : 8 : paid for her use and at her request by Mathias Lansey of Chester County indents herself servant to said Mathias for four years from this date, customary dues.

April 28th.

William Rankin assigns *Richard Hudson* (a servant from Ireland in the snow Dublin's Prize) to James Morgan of Phila. County for five years from April 17th 1746. Consideration £17: to have customary dues; this done by Edward Shippen Esq.

April 29th.

William Rankin assigns *Patrick McDonnell* (a servant from Ireland in the snow Dublin's Prize) to Daniel Lippincot of Burlington county for four years from April 17th 1746. Consideration £17: customary dues.

William Rankin assigns *Michael Corcoran* (a servant from Ireland in the snow Dublin's Prize) to William Evans of Burlington County for four years from April 17th 1746. Consideration £17: customary dues.

April 30th.

Anthony Morris Jr. assigns *Paul Phillips* his servant to John Scoggins of Phila. bricklayer for the remainder of his time four years from Sept. 22nd 1745. Consideration £15: to have customary dues.

William Rankin assigns *Darby Clarke* (a servant from Ireland in the snow Dublin's Prize) to James Starr of Chester County yeoman, for four years from April 17th 1746. Consideration £18: customary dues.

Jonathan Hurst Jr. by consent of his mother Anne Hutchins indents himself apprentice to James Gottier of Phila. cooper, for eight years from this date, to have six months day schooling and six months evening schooling to learn to read, write and cipher, to be taught the trade of a cooper, and at the end of his time to have two suits of apparel one of which is to be new.

William Rankin assigns *Dennis Gorman* (a servant from Ireland in the snow Dublin's Prize) to Isaac Roberts of Phila. bricklayer for four years from April 17th 1747. Consideration £20 : customary dues.

April 29th.

William Rankin assigns *Lawrence McAnnaly* (a servant from Ireland in the snow Dublin's Prize) to John Llewellin for four years from April 17th 1746. Consideration £10 : customary dues. This done by Samuel Hassler Esq.

April 30th.

William Rankin assigns *John Walker* (a servant from Ireland in the snow Dublin's Prize) to William Rush of Lancaster County yeoman for four years from April 17th 1746. Consideration £17 : customary dues.

May 1st.

John Drum in consideration of £17 : paid for his passage from Ireland to William Rankin indents himself apprentice to Richard Hinds of Hunterdon County, blacksmith, for five years, eleven months and a half from this date, to be taught the trade of a blacksmith, and at the end of his time to have the customary dues, and thirty shillings in money.

John Warner son of John Warner with consent of his father indents himself apprentice to John Peel, mariner, for six years from April 29th 1746, to be taught the art or mystery of a mariner, and at the end of his time to have two suits of apparel, one whereof to be new.

May 2nd.

William Rankin assigns *Anne Corny* (a servant from Ireland in the snow Dublin's Prize) to John Heathcot of Phila. butcher, for four years from April 17th 1746. Consideration £12 : customary dues.

John Peter Lambert with consent of his mother Anne Bury indents himself servant to Casper Wistar of Phila. for twelve years from this date. Consideration £9 : 9 paid

Stedman & Robertson for his passage from Holland, to be taught to read and write English, and to have customary dues.

May 3rd.

James Payne assigns *Michael Wooldrige* his servant to Adam Hoops of Lancaster County for the remainder of his time seven years and five months from Oct. 23rd 1745. Consideration £18 : to be taught the trade of a cooper and have customary dues.

John McLaughlin in consideration of £10 : paid to William Whelldon for the remainder of his time by James Lord of Gloucester Co. yeoman indents himself servant to said James Lord for three years, eleven months, 4 days from this date to have 3 months schooling to learn to read and write and at the end of his time to have customary dues.

William Rankin assigns *William Boat* (a servant from Ireland in the snow Dublin's Prize) to John Baldwin of Bucks County, shoemaker, for four years from April 17th 1746. Consideration £21 : customary dues.

William Rankin assigns *Charles Daly* (a servant from Ireland in the snow Dublin's Prize) to Evan Thomas of Phila. county, yeoman, for four years from April 17th 1746. Consideration £17 : 10/ customary dues.

May 5th.

William Rankin assigns *John Fitzpatrick* (a servant from Ireland in the snow Dublin's Prize) to Michael Huling of Phila. shipwright, for four years from April 17th 1746. Consideration £18 to have customary dues.

May 6th.

Maria Rody with consent of her mother-in-law Catherine Rody and in consideration of £7 : paid said Catherine by Nicholas Crone of Bucks County, indents herself servant to said Nicholas for seven years and a half from this date to have customary dues.

John O'bryan of Phila. yeoman, in consideraiton of £15 : indents himself servant to William Barge of Phila. county,

miller, for four years from March 11th 1745/6 customary
dues.

William Barge assigns *John O'bryan* his servant to Joseph
Farmer of Phila. county yeoman for the remainder of his
time four years from March 11th 1745/6 consideration £18;
customary dues.

William Rankin assigns *Daniel Donaghy* (a servant from
Ireland in the snow Dublin's Prize) to John Yoder of
Phila. County for four years from April 17th 1746.
Consideration £20: customary dues.

Willian Rankin assigns *Lawrence Ormsby* (a servant from
Ireland in the snow Dublin's Prize) to Robert Jewell of
Phila. ropemaker for four years from April 17th 1746.
Consideration £17: customary dues.

May 7th.

George Woods in consideration of £17: paid for his passage from Ireland in the snow Dublin's Prize indents himself servant to Henry Keely of Salem county for four years
and eleven months, to be taught husbandry and to have
customary dues.

Nathaniel Falkner indents himself apprentice to Joseph
Rivers of Phila. mariner, for seven years from this date
to be taught the art of navigation, and at the end of the
time to have one new suit of apparel.

William Rankin assigns *Michael Cosgrave* (a servant from
Ireland in the snow Dublin's Prize) to Abraham Coffin of
Phila. county, yeoman, for four years from April 17th
1746.   Consideration £10: customary dues.

Samuel Read assigns *George Clackstone* for the remainder
of his time, to Kendal Coles of Gloucester County, West
Jersey, for six years from May 21st 1744.   Consideration
£17: customary dues.

William Rankin assigns *Timothy Follier* (a servant from
Ireland in the snow Dublin's Prize) to Michael Silk of
Phila. plasterer, for four years from April 17th 1746.   Con-
sideration £20: customary dues.

William Rankin assigns *Mary Radcliff* (a servant from

Ireland in the snow Dublin's Prize) to Francis Manie of
Phila. sailmaker, for four years from April 17th 1746.
Consideration £14: customary dues.

May 8th.

Archibald Arskin with consent of his father John Arskin
indents himself apprentice to William McCrea of Phila.
ship joiner, for five years from May 1st 1746, to be taught
the trade of a ship joiner, and at the end of his time to
have one new suit of apparel, &c.

Jacob Hollingsworth indents himself apprentice to Lawrence Garret of Phila. County, cordwainer, for two years
four months and twenty-one days from this date, to be
taught the trade of a cordwainer and when free to have one
complete suit of new apparel, &c.

May 10th.

William Rankin assigns *John Dennison* (a servant from
Ireland in the snow Dublin's Prize) to James Pryor of
Chester County, yeoman, for four years from April 17th
1746. Consideration £16: customary dues.

William Rankin assigns *Arthur Bryan* (a servant from
Ireland in the snow Dublin's Prize) to Thomas Hallowell of
Phila. bricklayer, for four years from April 17th 1746.
Consideration £17: customary dues.

William Rankin assigns *Richard Sargent* (a servant from
Ireland in the snow Dublin's Prize) to Samuel Rhoads of
Phila. carpenter, for four years from April 17th 1746.
Consideration £20: customary dues.

May 12th.

Robert Murphy in consideration of £17: paid for his
passage from Ireland indents himself servant to Joseph
Conyers of Phila. mariner, for four years, eleven months
and five days from this date, to be taught the art of navigation and when free to have given him one mariners compass, scale and quadrant, and one new suit of apparel
besides his old ones.

May 14th.

William Rankin assigns *James Murphy* (a servant from Ireland in the snow Dublin's Prize) to Francis Dunlap of Salem County, yeoman, for four years from April 17th 1746. Consideration £17: customary dues.

William Rankin assigns *Darby Glancy* (a servant from Ireland in snow Dublin's Prize) to Francis Dunlap of Salem county, yeoman, for four years from April 17th 1746. Consideration £17: customary dues.

William Rankin assigns *Richard Barrett* (a servant from Ireland in the snow Dublin's Prize) to George Walker of Chester county, yeoman, for four years from April 17th 1746. Consideration £17: customary dues.

William Powell with consent of his father Thomas Powell of Phila. county, yeoman, indents himself apprentice to Joseph Watkins of Phila. house-carpenter, for seven years from March 1st 1745, to be taught the trade of a carpenter, customary dues.

May 15th.

James McCabe in consideration of £15: paid to John Williams of Phila. cordwainer by James Cusick, blockmaker, for his use and at his request indents himself servant to James Cusick for three years and nine months from this date, customary dues.

John Hamilton in consideration of £14: paid Robert Chrysty by Alexander Forbes of Phila. for the remainder of his time, indents himself servant to said Alexander for six years and fifteen days from this date; to have customary dues.

May 17th.

William Rankin assigns *James Bradley* (a servant from Ireland in the snow Dublin's Prize) to George Rock of Maryland, merchant, for four years from April 17th 1746. Consideration £15: customary dues.

William Rankin assigns *Charles Delay* (a servant from Ireland in the snow Dublin's Prize) to George Rock of

Maryland, merchant, for four years from April 17th 1746. Consideration £15: customary dues.

William Rankin assigns *James McCay* (a servant from Ireland in the snow Dublin's Prize) to George Rock of Maryland merchant, for four years from April 17th 1746. Consideration £15: customary dues.

William Rankin assigns *Michael Dowd* (a servant from Ireland in the snow Dublin's Prize) to George Rock of Maryland, merchant, for seven years from April 17th 1746. Consideration £15: customary dues.

William Rankin assigns *John Steel* (a servant from Ireland in the snow Dublin's Prize) to Joseph England of Chester County, yeoman, for four years from April 17th 1746. Consideration £10: customary dues.

May 19th.

James Kelly, with consent of his father Edward Kelly, indents himself apprentice to Joseph Saull of Phila. chairmaker, for eight years and seven months from May 21st 1746, to be taught the trade of a chairmaker and spinningwheel maker, and to read, write and cipher, customary dues

William Holland with consent of his father Thomas Holland, indents himself apprentice to Thomas Gant of Phila. joiner, for four years and nine months from this date, to be taught the trade of a joiner, his father to find him in apparel the first year, and his master the remainder of his time, to have six weeks night schooling every winter to be paid for by his father.

Leonard Fisslar, in consideration of £25: paid to his father Felix Fisslar by John Knight of Phila. baker, indents himself servant to John Knight for three years from May 16th 1746, the said master to give him during his servitude three new pairs of shoes and stockings, and at the end of his time one new suit of apparel besides his old ones.

William Rankin assigns *Clevell Ormsby* (a servant from Ireland in the snow Dublin's Prize) to Adam Rhoads of Phila. carpenter, for four years from April 17th 1746. Consideration £18: customary dues.

William Rankin assigns *James McDonald* (a servant from Ireland in the snow Dublin's Prize) to George Cunningham of Phila. barber, from April 17th 1746. Consideration £16: 4/ customary dues.

Thomas David assigns *John Andrews* his servant to William Jacobs Esq. for the remainder of his time seven years from Nov. 2nd 1739. Consideration £2.

May 23rd.

John Stephens assigns *William Spence* his servant to Andrew Beers of Phila. County mason, for the remainder of his time three years from May 28th 1745. Consideration £14.

May 24th.

Jacob Grave, Jr., with consent of his father Jacob Grave, indents himself to John Hart, bricklayer, for four years from this date, to be taught the trade of a bricklayer, and at the end of his time to have one complete suit of new broadcloth clothes, besides his old ones. Twenty shillings in money and a trowel and stone hammer.

Henry Campbell in consideration £5: indents himself servant to George Fling of Phila. county for one year from this date to serve in the province of Penna. to have given him during his servitude two new shirts, one new pair of trousers, one new pair of shoes and stockings, but no freedom dues. The £5: was paid to Michael Carie.

May 26th.

Jacob Chilton in consideration of £9: 2: paid by Samuel Cheesman to Thomas Overy for his use and at his request indents himself servant to Samuel Cheesman for one year from this date; is to make six pairs of shoes every week during his servitude, no clothes or freedom dues.

May 27th.

William Wright in consideration £10: paid for his use by Christopher Parry of Phila. cutler, indents himself servant to said Christopher for three years from this date, customary dues.

May 28th.

Peter Stevens of Talbot County in Maryland indents himself apprentice to Isaac Roberts of Phila. bricklayer, for four years and seven months from this date, to be taught the trade of a bricklayer and to be found in apparel by said Isaac (shoes and stockings excepted) and at the expiration of the said term to have one new suit of apparel besides his old ones.

Edward Parrish of the province of Maryland with consent of his mother indents himself apprentice to Isaac Roberts of Phila. bricklayer for six years and nine months from this date, to be taught the trade of a bricklayer, and to have customary dues.

Jacob Newman assigns *Conried Abel* his servant to Nicholas P—— of Phila. taylor, for the remainder of his time eight years from Nov. 11th 1745. Consideration £9 : 15/ customary dues.

James Crawford assigns *John Gray* (a servant from Ireland in the snow Martha) to Thomas Overing of Phila. cordwainer, for six years from May 19th 1746. Consideration £15 : customary dues.

James Crawford assigns *Hannah Welsh* (a servant from Ireland in the snow Martha) to Peter Townsend of Chester County yeoman, for four years from May 19th 1746. Consideration £14 : customary dues.

James Crawford assigns *James Graham* (a servant from Ireland in the snow Martha) to Moses Coates of Chester county, yeoman, for four years from May 19th 1746. Consideration £14 : customary dues.

Conyngham and Gardner assign *Charles McLaughlin* (a servant from Ireland in the snow Martha) to Thomas David of Phila. County for seven years from May 19th 1746. Consideration £15 : customary dues.

Daniel O'Barr (from Ireland in the snow Martha) in consideration £15 : paid for his passage, indents himself apprentice to Thomas Grave of Phila. for seven years from this date, to be taught the trade of a hatter and to have customary dues.

Thomas Grave assigns *David O'Barr* his apprentice to Thomas Doyle of the borough of Lancaster, hatter, for seven years from date, to be taught the trade of a hatter, and to have customary dues.

James Crawford assigns *Patrick O'Hassan* (a servant from Ireland in the snow Martha) to Robert Edge of Phila. County farmer, for four years from May 19th 1746. Consideration £14: customary dues.

John McMullan assigns *Margaret Boyd* (a servant from Ireland in the snow Martha) to David Lindsay of Bucks County yeoman, for three years from May 19th 1746. Consideration £14: customary dues.

Conyngham & Gardner assign *William Corny* (a servant from Ireland in the snow Martha) to John Cook of Chester County yeoman, for seven years from May 19th 1746. Consideration £10: customary dues.

Conyngham & Gardner assign *Alexander Stewart* (a servant from Ireland in the snow Martha) to John Allison of Lancaster County, yeoman, for four years from May 19th 1746. Consideration £15: customary dues.

May 29th.

Henry Campbell in consideration of £15: paid for his use by Nicholas Gale of Phila. victualler, indents himself servant to the said Nicholas for three years and a half from this date, to have customary dues.

Authur Howard indents himself an apprentice to Nicholas Fennell of Phila. cordwainer, for five years and a quarter from this date to be taught the trade of a cordwainer and have customary dues, this done with consent of his last Master Richard Murray.

James Davison assigns *Ephraim Boggs* (a servant from Ireland in the snow Martha) to John Johnson of Phila. tallow-chandler, for four years and a half from May 19th 1746. Consideration £15: customary dues.

John Burns assigns *James O'Rogherty*, (a servant from Ireland in the snow Happy Return) to John Stephens of

Phila. innholder, for four years from May 21st 1746. Consideration £16 : customary dues.

John Burns assigns *Daniel Welsh* (a servant from Ireland in the snow Happy Return) to Richard Miller of Phila. flatman, for four years from May 21st 1746. Consideration £15 : customary dues.

Conynghara & Gardner assign *Mary Brown* (a servant from Ireland in the snow Martha) to John Steenson of Phila. for four years from May 19th 1746. Consideration £24 : customary dues.

May 30th.

John McMullan assigns *John O'Neal* (a servant from Ireland in the snow Martha) to Andrew Farrell of Phila. tanner, for four years from May 19th 1746. Consideration £10 : 10 : customary dues.

Conynghan & Gardener assigns *Mary McConagall* (a servant from Ireland in the snow Martha) to Daniel Hoops of Chester county yeoman, for four years from May 19th 1746. Consideration £14 : 10/ customary dues.

May 31st.

John Burne assigns *Edmund O'Harken* (a servant from Ireland in the snow Happy Return) to Archibald Alexander of Phila. county yeoman, for four years from May 21st 1746. Consideration £15 : customary dues.

John McMullan assigns *Hugh Boyd* (a servant from Ireland in the snow Martha) to Hugh Mearns of Bucks County, yeoman, for three years and a half from May 19th 1746. Consideration £11 : 17: customary dues.

George O'Kill assigns *Patrick Safen* (a servant from Liverpool in the snow Emisle) to Samuel Read of Phila. baker, for four years from May 22nd 1746. Consideration £20 : customary dues.

"ACCOUNT OF SERVANTS BOUND AND ASSIGNED BEFORE JAMES HAMILTON, MAYOR OF PHILA-DELPHIA."

CONTRIBUTED BY GEORGE W. NEIBLE, CHESTER, PENNA.

June 2nd.

Edward Turner assigns *John Branson* his servant to Foster Parks of Phila. laborer, for the remainder of his time five years from Oct. 2nd. 1743. Consideration £17: customary dues.

June 3rd.

Conyngham & Gardner assign *Robert Toplin* (a servant from Ireland in the snow Martha) to Francis Johnson of Phila. baker, for seven years from May 19th 1746. Consideration £16: customary dues.

Conyngham & Gardner assign *Daniel Stewart* (a servant from Ireland in the snow Martha) to Joshua Humphreys of Phila. county yeoman, for four years and a half from May 19th 1746. Consideration £14: customary dues.

June 4th.

James Templeton assigns *Duncan Mc Vea* (a servant from Ireland in the briggt. Couli Kan) to Thomas Griffith of Phila. county, yeoman, for four years from Nov. 1st 1745. Consideration £16:10/ customary dues.

James Crawford assigns *William Wasson* (a servant from Ireland in the snow Martha) to Hugh Mathews of Phila. county, doctor, for four years from May 19th 1746. Consideration £14.10/ customary dues.

William Pierce, a free mulatto man, indents himsel' apprentice to James Casick of Phila. blockmaker, for six years from this date, to be taught the trade of blockmaker and have customary dues.

June 5th.

Conynyham & Gardner assign *Hugh McLaughlin*, (a servant from Ireland in the snow Martha) to Isacc Whitelock of Lancaster for four years from May 19th 1746. Consideration £14: customary dues.

Thomas Doyle assigns *Clement Power* his apprentice to Farrell Riely of Phila. hatter, for the remainder of his time seven years from Jan. 18th 1744/5 Consideration £8: customary dues.

James Crawford assigns *Michael Clark* (a servant from Ireland in the snow Martha) to Ephraim Sitle of Lancaster County for four years from May 19th 1746. Consideration £13:15/ customary dues.

Jane Brown in consideration of £11: paid John Faris by John Dongale at her request indents herself servant to John Dongale for four years from this date, to have customary dues.

Bridget O'Hanly in consideration of £7:10/ paid to Gerard Nellson by John Dongale of Phila. at her request indents herself servant to said Dongale for two years and a half from this date, no freedom dues.

June 7th.

Archibald McKeghan, in consideration of £13:10/ paid for his passage from Ireland in the snow Happy Return indents himself servant to John Foulke of the borough of Lancaster, tanner, for four years from May 21st 1746, to be taught the trade of a tanner and have customary dues.

Robert Pendar, in consideration £15: paid at his request by Lodwick Hann of West Jersey, yeoman, indents himself servant for one year from this date, to be employed in keeping a school only, and to have a house found for him and his family, but no other accomodations.

James Crawford assigns *Margaret Usher* (a servant from Ireland in the snow Martha) to serve James McVaugh for four years from May 19th 1746, customary dues, this done before Samuel Hasell Esq. June 3rd. 1746.

Bryan Boyl (a servant from Ireland in the snow Happy Return) in consideration £12:10/ paid for his passage from Ireland to James Mitchell, indents himself apprentice to James Reynolds, mastmaker, to be taught the trade of a mastmaker and have customary dues.

James Mitchell assigns *James McCauley* (a servant from Ireland in the snow Happy Return) to William Cunningham of Lancaster County, yeoman, for seven years from May 21st, 1746.   Consideration £13:10/ customary dues.

Bryan O'Mullan (a servant from Ireland in the snow Happy Return) in consideration of £8: paid for his passage indents himself servant to George Graham of Phila. trader, for three years from this date, customary dues and one new suit.

June 9th.

George Ryal assigns *Mary Guerry* his servant to Thomas Broome of Phila. brickmaker, for the remainder of her time two years, three months and seventeen days from Aug. 12th 1745.   Consideration £6: customary dues.

James Mitchell assigns *Robert McCarroll* (a servant from Ireland in the snow Happy Return) to Charles Edgar of Phila. merchant for four years from May 21st 1746.   Consideration £10: customary dues.

Conyngham & Gardner assign *Anne Carroll* (a servant from Ireland in the snow Happy Return) to Charles Edgar of Phila. merchant for four years from May 21st 1746. Consideration £10: customay dues.

James Crawford assigns *Donald Seffert,* (a servant from Ireland in the snow Martha) to Samuel Scott of Lancaster County, yeoman, for six years from May 19th 1746.   Consideration £13: customary dues.

Samuel Cummins assigns *Patrick Montgomery* (a servant from Ireland in the ship Katherine) to Samuel Scott of Lancaster county for four years from May 29th 1746.   Consideration £13: customary dues.

Conyngham & Gardner assign *Margaret Larkan* (a servant from Ireland in the ship Katherine) to Patrick Morrough of Phila. County, yeoman, for four years from May 29th 1746. Consideration £14: customary dues.

Samuel Cummins assigns *Patrick Carlin* (a servant from Ireland in the ship Katherine) to Samuel Scott of Lancaster county for four years and a half from May 29th 1746. Consideration £13.10/ customary dues.

Conyngham & Gardner, *Mary O'Mullan* (a servant from Ireland in the ship Katherine) to Thomas Watson of Lancaster County, yeoman, for four years from May 29th 1746. Consideration £13: customary dues.

Conyngham & Gardner assign *Anne Battle* (a servant from Ireland in the ship Katherine to Thomas Watson of Lancaster County, yeoman, for four years from May 29th 1746. Consideration £13: customary dues.

June 10th.

Conyngham & Gardner assign *Charles Murray* (a servant from Ireland in the ship Katherine) to Evan Evans of Chester County for four years and a half from May 29th 1746. Consideration £15:10/: customary dues.

June 11th.

William McNemee assigns *James Keaven* (a servant from Ireland in the ship Katherine) to John Hunt of West Jersey for three years and a half from May 29th 1746. Consideration £15: customary dues.

Anthony Siddon assigns *John Russel* his servant to Rees Williams of Chester County yeoman, for the remainder of his time four years from June 25th 1745. Consideration £13: customary dues.

John Parrock assigns *Alexander Patterson* (a servant from Ireland in the ship Katherine) to Thomas Atkinson of Burlington County for four years from May 29th 1746. Consideration £16: customary dues in behalf of Jane Ash.

William McNemee assigns *Anne McGonogale* (a servant from Ireland in the ship Katherine) to Michael Jirael of Phila. County trader, for two years from May 29th 1746. Consideration £8.

Conyngham & Gardner assign *Mary McCandles* (a servant from Ireland in the ship Katherine) to Richard Richardson of Chester County for four years from May 29th 1746. Consideration £14 : customary dues.

Burton Daxson assigns *John Ahern* (a servant from Ireland in the Briggt. William) to William Young of Lancaster County yeoman for seven years from June 3rd. 1746. £16 : customary dues.

James Crawford assigns *Thomas Springham* (a servant from Ireland in the snow Martha) to Richard Richardson of Phila. county, yeoman, for four years from May 19th 1746. Consideration £16 : customary dues.

James Mitchell assigns *John Cairus* (a servant from Ireland in the snow Happy Return) to Andrew Boggs of Lancaster County yeoman, for four years from May 21st 1746. Consideration £14 : customary dues.

George Karr assigns *Charles Donelly* (a servant from Ireland in the snow Happy Return) to John Teass of Lancaster County yeoman, for four years from May 21st 1746. Consideration £12 : 10/ customary dues.

Thomas Karr assigns *Charles McSwiney* (a servant from Ireland in the snow Happy Return) to Henry Chambers of Lancaster County yeoman, for four years from May 21st 1746. Consideration £12 : customary dues.

Joseph Smith assigns *Lettice Jones* (a servant from Ireland in the ship Katherine) to Robert Smith of Lancaster County yeoman, for four years from May 29th 1746. Consideration £14 : customary dues.

Joseph Smith assigns *Oliver Jones* (a servant from Ireland in the ship Katherine) to Andrew Caldwell of Lancaster county, yeoman, for four years from May 29th 1746. Consideration £14: customary dues.

Conyngham & Gardner assign *Bryan Hammil* (a servant from Ireland in the ship Katherine) to George Entrican of Chester County, for seven years from May 29th 1746. Consideration £14 : customary dues.

Conyngham & Gardner assign *John McAlister* (a servant

from Ireland in the ship Katherine) to James Guthry of New Castle County for seven years from May 29th 1746. Consideration £13. Customary dues.

June 12th.

John Carrol in consideration of £14: paid William Crawford for his passage from Ireland in the ship Katherine indents himself servant to William Crosswhaile of Phila. peruke maker, for five years from May 29th 1746, to be taught the trade or mystery of a peruke maker and have customary dues.

John Gray assigns *Elinor Heley* (a servant from Ireland in the ship Katherine) to Samuel Coates of Chester County yeoman for four years and a half from May 29th 1746. Consideration £14: customary dues.

William McCrea assigns *William Stewart* (a servant from Ireland in the snow Happy Return) to John Atchison of Lancaster County, yeoman, for three years from May 21st 1746.

Henry Campbell in consideration of £20: paid at his request by Mary Shewbart of Phila. widow indents himself servant to Mary Shewbart for four years from this date, customary dues.

Burton Daxson assigns *Timothy Brian* (a servant from Ireland in the Briggt. William) to James Cooper of Burlington County yeoman for four years from June 3rd. 1746. Consideration £16: customary dues.

John Morrison assigns *William Campbell* (a servant from Ireland in the ship Katherine) to William Watt of Lancaster County, yeoman, for three years and a half from May 29th 1746. Consideration 5/:, customary dues.

William Crawford assigns *John Thompson* (a servant from Ireland in the ship Katherine) to Anthony Thompson of Phila. County, yeoman, for three years and a half from May 29th 1746. Consideration £17: customary dues.

John Brown with consent of his father Thomas Brown, brewer, doth bind himself apprentice to David Elwell of

Phila. house-carpenter, for six years from May 16th 1746, to be taught the trade of a house carpenter to have liberty to go to night school every winter at his father's expence, and at the end of his time to have one new suit of clothes, besides his old ones.

June 13th.

Samuel Watt assigns *John Robinson* (a servant from Ireland in the snow Martha) to David Davis of Phila. mariner, for six years from May 19th 1746. Consideration £14: customary dues.

June 14th.

Hugh Thomas assigns *Thomas Townsend* his servant to Thomas Tillberry of Phila. county, yeoman, the remainder of his time fifteen years and a half from April 19th 1734. Consideration 5/: customary dues.

Thomas Tillbury assigns *William Garnett* his servant to Hugh Thomas of Phila. County, yeoman, for the remainder of his time four years from July 2nd. 1745. Consideration 5/:, customary dues.

William Humphrys assigns *Martin Kelly* (a servant from Ireland in the ship Delaware) to Richard Buller of Chester County, yeoman, for four years from June 5th 1746. Consideration £15: customary dues.

William Humphreys assigns *James Gainier* (a servant from Ireland in the ship Delaware) to Thomas Quant of New Castle County, yeoman, for four years from June 5th 1746. Consideration £15: customary dues.

William Humphreys assigns *Patrick Begg* (a servant from Ireland in the ship Delaware) to Thomas Quant of New Castle County, yeoman, for four years from June 5th 1746, consideration £15: customary dues.

William Humphreys assigns *Thomas Johnson* (a servant from Ireland in the ship Delaware) to James Hunter of Chester County, yeoman, for four years from June 5th 1746. Consideration £15: 10/ customary dues.

William Hogan in consideration £18: paid to William Humphreys for his passage from Ireland in the ship Delaware by Alexander Alexander of Phila. blacksmith indents himself servant to Alexander Alexander for five years from this date, to be taught his trade, customary dues.

Grove Gillis assigns *John McKinley* (a servant from Ireland in the ship Katherine) to Anthony Wayne of Chester County yeoman, for seven years from May 29th 1746. Consideration £12 : 5/ customary dues.

William Humphreys assigns *Barnaby Egan* (a servant from Ireland in the ship Delaware) to William Wheldon of Phila. victualler, for five years from June 5th 1746. Consideration £15 : customary dues.

William Humphreys assigns *Michael Caughlan* (a servant from Ireland in the ship Delaware) to William Wheldon of Phila. victualler for four years from June 5th 1746. Consideration 15: customary dues.

June 16th.

Robert Breaden assigns *Daniel McGowan* (a servant from Ireland in the snow Happy Return) to William Lockard of Chester County, for four years and a half from May 26th 1746, customary dues, assigned before Edward Shippen Esq.

William Humphreys assigns *John Burgess* (a servant from Ireland in the ship Delaware) to John Ladeley of Phila. county, yeoman, for four years from June 5th 1746. Consideration £16 : Customary dues.

William Hall with consent of his uncle Robert Toms (his father and mother being dead indents himself apprentice to Abraham Mitchell of Phila. hatter, for eight years from March 1st 1745, to be taught the trade of a hatter, to have nine months schooling in winter evenings, and customary dues.

William Humphreys assigns *Morris Fonler* (a servant from Ireland in the ship Delaware) to Patrick McCamish of Phila. bricklayer, for four years from June 5th 1746. Consideration £14 : 10/ Customary dues.

Patrick Moran in Consideration of £15 : 10/ paid William Humphreys for his passage from Ireland, indents himself apprentice to David Davis of Chester county, weaver, for seven years from June 5th, 1746, to be taught the trade of a weaver, and have customary dues.

William Humphreys assigns *Patrick Coyle* (a servant from Ireland in the ship Delaware) to William Branson of Phila. Merchant, for four years from June 5th 1746. Consideration £24 : Customary dues.

William Humphreys assigns *Michael Dardie* (a servant from Ireland in the ship Delaware) to William Branson of Phila. Merchant, for four years from June 5th 1746. Consideration £24 : to have customary dues.

William Humphreys assigns *John Walsh* (a servant from Ireland in the ship Delaware) to John Bowen of Chester County yeoman, for four years from June 5th 1746 : Consideration £14 : Customary dues.

William Humphreys assigns *Thomas Walsh* (a servant from Ireland in the ship Delaware) to James Trego of Chester County, yeoman, for four years from June 5th 1746, customary dues, consideration £14 :

William Humphreys assigns *Mathew Steel* (a servant from Ireland in the ship Delaware) to Thomas Bowen of Chester County, yeoman, for four years from June 5th 1746. Consideration £14 : Customary dues.

William Humphreys assigns *John Bryan* (a servant from Ireland in the ship Delaware) to Peter Tyson of Phila. County yeoman, for four years from June 5th 1746. Consideration £15 : Customary dues.

William Humphreys assigns *Philip Donahue* (a servant from Ireland in the ship Delaware) to Samuel Lloyd of Kent County on Delaware yeoman, for four years from June 5th 1846. Consideration £15 : Customary dues.

William Humphreys assigns *Patrick McEvey* (a servant from Ireland in the ship Delaware) to Daniel Lowry of Lancaster County, yeoman, for four years from June 5th 1746. Consideration £15 : to have customary dues.

William Humphreys assigns *Robert Walker* (a servant from Ireland in the ship Delaware) to Lazarus Lowry of

Lancaster County yeoman, for four years from June 5th 1746. Consideration £15: to have customary dues.

June 17th.

William Humphreys assigns *Dennis Quirk* (a servant from Ireland in the ship Delaware) to John Kelly of Lancaster County, yeoman, for four years from June 5th 1746. Consideration £15:—Customary dues.

William Humphreys assigns *Dennis Conran* (a servant from Ireland in the ship Delaware) to James Lowry of Lancaster county, trader, for four years from June 5th 1746. Consideration £15: Customary dues.

Robert Campbell in consideration of £17: paid James Crawford for his passage from Ireland by Mr. Moore of Jamaica, mariner, indents himself apprentice to William Moore for six years from May 19th 1746, to be taught the mystery of a mariner and have customary dues.

Burton Daxton assigns *Sarah Bluet* (a servant from Ireland in the brig⁺ William) to Judah Foulke of Phila. for four years from June 3rd 1746. Consideration £15: Customary dues.

William Humphreys assigns *Patrick Fitzpatrick* (a servant from Ireland in the ship Delaware) to George Fudge of Phila. bricklayer, for four years from June 5th 1746. Consideration £15: Customary dues.

June 18th.

William McCrea assigns *Hugh Meenagh* (a servant from Ireland in the ship Catharine) to John McCool of Chester county yeoman, for four years from May 29th 1746. Consideration £14: customary dues.

William Humphreys assigns *Philip Bryan* (a servant from Ireland in the ship Delaware) to Evan Lloyd of Chester County yeoman, for five years from June 5th 1746. Consideration £15: customary dues.

June 19th.

William Humphreys assigns *Dennis Bryan* (a servant from

Ireland in the ship Delaware) to David Jenkin of Chester
County yeoman, for four years from June 5th 1746.   Consideration £15 :   customary dues.

Thomas Brady in consideration of £15 :   paid for his
passage from Ireland in the ship Delaware to William
Humphreys indents himself apprentice to Samuel John of
Chester County yeoman, for six years from June 5th 1746,
to be taught the trade of a weaver and to have customary
dues.

Burton Daxson assigns *James Kearney* (a servant from
Ireland in the brigt William) to George Wood of Chester
County for seven years from June 3rd. 1746 :   Considera-
tion £14 : 10/:   Customary dues

George Black son of Elizabeth Black widow, with consent
of his mother who signs his indenture binds himself apprentice to Hugh Hodge of Phila. tobacconist, for fifteen years
and four months from this date to be taught the trade of a
tobacconist in all its branches, to have three quarters of a
year day schooling and one quarter night schooling to learn
to read and write and customary dues.

William Humphreys assigns *Patrick McGuire* (a servant
from Ireland in the ship Delaware) to Joseph Wills of
Chester County, yeoman, for seven years from June 5th
1746.   Consideration £14 :   to have customary dues.

John Dawson assigns *Patrick Doran* (a servant from Ireland in the ship Katherine) to John Kalteringer of Phila.
taylor, for three years from May 29th 1746.   Consideration
£13 :   Customary dues.

June 20th.

Martha Cooper with consent of her father Thomas Cooper
who was present, indents herself servant to James Trueman
of Phila. Cooper, for six years from June 14th 1746, to be
taught plain work and housewifry, to have six months day
schooling and six months night schooling, to learn to read
and write, and at the end of her time to have one new suit
of apparel, besides her old ones, and three pounds in money.

Francis Valiant with consent of his master Samuel Garri-
gine who hath received of Capt. Charles Willing six pounds
for the remainder of his time indents himself apprentice to
Charles Willing for three years from this date, to be taught
the mystery of a Mariner, customary dues.

June 21st.

William Humphreys assigns *Thomas Carey* (a servant from
Ireland in the ship Delaware) to Robert Anderson of Bucks
County, yeoman, for four years from June 5th 1746. Con-
sideration £13.10/: Customary dues.

John Mathews son of *Robert Mathews* brewer, with consent
of his father indents himself apprentice to John Jones of
Phila. blacksmith, for six years and five months from this
date, to be taught the trade of a blacksmith, to have three
quarters night schooling at his father's expense, and customary dues.

William Humphreys assigns *Paul Mahony* (a servant from
Ireland in the ship Delaware) to John Lawton and Simon
Sherlock of Phila. shipwrights, for four years from June
5th. 1746. Consideration £21: customary dues.

William Humphreys assigns *William Foe* (a servant from
Ireland in the ship Delaware) to John Reardon of Phila.
Cordwainer, for four years from June 5th 1746. Considera-
tion £20: customary dues.

William Humphreys assigns *Bartholomew Dorham* (a servant from Ireland in the ship Delaware) to William Crad-
dock of Phila. taylor, for four years from June 5th 1746.
Consideration £18: customary dues.

June 23rd.

Conyngham & Gardner assigns *Moses Fisher* (a servant
from Ireland in the ship Katherine) to James Galbreith and
Robert Harris of Lancaster County, gentlemen, for five
years from May 29th 1746. Consideration £8: customary
dues.

Conyngham and Gardner assign *Anne McAfee* (a servant
from Ireland in the ship Katherine), to James Galbreith and

Robert Harris of Lancaster County gentlemen, for five years
from May 29th 1746.   Consideration £8: customary dues.

Mary Smith, with consent of her mother who signs her
indenture, indents herself apprentice to James Finley and
Margaret his wife for fourteen years from this date, to be
taught to read and write, and to sew plain work, and have
customary dues.

William Humphreys assigns *Daniel O'Daniel* (a servant
from Ireland in the ship Delaware) to John Johnson of
Bucks County, yeoman, for four years from June 5th 1746.
Consideration £17.10/ Customary dues.

Daniel Hiraghty (a servant from Ireland in the ship Delaware) in consideration £15: paid William Humphreys
indents himself a servant to John Evans of Phila. County,
taylor, for six years from June 5th 1746, to be taught the
trade of a taylor, and to have customary dues.

June 24th.

John Kelly in consideration of £18:   paid for his passage
from Ireland to William Humphreys by John Hallowell of
Phila. cordwainer, indents himself servant to said Hallowell
for five years from June 5th 1746, to be taught the trade of
a shoemaker and have customary dues.

William Humphreys assigns *Michael Lee* (a servant from
Ireland in the ship Delaware) to John Hambelton of Chester
County, yeoman, for four years from June 5th 1746.   Con-
sideration £15: customary dues

Timothy Buzard, with consent of his father Jacob Buzard
who was present, and in consideration of £15: paid to his
father, indents himself servant to George Harding of Phila.
skiner, for fourteen years from May 28th 1746, to be taught
to dress buck skins, and to have two winters schooling at
night, when he is twelve years old to learn to read and
write, and customary dues.

"ACCOUNT OF SERVANTS BOUND AND ASSIGNED
BEFORE JAMES HAMILTON, MAYOR OF PHILA-
DELPHIA."

CONTRIBUTED BY GEORGE W. NEIBLE, CHESTER, PENNA.

June 25th.

James Shute son of Jacob Shute of Philada., cooper with
consent of his parents indents himself apprentice to Robert
Adams of said city, cooper, for five years from June 23rd
1746, to be taught the trade of a cooper, to have two months
night schooling in every winter, during the said term, and
at the end of his time to have one new suit of apparel besides
his old ones, and £10 : in money.

Thomas Shute of Phila. attorney to Joseph Shute of Carolina, merchant, binds a negro boy of Joseph Shute named
Carolina, apprentice to John Garrigues of Phila. cooper, for
five years from June 9th 1746, to be taught the trade of a
cooper, but not to be found in clothes by said Garrigues.

James Shirley son of Mary Buckley of Gloucester County
with consent of his mother indents himself apprentice to
William Crossthwaite of Phila. peruke maker, for seven
years from this date, is to be taught the trade of a peruke
maker, to have three months half day schooling to learn to
read and write for the first three years and at the end of his
time the customary dues.

William Humphreys assigns *Thomas Brady* (a servant
from Ireland in the ship Delaware) to Robert Jones Jr. of
Phila. county, yeoman, for five years from June 5th 1746.
Consideration £13 : customary dues.

William Humphreys assigns *Patrick Kearnan* (a servant
from Ireland in the ship Delaware) to Robert Jones of

Chester County, yeoman, for four years from June 5th
1746. Consideration £14 : 10/ to have customary dues.

William Humphreys assigns *Michael Herbert* (a servant
from Ireland in the ship Delaware) to John Singleton of
Phila. lawyer, for four years from June 5th 1746. Consideration £14 : 10/ customary dues.

June 26th.

George House, Isaac Jones and Peter Robertson, overseers of the poor of the city of Phila., bind *Walter Savage*,
an orphan apprentice to William Morris of Lancaster County,
ffuler, for twelve years from this date, to be taught to read,
and have customary dues.

Burton Daxson assigns *Francis Henderson* (a servant from
Ireland in the brigt. William) to William Gilkinson of Ches-
ter County, yeoman, for four years from June 3rd. 1746.
Consideration £13 : customary dues.

June 28th.

Samson Davis with consent of his mother Christian Davis
binds himself apprentice to John Hall of Phila. County,
blacksmith, for five years and eight months from June
27th 1746, to have six months winter nights schooling,
and when free the customary dues and £10 : in money.

William McCrea assigns *Philip McLaughlan* (a servant
from Ireland in the snow Martha) to William Peters of
Phila. gentleman, for four years from May 19th 1746.
Consideration £17 : 10/ customary dues.

William Humphreys assigns *Edward Neal* (a servant from
Ireland in the ship Delaware) to Richard Bevan of Phila.
county, yeoman, for four years from June 5th 1746. Consideration £14 : to have customary dues.

June 30th.

Thomas Claybourn with the consent and approbation of
his friends John Searl and Samuel Carson indents himself
apprentice to Peter Hatton of Phila. cooper, for five years

from April 1st 1746. to be taught the trade of a cooper and have customary dues.

Elinor Coughlan, in consideration £14 : paid Burton Daxson for her passage from Ireland in the brigt. William, indents herself servant to Lawrence Little of Phila. county yeoman, for four years from June 8d. 1746, to have customary dues.

Mary Planket widow, binds her daughter *Mary Planket* to Gideon Brasmon and Katherine his wife for ten years and five months from this date and give £8 : with her, the said infant to be taught to read, write and sew linen, and at the end of her time to have given to her two complete suits of apparel, one of which is to be new.

Charles Edgar assigns *John Healy* (a servant from Ireland in the ship Delaware) to Nathan Seevie of Chester county yeoman for four years from June 5th 1746. Consideration £15 : customary dues.

July 1st.

John Roe in consideration of £21 : 10/ paid by William Wheldon of Phila. victualler, to Dr. Thomas Greene for his use and at his request indents himself servant to William Wheldon for four years from this date, no freedom dues.

July 2nd.

Joseph Smith assigns *Elizabeth McNalton* (a servant from Ireland in the ship Katherine) to Peacock Bigger of Phila. coppersmith, for four years from May 29th 1746. Consideration £14 : customary dues.

July 3d.

Conyngham and Gardner assign *Thomas Mullen* (a servant from Ireland in the ship Katherine) to Charles Mullen or West Jersey yeoman, for four years from May 29th 1746. Consideration £14 : customary dues.

William Humphreys assigns *George Vance* (a servant from Ireland in the ship Delaware) to John Moore of Phila. yeo-

man for four years from June 5th 1746.   Consideration
£14 : 10/ customary dues.

James Eldridge son of Elizabeth Norton of Cape May with
consent of his mother signified by —————— indents himself
apprentice to Augustine Allman of Phila. cordwainer, for
six years and four months from this date, to be taught the
trade of a shoemaker and have customary dues.

July 4th.

William Humphreys assigns *John Egan* (a servant from
Ireland in the ship Delaware) to Abraham Coates of Phila.
county for four years from June 5th 1746.   Consideration
£16 : customary dues.

Cornelius McDermott in consideration of £7 : paid for his
use by Joseph Love of Virginia, trader, indents himself a
servant to said Joseph for one year from this date to have
one shirt, one pair shoes, one jacket and two pair moccasins
all new, as they become necessary.

July 5th.

Benjamin Sashley in consideration of £8 : paid for his
passage from Ireland by Archibald Thorp of Phila. cordwainer, indents himself a servant to the said Archibald for
one year from June 18th 1746, no apparel nor freedom dues.

July 8th.

William Adams assigns *Philip Lenehan* his servant for the
remainder of his time to Richard Smith of Phila. porter,
for four years from August 29th 1743.   Consideration £9 :
customary dues.

William Davenport in consideration £10 : paid Edward
Dowers for his passage from Liverpool by Voisall Chubb of
Phila. merchant, indents himself servant to said Voisall
Chubb for three years from this date, to have customary dues.

July 11th.

Samuel McCall assigns *Joseph Davison* his servant for the
remainder of his time to William Arbour of Phila. yeoman

for four years from June 15th 1745. Consideration £19: to have customary dues.

July 12th.

George Guion assigns *John Kennan* (a servant from Ireland in the snow Happy Return) to George Craughon of Lancaster County, trader, for four years from June 5th 1746. Consideration £14: customary dues.

July 14th.

Conyngham and Gardner assign *Dougal Boyd* (a servant from Ireland in the Belinda) to Samuel Vernon of Phila. County yeoman, for five years from July 3d. 1746. Consideration £14: customary dues.

July 15th.

James Campbell with consent of his mother Anne Green indents himself apprentice to Stephen Armit of Phila. joiner, for four years and thirteen days from this date, to be taught the trade of a joiner, his master to give him in the first year of his apprenticeship two new pairs of stockings and shoes, and to find him in every kind of apparel during the rest of his time, to have liberty to go to school three months in winter evenings and customary dues.

Conyngham and Gardner assign *Daniel Brown* (a servant from Ireland in the Belinda) to William Woppler of Lancaster County gentleman, for four years from July 3rd 1746. Consideration £15. customary dues.

Conyngham and Gardner assign *Margaret Rorty* (a servant from Ireland in the Belinda) to Edward William of Phila. County yeoman, for four years from July 3rd. 1746. Consideration £13 : 10/ customary dues.

Conyngham and Gardner assign *Margaret Right* (a servant from Ireland in the Belinda) to Edward Goff of Chester County yeoman, for four years from July 3rd. 1746. Consideration £12 : 10/ customary dues

Conyngham and Gardner assign *Thomas Right* (a servant from Ireland in the Belinda) to Edward Goff of Chester

County yeoman, for five years from July 3rd. 1746. Consideration £12 : 10/ customary dues.

Conyngham & Gardner assign *Bridget McHendry* (a servant from Ireland in the Belinda) to Joseph Paxton of Trenton, merchant, for five years from July 3rd. 1746. Consideration £15 : customary dues.

Conyngham and Gardner assign *John Smith* (a servant from Ireland in the Belinda) to Thomas Hootton of Trenton, tavernkeeper, for five years from July 3rd. 1746. Consideration £14 : customary dues.

Conyngham and Gardner assign *Sarah Right* (a servant from Ireland in the Belinda) to George Walker of Chester County yeoman, for six years from July 3d. 1746. Consideration £13 : customary dues.

Conyngham and Gardner assign *George Atchison* (a servant from Ireland in the Belinda) to George Gibson of the Borough of Lancaster for five years from July 3d. 1746. Consideration £14 : customary dues.

Burton Daxson assigns *Timothy Scannell* (a servant from Ireland in the brigt. William) to William Spafford of Phila. City, mariner, for seven years from June 3rd. 1746. Consideration £16 : customary dues.

Conyngham and Gardner assign *Anne Rorty* (a servant from Ireland in the Belinda) to Hamilton Rogers of Bucks County, yeoman, for four years from July 3rd. 1746. Consideration £12 : 10/ customary dues.

July 16th.

Thomas Deane now of Phila. indents himself apprentice to Michael Caris of Phila. jeweler, for three years from June 1st 1746. to be taught the trade of a jeweler, and when free to have the customary dues.

Edmund Bourk assigns *Matthew McCully* his servant for the remainder of his time three years from October 31st 1745, to John Reardon of Phila., cordwainer. Consideration £14; customary dues.

Charles Dennison in consideration of £13: paid for his passage from Ireland to Walter Goodman by Samuel Flower of Chester County indents himself servant to Samuel Flower for four years from June 3rd. 1746, customary dues.

Patrick Patterson in consideration of £13: paid Walter Goodman for his passage from Ireland by Capt. Samuel Flower of Chester County indents himself servant to Samuel Flower for four years from June 3rd. 1746, to have customary dues.

Burton Daxon assigns *Edward Murphy* (a servant from Ireland in the brigt. William) to Samuel Flower of Chester County for four years from June 3rd. 1746. Consideration £13. customary dues.

Burton Daxon assigns *Catherine Carthy* (a servant from Ireland in the brigt. William) to Samuel Flower of Chester County for four years from June 3rd. 1746. Consideration £13: customary dues.

Burton Daxon assigns *Owen Sullivan* (a servant from Ireland in the brigt. William) to Samuel Flower of Chester County for four years from June 3rd. 1746. Consideration £13: customary dues

Burton Daxon assigns *William Daly* (a servant from Ireland in the brigt. William) to Samuel Flower of Chester County for four years from June 3rd. 1746. Consideration £13: customary dues.

Burton Daxon assigns *John Falls* (a servant from Ireland in the brigt. William) to Samuel Flower of Chester County for four years from June 3rd. 1746, customary dues.

July 17th.

Conyngham and Gardner assign *Thomas Mitchell* (a servant from Ireland in the Belinda) to Benjamin Davis of Phila. County for four years from July 3rd. 1746. Consideration £15: customary dues.

David Lindsay with consent of his mother Bershaba binds himself apprentice to Jacob Shoemaker of Phila. turner, for six years from this date to be taught the trade of a turner

to have five months evening or half day schooling and when
free to have one new suit of apparel besides his old ones.

July 18th.

William Humphreys assigns *Peter Karvin* (a servant from
Ireland in the ship Delaware) to Colen Johnston of Phila.
taylor, for four years from June 5th 1746.   Consideration
£20 : customary dues.

Conyngham and Gardner assign *John Burr* (a servant
from Ireland in the Belinda) to John Towers of Phila.
skinner, for seven years from July 3d. 1746.   Consideration
£14 : customary dues.

Conyngham and Gardner assign *Mary McBride* (a servant
from Ireland in the Belinda) to John Hunt of Burlington
County yeoman, for four years from July 3rd. 1746.   Consideration £13 : 15 customary dues.

July 19th.

John Trainer in consideration of £30 : paid to him by
Frederick Wambold of Phila. County, yeoman, indents
himself servant to said Frederick Wambold for three years
from this date, to be found in apparel to have when free
three axes, but no freedom dues.

Conyngham and Gardner assign *Christopher McKinney*
(a servant from Ireland in the Belinda) to Thomas Morris
of Chester County yeoman, for four years from July 3rd.
1746.   Consideration £12 : customary dues.

Conyngham and Gardner assign *John O'Donnell* (a servant
from Ireland in the Belinda) to Joshua Morris of Phila.
county, yeoman, for four years from July 3d. 1746.   Consideration £12 : 15/ to have customary dues.

July 21st.

John McKoun with consent of his uncle Finley McKoun
and in consideration of £8 : paid Conyngham and Gardner
for his passage from Ireland indents himself servant to Jonas
Osbourn of Phila. lace-weaver, for ten years and a half from

this date to be taught to read, write, and cipher as far as
the rule of three and the art or mystery of a lace-weaver,
and at the end of his time to have the customary dues.

July 22nd.

John Branigan with consent of his uncle Finley McKoun
and in consideration £5 : 7/ paid Conyngham and Gardner
for his passage from Ireland indents himself servant to Jonas
Osbourn of Phila. lace-weaver for eleven years and a half
from this date to be taught to read, write and cipher as far
as the rule of three, and the art or mystery of a lace-weaver,
and when free to have the customary dues.

William Gammon with consent of his father William Gammon indents himself apprentice to Edward Windor of Phila.
pavier for six years from this date, to be taught to write and
cipher as far as the rule of three, and the trade of a pavier,
and when free to have customary dues.

Elizabeth Hamilton with consent of her mother Rebecca
indents herself apprentice to Susanna Fassell for twelve
years four months and fifteen days from June 24th 1746, to
be taught housewifry and to read and write and when free
to have the customary dues.

Conyngham and Gardner assign *David Linch* (a servant
from Ireland in the Belinda) to Robert Whartentby of Phila.
County yeoman, for five years from July 3rd. 1746. Consideration £16., to have customary dues.

July 23rd.

Michael Crapp with consent of his father Simon Crapp
and in consideration of £2 : paid his said father by Jacob
Maack of Phila. shopkeeper, indents himself servant to said
Jacob for seven years and five months from this date, when
free to have customary dues and £3 : in money.

Thomas Norrington assigns *Hugh Carbery* his servant for
the remainder of his time to John Justis of Phila. County
yeoman, for six years from May 11th 1745. Consideration

£14: customary dues and the said Hugh releases the covenant whereby he was to be taught the trade of a loaf bread maker.

July 25th.

William Hughs assigns *Mary Catharine Herth* his servant to Peter Vanaken jr. of Bucks County yeoman for the remainder of her time for eight years from March 13th 1741/2. Consideration £11: customary dues.

July 26th.

Edward Layne in consideration of £14: in hand paid indents himself servant to William Peters of Phila. gentleman for one year from this date to have given him one pair of shoes and one hat, but no freedom dues.

Michael Frederick in consideration of £24: in hand paid by Marcus Kuyhl of Phila. baker, indents himself servant to the said Marcus for two years from this date, not to have any freedom dues.

July 28th.

George Rock assigns *James Bradley* his servant for the remainder of his time for four years from April 17th 1746, to John Langdate of Phila. Consideration £15: customary dues.

William Topham with consent of his father Matthias Topham indents himself apprentice to Eden Haydock of Phila. glazier for six years and eleven months from this date, to be taught the trade of a glazier, plumber and painter, and to read, write and cipher as far as the rule of three; freedom dues.

Jacob Pinckney of Phila. hatter, indents himself servant to Abraham Mitchell of Phila. hatter for two years from this date Consideration sundry sums of money paid for his use, to be found in apparel, and when free to have ten pounds in money, but no freedom dues.

July 29th.

Robert Worrell assigns *Shadrick Sord* his servant to John Elliot of Phila. cordwainer, for the remainder of his

time four years from May 19th 1744.   Consideration £16 :
customary dues.

July 30th.

George House, Isaac Jones and Peter Robertson, overseers of the poor of Phila. bind *Susanna Whitfield* an apprentice to Ruth Adams of Phila. shopkeeper for eight years
and ten months from this date, to be taught to read and
write and sew plain work and housewifry and when free to
have two suits of apparel one whereof to be new.

William Humphreys assigns *Robert Crawford* (a servant
from Ireland in the ship Delaware) to Robert Hows of Phila.
Surveyor for four years from June 5th 1746.   Consideration £14 : customary dues.

Robert Stevenson assigns *Patrick Kennedy* (a servant from
Ireland in the Belinda) to John Jones of Phila. pilot for ten
years from July 3rd, 1746.   Consideration £13 : customary
dues.

July 31st.

Mathew Garrigues jr. son of Mathew Garrigues indents
himself apprentice with consent of his father, to John Garrigues of Phila. cooper for fifteen years and nine months from
this date, to be taught the trade of a cooper, to read, to
write and to have customary dues.

August 1st.

William Blanchfield assigns *Morgan McMahon* his servant
to Richard Smith of Phila. butcher, for the remainder of
his time, for two years and nine months from January 18th
1745.   Consideration £8 : customary dues.

William Thomas in consideration of £20 : paid by George
Walker of Chester County, yeoman, to Mathias Larney at
his request indents himself a servant to the said George
Walker for six years from this date to have customary dues.

August 4th.

Barnaby Egin in consideration of £15 : paid at his request
by Thomas Griffith of Phila. hatter, indents himself appren-

tice to Thomas Griffiths for seven years from this date,
to be taught the trade or mystery of a hatter, and have
customary dues.

August 5th.

Conyngham and Gardner assign *Daniel O'Mullan* (a servant
from Ireland in the Belinda) to John Wells of Gloucester
County yeoman, for four years from July 3rd. 1746.   Consideration £14: customary dues.

August 6th.

John Davis of Phila mariner, indents himself apprentice
to Michael Sisk of the said city plasterer, for three years
from this date, to have given him three quarters schooling
at an evening school, to learn to read and write, and
when free the customary dues.

August 7th.

William Geddes assigns *James Carey* (a servant from Ire-
land in the snow Chester) to James Cummins of Bucks
County, yeoman, for four years from August 3rd. 1746.
Consideration £14: 15/ customary dues.

William Geddes assigns *Bryan Burks* (a servant from Ireland in the snow Chester) to Joseph Obourn of Phila.
tallow-chandler, for five years from August 3rd. 1746.
Consideration £16: to have customary dues.

George Hatfield assigns *Catherine Shueman* his servant for
the remainder of her time eleven years from October 6th
1740, to Edward Warner of Phila house-carpenter.   Consideration £16: customary dues.

William Wheldon assigns *John Roe* his servant for the
remainder of his time four years from July 1st 1746 to
Thomas Potts of Phila. County, iron master.   Consideration half a ton of bar iron, to have customary dues.

Abigail Petro assigns *Mary Magrogan* her servant for the
remainder of her time seven years from October 5th 1745,

to John Bell of Chester County.   Consideration £11 : 10/
customary dues.

August 8th.

William Geddes assigns *John Reiley* (a servant from Ireland in the snow Chester) to Oliver Williams of Phila.
skinner, for four years from August 3rd 1746.   Consideration £17 : customary dues.

August 9th.

Nathaniel Ambler assigns *George Keate* (a servant from
Ireland in the snow George) to Alexander Alexander of
Phila. blacksmith, for seven years from August 2d. 1746.
Consideration £16 : customary dues.

August 11th.

William Humphreys assigns *Thomas Martin* (a servant
from Ireland in the ship Delaware) to Joseph Shippen and
Jonathan Robeson for four years from June 5th 1746.   Consideration £15 : customary dues.

William Humphreys assigns *Ferdinando O'Neil* (a servant
from Ireland in the ship Delaware) to Joseph Shippen and
Jonathan Robeson for four years from June 5th 1746.
Consideration £15 : customary dues.

Nathaniel Ambler assigns *Thomas Stapleton* (a servant from
Ireland in the snow George) to William Sandwith of Phila.
tallow-chandler, for four years from August 2nd. 1746.
Consideration £18 : customary dues.

John Reardon assigns *Mathew MCalley* his servant for the
remainder of his time three years from October 31st 1745,
to Alexander Moore of Phila. peruke-maker.   Consideration £14 : customary dues.

Peter Sponers late of Maryland indents himself apprentice
to John Reardon of Phila. cordwainer, for five years from
this date to have three quarters evening schooling to learn
to read and write, to be taught the trade of a cordwainer,
to have customary dues.

George Blair for Thomas Walker and company assigns *Andrew McKeesan* (a servant from Ireland in the snow Chester) to Arnold Pendar of Chester County yeoman, for four years from August 3rd 1746. Consideration £15: customary dues.

Blair and Irvine assign *William Couples* (a servant from Ireland in the snow Chester) to Alexander Mabane of Lancaster county yeoman, for four years from August 3rd. 1746. Consideration £15: customary dues.

Nathaniel Ambler assigns *Luke Sexton* (a servant from Ireland in the snow George) to Robert Dawson of Phila. shop-keeper for four years from August 2nd. 1746. Consideration £16: customary dues.

William Humphreys assigns *Francis O'Neill* (a servant from Ireland in the ship Delaware) to Joseph Shippen and Jonathan Robeson for four years from June 5th 1746. Consideration £15: customary dues.

William Humphreys assigns *Hugh Goohegan* (a servant from Ireland in the ship Delaware) to Joseph Shippen and Jonathan Robeson for four years from June 5th 1746. Consideration £15: customary dues.

George Patterson assigns *Elizabeth Recey* (a servant from Ireland in the snow Chester) to Samuel Cheesman of Phila. cordwainer, for four years from August 3rd. 1746. Consideration £14: customary dues.

George Wakely assigns *Esther Wakely* (a servant from Ireland in the snow George) to Methusaleth Davis of Chester County yeoman, for four years from Aug. 2d. 1746. Consideration £14: customary dues.

George Wakely assigns *Susannah Sanders* (a servant from Ireland in the snow George) to John Moland of Phila. county for four years August 2nd 1746. Consideration £14: customary dues.

George Patterson assigns *Robert Conn* (a servant from Ireland in the snow Chester) to John Jones of Germantown, tanner, for four years from August 3rd, 1746. Consideration £16: customary dues.

Nathaniel Ambler assigns *Charles Smith* (a servant from Ireland in the snow George) to George Bradley of Phila. shopkeeper for four years from August 2nd 1746. Consideration £18 : customary dues.

Nathaniel Ambler assigns *James Hogan* (a servant from Ireland in the snow George) to Benjamin Engle of Germantown, tanner, for seven years from August 2nd 1746. Consideration £15 : customary dues.

August 12th.

Nathaniel Ambler assigns *Miles Aske* (a servant from Ireland in the snow George) to Jonathan Darell of Phila. potter, for seven years from August 2nd. 1746. Consideration £16 : customary dues.

George Blair (for Thomas Walker and Co.) assigns *Thomas Mucklegun* (a servant from Ireland in the snow Chester) to Andrew McClemont of Kent County for four years from August 3rd. 1746. Consideration £16 : customary dues.

George Blair for David Cowpland, assigns *Philemy Boylan* (a servant from Ireland in the snow Chester) to John Dobbins of Phila. blacksmith, for five years from August 3rd. 1746. Consideration £17 : customary dues.

George Wakely assigns *William Fox* (a servant from Ireland in the snow George) to John Davis of Chester County yeoman, for seven years from August 2nd. 1746. Consideration £15 : customary dues.

Nathaniel Ambler assigns *Michael Malone* (a servant from Ireland in the snow George) to Thomas Robinson of Phila. blacksmith, for six years from August 2nd 1746. Consideration £17 ; customary dues.

Mary Hamilton in consideration of £10 : paid Abram Shelly by James Webb of Lancaster County, mason, indents himself servant to the said James for four years from this date, when free to have customary dues.

Nathaniel Ambler assigns *Dennis Dunn* (a servant from Ireland in the snow George) to Joseph Walton of Phila.

County for four years from August 2nd. 1746.   Consideration £18 : customary dues.

August 13th.

James Cleaver in consideration of his passage from Ireland
in the snow Martha indents himself servant to James Crawford for three years from this date, to have customary dues.

John Littledale indents himself servant to Joseph Kaighin
of Gloucester County yeoman, for two years from this date.
Consideration £7 : 3 : advanced and paid for his use and at
his request, no freedom clothes.

Anne Betty assigns *Nicholas Hays* (a servant from Ireland
in the snow Chester) to William Scott of Phila. taylor, for
four years from August 3rd. 1746.   Consideration £18 :
customary dues.

Nathaniel Ambler assigns *Bryan Kelly* (a servant from
Ireland in the snow George) to·John Dougharty of Chester
County, yeoman, for four years from August 2nd. 1746.
Consideration £17 : customary dues.

George Patterson assigns *Andrew Neelson* (a servant from
Ireland in the snow Chester) to Daniel Craig of Bucks
county yeoman, for four years from August 3rd. 1746.
Consideration £16 : 10/ customary dues.

"ACCOUNT OF SERVANTS BOUND AND ASSIGNED BEFORE JAMES HAMILTON, MAYOR OF PHILA-DELPHIA."

CONTRIBUTED BY GEORGE W. NEIBLE, CHESTER, PENNA.

August 14th.

Peter Conolly indents himself apprentice to Samuel Evans of Phila. mason and bricklayer, for four years and a half from this date, to be taught the trade of bricklayer and mason, and when free to have customary dues, and to the exc. for the said Samuel Evans.

Hugh Diver, in consideration of £14: paid James Carr at his request indents himself servant to Maurice and Edmund Nihil of Phila. brewers for three years wanting four days from this date, customary dues.

Nathaniel Ambler assigns *John Martin* (a servant from Ireland in the snow George), to William Adiddle of Phila. County yeoman, for four years from August 2nd. 1746. Consideration £19: customary dues.

August 15th.

Conyngham and Gardner assign *Alexander McCallister,* (a servant from Ireland in the Belinda) to Joseph Nicholls of New Castle county yeoman, for two years from July 3rd. 1746. Consideration £7: customary dues.

George Wakely assigns *Anne Ellis* (a servant from Ireland in the snow George) to Samuel Vanburkilow of Phila. cordwainer, for four years from August 2nd. 1746. Consideration £15: customary dues.

George Patterson assigns *Sarah Crafeart* (a servant from Ireland in the snow Chester) to James Johnson of Lancaster

county, yeoman, for four years from August 3rd. 1746.
Consideration £14: customary dues.

Archibald Campbell in consideration of £14: paid Conyngham and Gardner for his passage, indents himself servant
to Jeremiah Vastinie for three years and two months from
this date to be taught to read, and have customary dues.

Blair and Irvine assign *Daniel Brady* (a servant from Ireland in the snow Chester) to William Hudson of Phila. for
four years from August 3rd. 1746. Consideration £19:
customary dues.

John Behman son of Nathaniel Behman with consent of
his father who signs his indenture, indents himself apprentice to Archibald Thorp of Phila. cordwainer, for fifteen
years and a half from this date, to be taught to read write
and cypher as far as the rule of three, and the trade of a
cordwainer, when free to have customary dues.

Nathaniel Ambler assigns *John Coply* (a servant from Ireland in the snow George) to Alexander Morgan of Gloucester County yeoman, for four years from August 2nd 1746.
Consideration £16: customary dues.

Nathaniel Ambler assigns *John Coffee* (a servant from Ireland in the snow George) to Thomas Griffith of Chester
county yeoman, for six years from August 2nd. 1746. Consideration £15: customary dues.

Nathaniel Ambler assigns *John McCawley* (a servant from
Ireland in the snow George) to John Tyson of Phila. county
yeoman, for four years from August 2nd. 1746. Consideration £7: 10/ customary dues.

Blair and Irvine assign *Neal O' Neil* (a servant from Ireland
in the snow Chester) to Barak Wright of Germantown, tanner, for four years from August 3rd. 1746. Consideration
£16: customary dues.

Nathaniel Ambler assigns *Owen Kerigan* (a servant from
Ireland in the snow George) to Bernard Reiser of Phila.

county yeoman, for six years from August 2nd. 1746. Consideration £16 : customary dues.

William Harris assigns *Mary Hear* (a servant from Ireland in the snow Chester) to David Chambers of Phila. shopkeeper, for four years from August 3rd. 1746. Consideration £14 : customary dues.

John Heaton indents himself apprentice to David Cane of Phila. joiner, for eighteen months from this date, to be taught the trade of a chairmaker, to have during his apprenticeship two new shirts, one new jacket and pair new shoes, but no freedom dues.

Michael Ark in consideration of £16 : paid Nathaniel Ambler for his passage from Ireland indents himself servant to John Ristine of Phila. county, tanner, for six years from August 2nd. 1746, to be taught the trade of a tanner and have customary dues.

Thomas Duke in consideration £15 : 15/. paid Nathaniel Ambler for his passage from Ireland indents himself servant to Baltel Roser of Phila. county, tanner for five years from August 2nd 1746, to be taught the trade of a tanner and have customary dues.

James Ray for divers good consideration indents himself apprentice to Conrad Waldegar of Phila. butcher for six years from this date, to be taught the trade of a butcher and have customary dues.

Nathaniel Ambler assigns *Owen Reily* (a servant from Ireland in the snow George) to Silas Parvin of Phila. shallopman, for four years from August 2nd. 1746. Consideration £15 : customary dues.

Nathaniel Ambler assigns *Robert Jones* (a servant from Ireland in the snow George) to Silas Parvin of Phila. shallopman, for four years from August 2nd 1746. Consideration £15 : customary dues.

Nathaniel Ambler assigns *Dennis Callaghan* (a servant from Ireland in the snow George) to Lewis Davis of Chester county yeoman, for five years from August 2nd 1746. Consideration £14 : 10/ customary dues.

Georgu Wakely assigns *Thomas Riely* (a servant from Ireland in the snow George) to Joseph Williams of Phila. county yeoman for four years from August 2nd 1746. Consideration £15 : customary dues.

August 19th.

Nathaniel Ambler assigns *John Clark* (a servant from Ireland in the snow George) to Henry Crooks of Bucks County yeoman, for five years from August 2nd 1746. Consideration £16 : customary dues.

Anne Betty assigns *Charles McGauren* (a servant from Ireland in the snow Chester) to Isaac Whitelock of Lancaster, tanner, for four years from August 3rd 1746. Consideration £15 : customary dues.

Nathaniel Ambler assigns *John Gory* (a servant from Ireland in the snow George) to Thomas Norrington of Phila. baker, for five years from August 2nd 1746. Consideration £15 : customary dues.

William Cunningham indents himself servant to Robert Mathews of Phila. brewer for three years from this date, to have given him three pairs of new shoes and two pairs of new stockings during his servitude but no freedom dues. Consideration paying for his passage.

August 20th.

Nathaniel Ambler assigns *Garret Murray* (a servant from Ireland in the snow George) to Richard Pritchard of Chester County, blacksmith, for four years from August 2nd 1746. Consideration £18 : 10/ customary dues.

August 21st.

James Cunningham, with consent of his father George Cunningham who was present, indents himself apprentice to William Greenway of Phila. mariner, for six years from this date, to be taught navigation and the mystery of a sailor, and customary dues.

Anne Garraway by consent of her mother Abigail Frederick who signs her indenture in consideration of £3 : paid her mother, indents herself servant to Jacob Cooper of Phila. shopkeeper, for nine years and one month from this date, customary dues.

Alexander Williams late of Antequa indents himself apprentice to John Scull of the Northern Liberties, house carpenter, for four years, three months and a half from this date, to be taught the trade of house carpenter, and have customary dues.

August 22nd.

Nathaniel Ambler assigns *Hugh Gillan* (a servant from Ireland in the snow George) to James Fullerton of Somerset County in East Jersey, yeoman, for four years from August 2nd 1746. Consideration £17 : customary dues.

Nathaniel Ambler assigns *Thomas Caray* (a servant from Ireland in the snow George) to Peter McDowell of Somerset County in East Jersey, yeoman, for four years from August 2nd 1746. Consideration £15 : customary dues.

Martin McVeagh in consideration £8 : paid for his use and at his request indents himself servant to Samuel Hastings of Phila. shipwright for one year from this date, to have two new check shirts, and two pair of new shoes, during his servitude, but no freedom dues.

August 23rd.

Nathaniel Ambler assigns *James Wood* (a servant from Ireland in the snow George) to John Cleland of Lancaster County yeoman, for four years from August 2nd 1746. Consideration £15 : customary dues.

George Wakely assigns *James Boyle* (a servant from Ireland in the snow George) to Ephraim Leech of Phila. county yeoman, for four years from August 2nd 1746. Consideration £15 : customary dues.

Joseph Turner assigns *Thomas Knight*, late servant to Richard Trappell, to Edward Brooke of Phila. butcher, for five years from January 18th 1744, to be taught the trade of a butcher and have customary dues.

August 25th.

Nathaniel Ambler assigns *Thomas Conolly* (a servant from Ireland in the snow George) to Randall Malin of Chester County yeoman, for four years from August 2nd 1746. Consideration £15˙: 10/ customary dues.

Nathaniel Ambler assigns *Patrick Fitzgerald* (a servant from Ireland in the snow George) to Benjamin Watkin of Phila. county, yeoman, for four years from August 2nd 1746. Consideration £15 : 10/ customary dues.

Nathaniel Ambler assigns *Arthur Sacheverdrall* (a servant from Ireland in the snow George) to Patrick Ogilby of Bucks County yeoman, for four years from August 2nd 1746. Consideration £16 : customary dues.

Nathaniel Ambler assigns *Thomas Dillon* (a servant from Ireland in the snow George) to Benjamin Gilbert of Bucks County yeoman, for five years from August 2nd 1746. Consideration £16 : customary dues.

John McClean in consideration £16 : paid for his passage from Ireland indents himself apprentice to Farrel Reiley of Phila. hatter for five years from this date, to be taught the trade or mystery of a hatter and have customary dues.

August 27th.

Nathaniel Ambler assigns *Peter Perkins* (a servant from Ireland in the snow George) to David Jones of Lancaster County yeoman, for seven years from August 2nd 1746. Consideration £15 : customary dues.

Nathaniel Ambler assigns *Cormack Conolly* (a servant from Ireland in the snow George) to David Jones of Lancaster county yeoman, for four years from August 2nd 1746. Consideration £15 : customary dues.

Nathan Ambler assigns *Dominick Kelly* (a servant from Ireland in the snow George) to Evan Jones of Lancaster county yeoman, for five years from August 2nd 1746. Consideration £15 : customary dues.

Gabriel Mitchell in consideration £15 : paid George Wakely for his passage from Ireland indents himself servant to Evan Jones of Lancaster county, yeoman, for five years and eleven months from this date, customary dues.

Nathaniel Ambler assigns *Patrick Charles* (a servant from Ireland in the snow George) to Joseph Kaighin of Gloucester county, gentleman, for five years from August 2nd 1746. Consideration £15 : customary dues.

James Goodwin in consideration of £10 : 10/ paid Henry Kellso for his passage from Ireland indents himself servant to Moses Foster of Phila. chaise-maker for five years from this date, to be taught the trade of a harness maker and have customary dues.

August 29th.

John Parrock assigns *Hugh Williams* (a servant from Ireland in the ship Katherine) to Samuel Read of Phila. baker, for seven years from May 29th 1746. Consideration £16 : customary dues.

Margaret Templeton in consideration £7 : paid for her use and at her request by John Frew of Chester county yeoman, indents herself servant to John Frew for two years from this date, to be found in apparel during her servitude, but no freedom dues.

John Slowman Taylor in consideration £20 : paid for his use and at his request by Hugh Davids of Phila. cordwainer indents himself servant to Hugh Davids for four years from this date, to have customary dues.

Nathaniel Ambler assigns *Patrick Johnson* (a servant from Ireland in the snow George) to Thomas Moorey of Somerset County in East Jersey, yeoman, for four years from August 2nd 1746. Consideration £15 : customary dues.

Nathaniel Ambler assigns *Robert Grant* (a servant from Ireland in the snow George) to Thomas Moorey of Somerset County in East Jersey yeoman, for four years from August 2nd 1746. Consideration £15 : customary dues.

August 30th.

William Anderson in consideration of £16 : 5 : paid James Moore for his passage from Ireland, indents himself servant to Robert Casky of Bucks County yeoman, for four years from this date to have customary dues.

George Patterson assigns *Sarah Sleans* (a servant from Ireland in the snow Chester) to Rebecca Leech of Phila. County widow, for four years from August 3rd 1746. Consideration £14 : customary dues.

George Patterson assigns *Anne Canide* (a servant from Ireland in the snow Chester) to Simon Evans of Phila. house-carpenter, for five years from August 3rd. 1746. Consideration £14 : customary dues.

Nathaniel Ambler assigns *James Johnston* (a servant from Ireland in the snow George) to Joseph Morgan of Gloucester County yeoman, for five years from August 2nd 1746. Consideration £15 : 18/ customary dues.

John McCowen in consideration £10 : 10/ paid James Moore for his passage from Ireland indents himself servant to John Wogan of Lancaster county yeoman, for three years from this date, customary dues.

Nathaniel Ambler assigns *Garret Cavenagh* (a servant from Ireland in the snow George) to Francis Battin of Gloucester County, yeoman, for four years from August 2nd 1746. Consideration £15 : customary dues.

Nathaniel Ambler assigns *Laughlin Dunn* (a servant from Ireland in the snow George) to James Treviller of Chester county, yeoman, for four years from August 2nd 1746. Consideration £15 : customary dues.

James Parker assigns *Robert M. Cook* (a servant from Ireland in the ———) to Arthur Nesmith of Chester county yeoman, for seven years from August 1746. Consideration £12: customary dues.

September 2nd.

Richard Miller assigns *Daniel Welsh* his servant for the remainder of his time four years from May 21ˢᵗ 1746, to Othniel Tomlinson of Salem County yeoman. Consideration £16: customary dues.

William Spense in consideration £9: paid Andrew Beer for his use and at his request indents himself servant to Alexander Gibbony of the borough of Lancaster bricklayer, for one year and nine months from this date no freedom dues.

Daniel McKendry in consideration of £14: paid Robert Blair for his passage from Ireland indents himself servant to Thomas McMollin of Chester County, weaver, for five years and a half from this date, to be taught the trade of a weaver, and have customary dues.

Nathaniel Ambler assigns *Daniel Dawson* (a servant from Ireland in the snow George) to Robert Eastburn of Phila. blacksmith, for four years from Aug. 2ⁿᵈ 1746. Consideration £15: customary dues.

Andrew Hesley in consideration of £14: 10/ paid George O'kill for his passage from Ireland indents himself servant to . . . .

September 3rd.

Patrick Dougherty in consideration £14: paid Conyngham and Gardner for his passage from Ireland indents himself servant to James Todd of Phila. County taylor, for eight years from this date to be taught the trade of a taylor and have customary dues.

Nathaniel Ambler assigns *George Allen* (a servant from Ireland in the snow George) to John Smith of Phila. County yeoman, for six years from August 2ⁿᵈ 1746. Consideration £16: customary dues.

Thomas Robbs indents himself apprentice to John Blackwood of Phila. cordwainer, for five years from this date to be taught the trade of a shoemaker and to have customary dues.

John Hall in consideration £1: 10/ paid by Joshua Nicholson of Phila. taylor, assigns *Peter Flood* his apprentice to him the said Joshua for twelve years from February 3rd. 1745.

Isaac Conrow with consent of his mother Jane Hedges, widow, indents himself apprentice to Edward Fell of Chester County, weaver, for eight years and eight months from this date to be taught the trade of a weaver to read and write, and to have customary dues.

Robert Blair assigns *Daniel McClode* (a servant from Ireland in the brig Sally) to James Allison of Chester county yeoman, for four years from August 24th 1746. Consideration £16: customary dues.

John Doge in consideration £7: 11: 6 paid George O'kill for his passage from Ireland indents himself servant to Derick Tyson of Phila. county yeoman, for three years and one month from this date, customary dues.

September 4th.

Nathaniel Ambler assigns *Richard Kelly* (a servant from Ireland in the snow George) to John Granner of Chester county, yeoman, for seven years from August 2nd 1746. Consideration £15: customary dues.

September 5th.

Nathaniel Ambler assigns *Michael Hogan* (a servant from Ireland in the snow George) to Samuel Richardson of Phila. county yeoman for four years from August 2nd 1746. Consideration £15: customary dues.

Nathaniel Ambler assigns *John McCartney* (a servant from Ireland in the snow George) to Bryan Powell of Kent

County in Maryland, gentleman, for five years from August 2ⁿᵈ 1746. Consideration £16 : customary dues.

Nathaniel Ambler assigns *Edward Penbrook* (a servant from Ireland in the snow George) to Bryan Powell of Kent County in Maryland, gentleman, for four years from August 2ⁿᵈ 1746. Consideration £17 : customary dues.

Christopher Parry assigns *William Wright* his servant to William Darvill of Phila. baker, for the remainder of his time three years from May 27ᵗʰ 1746. Consideration £10 : 7 : 6. customary dues.

Nathaniel Ambler assigns *Bryan Dunkin* (a servant from Ireland in the snow George) to Nathaniel Delays of Gloucester County, yeoman, for four years from August 2ⁿᵈ 1746. Consideration £15 : customary dues.

September 6th.

Nathan Ambler assigns *John Johnson* (a servant from Ireland in the snow George) to John Scoggin of Phila. bricklayer for five years from August 2ⁿᵈ 1746. Consideration £16 : customary dues.

Elizabeth Lynn with the consent of her mother Bridget Lynn who signs her indenture, indents herself apprentice to Patrick Oneal of Phila. chair maker for seventeen years and nine months from June 6ᵗʰ 1746; customary dues.

Nathaniel Ambler assigns *Patrick Harkill* (a servant from Ireland in the snow George) to John Benson of Chester County yeoman, for four years from August 2ⁿᵈ 1746. Consideration £15 : 10/ customary dues.

Nathaniel Ambler assigns *Neal McCawley* (a servant from Ireland in the snow George) to George Walker of Chester county, yeoman, for five years from August 2ⁿᵈ 1746. Consideration £15 : 10/ customary dues.

John Morn in consideration of being taught the art or mystery of a ropemaker, indents himself apprentice to Henry Williamson of Phila. county, ropemaker, for seven years from August 2ⁿᵈ 1746; to have customary dues.

Nathaniel Ambler assigns *James Brow* (a servant from Ireland in the snow George) to Thomas Attinors (?) of Gloucester county, yeoman, for four years from August 2nd 1746.   Consideration £19 : customary dues.

Thomas Walker assigns *Peter Colwell* (a servant from Ireland in the snow Chester) to William Wallace of Phila. taylor, for four years from August 3rd. 1746.   Consideration £17 : customary dues.

Edward Bridy indents himself apprentice to Thomas Walker William Blair and Caleb Cowpland owners of the snow Chester, to serve on board said snow as a cooper, four years from this date to be taught navigation and have customary dues.

George Okill assigns *Robert McCree* (a servant from Ireland in the ship Griffin) to Renier Tyson of Phila. county, yeoman, for four years from August 25th 1746.   Consideration £14 : customary dues.

Elizabeth Kerr assigns *Janet McClane* her servant for the remainder of her time to Conrad Waldegar of Phila. butcher, for six years from September 20th 1745.   Consideration £6 : customary dues.

Robert Cochran assigns *Hugh Quin* (a servant from Ireland in the ship Griffith) to Thomas McKane of Chester County, innholder, for four years from August 25th 1746. Consideration £14 : 10/ customary dues.

Sarah White in consideration of £12 : paid for her passage from Ireland indents herself servant to James Shannon of Phila. county yeoman, for six years from this date, customary dues.

William Wright in consideration of £10 : 10/ paid for his use and at his request indents himself servant to Anthony Nicholas of Phila. blacksmith for four years from this date, to have customary dues.

John Irvine assigns *Thomas Waddal* (a servant from Ireland in the snow Chester) to John Fullerton of Phila. taylor, for four years from August 3rd 1746.   Consideration £19 : customary dues.

September 8th.

John Scoggin assigns *Timothy Castleton* his servant to James Stevens of Phila. baker, for the remainder of his time four years from Sept 22nd 1745.   Consideration £12 : customary dues.

Mary Givings by consent and approbation of her mother Mary Givings (?) indents herself apprentice to John Justis of Northern Liberties yeoman, for three years and ten months from this date, to be taught to read the Bible and have customary dues.

"ACCOUNT OF SERVANTS BOUND AND ASSIGNED BEFORE JAMES HAMILTON, MAYOR OF PHILADELPHIA."

CONTRIBUTED BY GEORGE W. NEIBLE, CHESTER, PENNA.

September 9th.

Thomas Rutter, with the consent of his mother Mary Catherine Pyewell indents himself apprentice to George Claypole of Phila. joiner, for six years and four months from this date, to be taught the trade of a joiner or cabinet maker, and William Pyewell to find him in clothes.

William Coleman assigns *Honour Magrah* (a servant from Ireland in the snow Martha) to John Jones of Phila. innholder, for four years from August 24th 1746. Consideration £10: customary dues.

Martha Skinner assigns *Eva* her servant for the remainder of her time to John George Shaver for six years and six months from October 14th 1743. Consideration £8: customary dues.

September 10th.

Tobias Nile assigns *Anne Fitzgerald* his servant for the remainder of her time to Anne Maltimore of Phila. for four years from December 22nd 1743. Consideration £3: customary dues.

Nathaniel Ambler assigns *John Slater* (a servant from Ireland in the snow George) to John Hillbourn of Phila., laborer, for four years from August 2nd 1746. Consideration £15: 10/ customary dues.

George House and other overseers of the poor bind *George Redman* (son of Katherine Bowman) an orphan an apprentice to Robert Lowry of Phila. laborer for eighteen years and a half from this date, to be taught to read and write and to have customary dues.

September 11th.

George O'Kell assigns *Andrew Heslep* (a servant from Ireland in the ship Griffin) to James Abraham of Phila. county, yeoman for six years from August 25ᵗʰ 1746. Consideration £14 : customary dues.

Jacob Gerr with consent of his father Bernard Gerr and in consideration of eleven pistoles paid for his passage from Holland indents himself servant to Samuel Shoemaker of Phila. merchant for nine years and five months from this date to be taught to read the Bible in the English language and when free to have customary dues.

Nathaniel Ambler assigns *Michael Gallagher* (a servant from Ireland in the snow George) to Patrick Kelly of Maryland yeoman, for four years from August 2ⁿᵈ 1746. Consideration £15 : customary dues.

September 12th.

Thomas Knight in consideration £15 : paid Joseph Turner for his use and at his request indents himself servant to Edward Brooks of Phila. victualler, for three years from September 1ˢᵗ 1746, customary dues.

September 13th.

Conyngham and Gardner assigns *Mary Winsly* (a servant from Ireland in the Brigt. Nancy) to Mathias Gamalise of Phila. county yeoman, for four years and a half from August 16ᵗʰ 1746. Consideration £5 : customary dues.

George Gibson in consideration of £5 : 8 : 6 paid for his use and at his request indents himself servant to Jeremiah Warder of Phila. hatter for six months from this date, no freedom dues.

George Patterson assigns *Jane Reay* (a servant from Ireland in the snow Chester) to Andrew Harris of Phila. county yeoman, for four years from August 3ʳᵈ 1746. Consideration £13 : 10/ customary dues.

Alexander Soles in consideration of £5: paid Stephen
Paschal indents himself apprentice to Jonathan Humphreys
of Phila. county, black-smith, for four years eight months
and twelve days from this date to be taught the trade of a
blacksmith and at the expiration of the said term to have
five pounds paid him in money and the customary dues.

September 15th.

John Erwin assigns *Anne Dallrymple* (a servant from Ireland in the snow George) to Thomas Doyle of the Borough
of Lancaster hatter, for four years from September 11ᵗʰ
1746. Consideration £14: customary dues.

John Erwin assigns *John Cunningham* (a servant from Ireland in the snow George) to Samuel Austin of Phila. joiner,
for four years from Sept. 11ᵗʰ 1746. Consideration £16:
customary dues.

John Greenway assigns *John Stockam* his servant for the
remainder of his time, six years from Sept. 12ᵗʰ 1743 to
John Garrigue of Phila. cooper, consideration £12: customary dues.

Samuel Vernor binds himself apprentice to John Bruno of
Phila. blockmaker, for six years from this date, to be taught
the trade of a blockmaker, to have two quarters schooling
at an evening school, to learn to write and cypher and customary dues.

John Erwin assigns *Jane McCambridge* (a servant from
Ireland in the snow Brigt. Sally) to Thomas Cuthbert
of Phila. shipwright for three years and a half from
Aug. 24ᵗʰ 1746. Consideration £11: to have customary
dues.

John Erwin assigns *William McCall* (a servant from Ireland in the snow George) to Thomas Hill of Bucks County
yeoman, for seven years from September 11ᵗʰ 1746. Consideration £16: customary dues.

Owen Jones assigns *John Conrad Monk* his servant for the
remainder of his time eight years from Sept. 3rd. 1743, to

Jacob Monk of Phila. County, yeoman, consideration £25 : customary dues.

John White assigns *Samuel Boon* his apprentice for the remainder of his time seven years and ten months from December 3ʳᵈ 1745 to Zachoriah Sims of Phila. cooper, consideration £5/ customary dues.

September 15th.

Rowland Judd in consideration of £28 : paiᵈ for his use and at his request indents himself servant to Thomas Stammers of Phila. County yeoman, for four years from this date to have the customary dues.

September 16th.

Joshua Fisher son of Jabez & Maud Fisher deceased indents himself apprentice to Thomas Shoemaker of Phila. house carpenter for five years and five months from July 16ᵗʰ 1746, to be taught the trade of a carpenter and have customary dues.

George Patterson assigns *Mary Carlton* (a servant from Ireland in the snow Chester) to Gunning Bedford of Phila. carpenter, for four years from August 3ʳᵈ 1746. Consideration £14 : customary dues.

John Erwin assigns *Mary Wide* (a servant from Ireland in the snow George) to George Kelly of Phila. blacksmith for four years from September 11ᵗʰ 1746. Consideration £15 : customary dues.

Patrick Chambers son of Mary Chambers with the consent of his mother indents himself apprentice to Hugh Hodge of Phila. tobacconist for thirteen years from this date, to be taught the trade of a tobacconist to have one years day schooling and when free the customary dues.

September 16th.

Conyngham and Gardner assign *George McConnel* (a servant from Ireland in the brigt. Nancy) to George Sanderson of the Borough of Lancaster, for seven years from Aug. 12th 1746.   Consideration £15 : customary dues.

September 17th.

John Erwin assigns *Matthew McVeagh* (a servant from Ireland in the snow George) to Henry Dalton of Phila. county yeoman, for seven years from Sept. 11th 1746.   Consideration £15 : 10/ customary dues.

John Erwin assigns *Colon Logan* (a servant from Ireland in the snow George) to Patrick McDonald of Phila. laborer, for four years and a half from Sept. 11th 1746.   Consideration £16 : customary dues.

George House and other overseers of the poor bind *Jacob Hartsell* an orphan, an apprentice to Frederick Dord of Phila. county yeoman for seventeen years from this date to be taught to read and write the German language, and have customary dues.

George House and other overseers of the poor bind *Esther Hartsell* an orphan, an apprentice to Frederick Snyder of Phila. county yeoman for twelve years from this date, to be taught to read and write the German language and have customary dues.

John Erwin assigns *Dominick McCullock* (a servant from Ireland in the snow George) to Stephen Jenkins of Phila. County for four years from Sept. 11th 1746.   Consideration £17 : 10/ customary dues.

John Elliot assigns *Shadrick Lord* his servant for the remainder of his time four years from May 19th 1744, to Samuel Vanbirkilow of Phila. cordwainer. Consideration £12 : 10/ customary dues.

John Erwin assigns *Richard Matchet* (a servant from Ireland in the snow George) to John Henderson of Monmouth County in East Jersey for seven years from Sept. 11th 1746. Consideration £15 : customary dues.

September 18th.

John Erwin assigns *Nathaniel Robison* (a servant from Ireland in the snow George) to Paul Miller of Brunswick Esq.

for four years from Sept. 11ᵗʰ 1746. Consideration £16: customary dues.

September 19th.

Jacob Sowder adm. of Margaret Sowder deceased, assigns *Hans Herelly* his servant to John Wistar of Phila. shopkeeper for the remainder of his time fourteen years from Dec. 30ᵗʰ 1742, to be taught to read and write and to have customary dues. Consideration £12:

September 20th.

John Erwin assigns *Anne Kerney* (a servant from Ireland in the snow George) to James Willson of Gloucester County, yeoman, for seven years from Sept. 11ᵗʰ 1746. Consideration £16: customary dues.

John Erwin assigns *John Crossby* (a servant from Ireland in the snow George) to James Wakely of Lancaster County yeoman, for seven years from Sept. 11ᵗʰ 1746. Consideration £14: 10/ customary dues.

Nathaniel Ambler assigns *James Boncher* (a servant from Ireland in the snow George) to Robert White of Bucks County yeoman, for seven years from August 2ⁿᵈ 1746. Consideration £15: 10/ customary dues.

September 22nd.

Benjamin Burk assigns Morgan Shee (a servant from Ireland in the Brigᵗ Rebecca) to Daniel Ashelman of Lancaster County yeoman, for six years from Sept. 21ˢᵗ 1746. Consideration £19: customary dues.

Benjamin Burk assigns *Mary Moor* (a servant from Ireland in the Brigt. Rebecca) to John Hallowell of Phila. shoemaker for five years from Sept. 20ᵗʰ 1746. Consideration £15: customary dues.

David Wells assigns *Elinor Murphy* (a servant from Ireland in the ship William and Mary) to Jacob Leech of Phila. county gentleman, for four years from Sept. 16ᵗʰ 1746. Consideration £14: 15/ customary dues.

September 23rd.

William Hill assigns *John Reardon* his servant for the remainder of his time four years and seven months from April 29th 1746, to Dennis Reardon of Gloucester County yeoman. Consideration £20 : customary dues.

Benjamin Burk assigns *Margaret Francis* (a servant from Ireland in the Brig[t] Rebecca) to Joseph Taylor of Chester County yeoman, for four years from Sept. 20th 1746. Consideration £14 : customary dues.

Benjamin Burk assigns *John Neal* (a servant from Ireland in the Brig[t] Rebecca) to Henry Burr of West Jersey yeoman, for five years from Sept. 20th 1746. Consideration £16 : customary dues.

George Patterson assigns *George McWhirter* (a servant from Ireland in the snow Chester) to Francis Richay of Bucks County yeoman for four years from August 3rd 1746. Consideration £16 : customary dues.

Benjamin Burk assigns *Elinor Moor* (a servant from Ireland in the Brigt. Rebecca) to William Hill of Chester County yeoman, for four years from Sept. 20th 1746. Consideration £15 : customary dues.

William & David McIlvaine assign *Patrick A. Demsey* (a servant from Ireland in the ship William and Mary) to John Pourdey of Bucks County yeoman, for four years from Sept. 16th 1746. Consideration £16 : customary dues.

September 24th.

Benjamin Burk assigns *James Gromell* (a servant from Ireland in the Brigt. Rebecca) to John Horsobing of Lancaster County yeoman for seven years from Sept. 20th 1746. Consideration £15 : customary dues and to be taught to read and write.

Benjamin Burk assigns *Mary Conely* (a servant from Ireland in the Brig[t] Rebecca) to Joseph Colburn of Phila. innholder, for four years from Sept. 20th 1746. Consideration £15 : customary dues.

John Erwin assigns *Agnes Cowley* (a servant from Ireland in the snow George) to George Patterson of Lancaster County yeoman, for four years from Sept. 11th 1746. Consideration £13:2/ customary dues.

John Erwin assigns *Robert Yeats* (a servant from Ireland in the snow George), to Abraham McConnor of Chester County, yeoman, for four years from Sept. 11th 1746. Consideration £15 : customary dues.

Samuel Boon with consent of his mother Elizabeth Sims indents himself apprentice to Oswald Eve of Phila. mariner for six years from Sept. 20th 1746, to be taught to read and write, and the art of navigation and to have when free customary dues.

Anthony Magner, with consent of his mother Barbara Butterfield indents himself servant to Darby Cassiday of Chester County for eighteen years from this date, to be taught to read and write and have customary dues.

John Lochron in consideration of £12 : paid Conyngham and Gardner for his passage from Ireland by Samuel Evans of Chester County indents himself servant to Samuel Evans for three years and a quarter from this date, no freedom dues.

September 25th.

William & David McIlvaine assign *James Woodside* (a servant from Ireland in the ship William and Mary) to Adam Farquhar of Phila. laborer for four years from Sept. 16th 1746. Consideration £16 : customary dues.

Manuel Pereira in consideration £16 : paid William Blair for his passage from Ireland in the ship William and Mary indents himself servant to John McFarran of Somerset County in East Jersey for four years from April 15th 1746, customary dues.

William and David McIlvaine assign *Arthur McNeal* (a servant from Ireland in the ship William and Mary) to Francis McConnell of Chester county yeoman, for four years and a half from Sept. 16th 1746. Consideration £16 : customary dues.

Luke Sexton in consideration of £16 : paid at his request
to George Emlen jr. and James Benzet adm. of Robert
Dawson deceased. indents himself servant to John Potts,
Indian trader for four years from August 2ⁿᵈ 1746: customary dues.

Marian Henry in consideration £9 : paid William Blair
for her passage from Ireland indents herself servant to
Joshua Humphreys of Phila. county yeoman for four years
from this date, customary dues.

Charles Henry with consent of his mother who signs his
indenture, indents himself servant to Joshua Humphreys of
Philadelphia county yeoman for sixteen years from this
date to be taught to read and write and have customary
dues.

September 26th.

Benjamin Burk assigns *Catherine Duggan* (a servant from
Ireland in the Brigᵗ Rebecca) to John Eachus of Chester
County yeoman, for four years from Sept. 21ˢᵗ 1746.   Con-
sideration £14: customary dues.

James Burke in consideration £14 : paid Archibald Montgomery for his passage from Ireland indents himself servant
to George Willson of Chester County, weaver, for seven
years from Sept. 21ˢᵗ 1746, to be taught the trade of a
weaver and to have customary dues.

James Burke assigns *Anne Francis* (a servant from Ireland in the Brigᵗ Rebecca) to Mathew Ingels of Phila. county
Fuller, for four years from September 20ᵗʰ 1746.   Consideration £14: 10/ customary dues.

September 27th.

Anne Ellis in consideration £15 : paid Robert Wakely for
her passage from Ireland indents herself servant to John
Sessly of Phila. mariner for four years from August 2ⁿᵈ
1746, customary dues.

Anne Sleighty in consideration nine pistoles paid Benjamin
Shoemaker for her passage from Holland indents herself

servant to Jacob Berr jr. of Lancaster County for three years from this date, to have freedom dues and one heifer.

Benjamin Burk assigns *Mary Grimes* (a servant from Ireland in the Brig' Rebecca) to William Wheldon of Phila. butcher, for four years from Sept. 20th 1746. Consideration £15 : customary dues.

Benjamin Burk assigns *Sarah Manly* (a servant from Ireland in the Brig' Rebecca) to Dennis Flood of Phila. taylor for four years from Sept. 20th 1746. Consideration £6 : customary dues.

George O'Kill assigns *Patrick Stewart* (a servant from Ireland in the ship Griffin) to James Craig of Bucks County yeoman, for four years from August 25th 1746. Consideration £14 : 10/ customary dues.

George O'Kill assigns *Robert Russell* (a servant from Ireland in the ship Griffin) to William Wright of Huntedan County in West Jersey yeoman for seven years from August 25th 1746. Consideration £13 : customary dues.

Benjamin Burk assigns *Honour Howdrick* (a servant from Ireland in the Brig' Rebecca) to John Detrick Bowman of Phila. county yeoman for four years from Sept. 20th 1746. Consideration £15 : customary dues.

Benjamin Burk assigns *Michael Sullivan* (a servant from Ireland in the Brig' Rebecca) to John Detrick Bowman of Phila. county yeoman for four years from Sept. 20th 1746. Consideration £15 : customary dues.

September 29th.

Anne Elizabeth Klevering in consideration of thirteen pistoles and a half paid Benjamin Shoemaker for her passage from Holland with consent of her father indents herself servant to Henry Van Aken his Exc. for seven years from this date to have customary dues.

John Henry Kalbfleish in consideration of nine pistoles paid Benjamin Shoemaker for his passage from Holland indents himself servant to Stephen Goodman of Phila. county his Exc. for two years from this date, to have customary dues.

Anna Elizabeth Derner in consideration fourteen pistoles paid Benjamin Shoemaker for her passage from Holland indents herself a servant to Joseph Redman of Phila. shopkeeper his Exc. for four years from this date to have customary dues.

Conrad Werner in consideration of nine pistoles paid Benjamin Shoemaker for his passage from Holland indents himself servant to Peter Reif of Phila. County his Exc. for four years from this date no freedom dues.

Catharine Dorothy Seeman in consideration nine pistoles paid Benjamin Shoemaker for her passage from Holland indents herself servant to Stephen Armit joiner her Exc. for three years from this date, customary dues.

John Baltzer Darner in consideration of fourteen pistoles paid Benjamin Shoemaker for his passage from Holland indents servant to John Witmer of Lancaster county his Exc. for three years from this date, customary dues.

Benjamin Burke assigns *Patrick Fitts Morris* (a servant from Ireland in the Brig^t Rebecca) to Humphrey Ellis of Chester county yeoman for six years from Sept. 20th 1746. Consideration £14 : 10/ customary dues.

Benjamin Burke assigns *Lawrence Scancle* (a servant from Ireland in the Brig^t Rebecca) to Samuel Morgan of Chester County yeoman for six years from Sept. 20th 1746. Consideration £15 : customary dues.

Benjamin Burke assigns *Austis Sullivan* (a servant from Ireland in the Brig^t Rebecca) to Nicholas Rapine of Phila. County yeoman for four years from Sept. 20th 1746. Consideration £14 : 10/ customary dues.

Magdelena Shontin in consideration ten pistoles paid Benjamin Shoemaker for her passage from Holland indents herself servant to Bernard ———, of Phila. County yeoman for three years and a half from this date, customary dues.

Benjamin Burke assigns *Julian Moor* (a servant from Ireland in the Brig^t Rebecca) to George Rider of Phila. county yeoman for four years from Sept. 20th 1746. Consideration £14 : 10/ customary dues.

Benjamin Burke assigns *Mary Scanlan* (a servant from Ireland in the Brig^t Rebecca) to William Rodman of Bucks County yeoman for four years from Sept. 20th 1746. Consideration £15 : customary dues.

Jacob Dowdle in consideration nine pistoles paid Benjamin Shoemaker for his passage from Holland indents himself servant to Valentine Crook of Lancaster tanner for two years and one month from this date, customary dues.

Gutlip Wainer in consideration ten pistoles paid Benjamin Shoemaker for his passage from Holland indents himself servant to Valentine Crook of Lancaster, tanner his Exc. for two years and one month from this date, customary dues.

Christina Baisner in consideration six pistoles paid Benjamin Shoemaker for her passage from Holland indents herself servant to Valentine Crook of Lancaster tanner his Exc. two years and a half from this date, customary dues.

Burket Baisner in consideration ten pistoles paid Benjamin Shoemaker for his passage from Holland indents himself servant to Charles Miers of Lancaster County yeoman his Exc. for two years and one month from this date, customary dues.

Anne Elizabeth Brohtsmenning in consideration nine pistoles paid Benjamin Shoemaker for her passage from Holland indents herself servant to Jacob Cowdrop of Phila. shipwright his Exc. for three years from this date, customary dues.

Anna Maria Seal in consideration thirteen pistoles and a half paid Benjamin Shoemaker for her passage from Holland indents herself servant to William Taylor of Phila. shipwright his Exc. for four years from this date, customary dues.

John Jurg Roht in consideration nine pistoles paid Benjamin Shoemaker for his passage from Holland indents himself servant to William Kass of Huntedon County in West Jersey yeoman his Exc. for three years from this date, customary dues.

Eva Roht in consideration fourteen pistoles and a half paid Benjamin Shoemaker for her passage from Holland indents herself servant to Leonard Van ———— of Phila.

County yeoman his Exc. for four years and a half from this date, customary dues.

Benjamin Burke assigns *Sarah Hermitage* (a servant from Ireland in the Brig* Rebecca) to George Cling of Chester county yeoman for four years from Sept. 20th 1746. Consideration £15: customory dues.

Anna Barbara Blickley with consent of her father who signs her indenture binds herself a servant to Jacob Sheromire of Germantown mason his Exc. for fifteen years from this date, to be taught to read the Bible, to knit and spin, and when free to have given her one spinning wheel and one woolen wheel.

Maria Elizabeth Cleverin in consideration ten pistoles paid Benjamin Shoemaker for her passage from Holland indents herself servant to Elizabeth Holton of Phila. widow her Exc. for eight years from this date when free to have customary dues and half a pistole.

Christopher Danner in consideration fourteen pistoles paid for his passage from Holland indents himself servant to Daniel Farree of Lancaster county yeoman his Ex. for three years and three quarters from this date, customary dues.

Peter Spence assigns *Mary McIntyre* (a servant from Ireland in the Brig* John) to John Adams of East Jersey yeoman for four years from Sept. 15th 1746. Consideration £13: 15/ customary dues.

Jacob Tigle in consideration ten pistoles paid Benjamin Shoemaker for his passage from Holland indents himself servant to George Widener of Phila. county yeoman for four years from this date to have customary dues and one two year old heifer.

John Henry Snyder, with consent of his father and in consideration £10: pistoles paid Benjamin Shoemaker for his passage from Holland indents himself servant to Dr. William Shippen of Phila. his Exc. for eight years from this date, customary dues.

Catharina Snyder with consent of her father and in consideration of four pistoles paid Benjamin Shoemaker for her passage from Holland indents herself a servant to Dr. William Shippen of Phila. his Exc. for thirteen years from this date, customary dues.

Catharina Boon in consideration twelve pistoles paid Benjamin Shoemaker for her passage from Holland indents herself servant to Joseph Marshall of Phila. bricklayer his Exc. for four years from this date, customary dues.

Jahn Jurg Gottschalk in consideration nine pistoles paid Benjamin Shoemaker for his passage from Holland indents himself servant to John Ecker of Lancaster County yeoman his Exc. for two years and three months from this date customary dues.

October 1st.

Benjamin Burk assigns *Cornelius Connor* (a servant from Ireland in the Brig* Rebecca) to John O'Daniel of Hunterdon County West Jersey for four years from Sept. 20th 1746. Consideration £15 : 10/ customary dues.

Benjamin Burke assigns *Ella Field* (a servant from Ireland in the Brig* Rebecca) to Robert Shields of Hunterdon County West Jersey for four years from Sept. 20th 1746. Consideration £15 : customary dues.

Juliana Seftelsin with consent of her father who was present in consideration nine pistoles paid for her passage from Holland indents herself servant to Aaron James of Chester County his Exc. for twelve years from this date, customary dues.

Benjamin Burk assigns *John Rourk* (a servant from Ireland in the Brig* Rebecca) to Isaac Knight of Phila. County yeoman for three years and a half from this date. Consideration £8 : sterling customary dues.

Benjamin Burk assigns *Patrick Fitzgerald* (a servant from Ireland in the Brig* Rebecca) to Nicholas Uplinger of Phila. County yeoman for five years from Sept. 20th 1746. Consideration £15 : customary dues.

Benjamin Burk assigns *Martin Lowry* (a servant from Ire-

land in the Brig^t Rebecca) to William Showler of Phila.
county yeoman for four years from Sept. 20th 1746. Consideration £15 : customary dues.

Michael Egolf in consideration fifteen pistoles paid Benjamin Shoemaker for his passage from Holland indents himself servant to Owen Jones of Phila. baker for five years
from this date, customary dues.

Richard Vaughn in consideration £15 : paid Archibald
Montgomery for his passage from Ireland indents himself
servant to Samuel Showler of Phila. County Miller his Exc.
for five years from this date, to be taught the trade of a
miller customary dues.

John Danner in consideration twelve pistoles paid Benjamin Shoemaker for his passage from Holland indents himself servant to Valentine Puff of Phila. County yeoman for
seven years and three quarters from this date, to have customary dues and one dollar.

Benjamin Burk assigns Darby Dowling (a servant from
Ireland in the Brig^t Rebecca) to James Cooper of Glou-
cester County yeoman for four years from Sept. 20th 1746.
Consideration £16 : customary dues.

Benjamin Burk assigns *Barnaby Lynch* (a servant from
Ireland in the Brig^t Rebecca) to James Coddy of Fredericks'
County in Virginia yeoman for four years from Sept. 20th
1746.   Consideration £15 : customary dues.

Benjamin Burk assigns *Thomas Shea* (a servant from Ireland in the Brig^t Rebecca) to William Bird of Phila. county
yeoman for four years from Sept. 20th 1746.   Consideration
£15 : customary dues.

Benjamin Burk assigns *James Fagan* (a servant from Ireland in the Brig^t Rebecca) to William Bird of Phila. County
yeoman for four years from Sept. 20th 1746.   Consideration
£15 : customary dues.

Benjamin Burk assigns *John Savage* (a servant from Ireland in the Brig^t Rebecca) to William Bird of Phila. county
yeoman, for four years from Sept. 20th 1746.   Consideration
£15 : customary dues.

Benjamin Buck assigns *Patrick Connor* (a servant from Ireland in the Brig^t Rebecca) to George Smith of Chester County yeoman for four years from Sept. 20th 1746. Consideration £15 : customary dues.

Benjamin Burk assigns *Thomas Lynch* (a servant from Ireland in the Brig^t Rebecca) to John Lesher of Philada. county yeoman for five years from Sept. 20th 1746. Consideration £15 : customary dues.

Benjamin Burk assigns William Paltmer (a servant from Ireland in the Brig^t Rebecca) to John Lesher of Phila. county yeoman for five years from Sept. 20th 1746. Consideration £15 : customary dues.

Benjamin Burk assigns *James Suill* (a servant from Ireland in the Brig^t Rebecca) to John Lesher of Phila. County yeoman, for four years from Sept. 20th 1746. Consideration £15 : customary dues.

Benjamin Burk assigns *James Purcell* (a servant from Ireland in the Brig^t Rebecca) to John Lesher of Phila. county yeoman for four years from Sept. 20th 1746. Consideration £15 : customary dues.

Benjamin Burk assigns *Hugh Connor* (a servant from Ireland in the Brig^t Rebecca) to John Lesher of Phila. County yeoman, for four years from Sept. 20th 1746. Consideration £15 : customary dues.

Anna Lenter in consideration her passage from Holland indents herself servant to Josiah Forster of Burlington County West Jersey his Exc. for two years from this date to have customary dues.

Christina Lenter with consent of her mother and in consid. eration of her passage from Holland indents herself a servant to Josiah Forster of Burlington County West Jersey his Exc. for six years from this date to have customary dues.

Catharine Lenter with consent of her mother and in consideration of her passage from Holland indents herself servant to Josiah Forster of Burlington County West Jersey his Exc. for eight years from this date, customary dues.

John Lenter with consent of his mother and in consideration of his passage from Holland indents himself to Josiah
Forster of Burlington County West Jersey for thirteen
years from this date to have customary dues.

October 2nd.

Barbara Fetterlin in consideration nine pistoles paid Benjamin Shoemaker for her passage from Holland indents
herself servant to Nicholas Custar of Phila. County yeoman for two years and a half from this date, to have customary dues.

Henry Claughan in consideration £15: paid Benjamin
Burk for his passage from Ireland indents himself servant
to Anthony Whitely of Phila. tavernkeeper for six years
from Sept. 20th 1746. to have customary dues.

Samuel Burden with consent of his parents indents himself apprentice to Isaac Lobdell of Phila. carpenter for six
years and three months from this date to have two quarters
schooling in the time of his apprenticeship, customary dues
and the trade.

Anna Falkenstine in consideration ten pistoles paid Benjamin Shoemaker for her passage from Holland indents
herself servant to Michael Hellingoff of Phila. potter for
three years from this date, to have customary dues.

October 3rd.

Thomas Broom assigns *Mary Guerry* his servant for the
remainder of her time to John Sanders of Phila. huntsman
for two years three months and seventeen days from August
12th 1745.   Consideration £3: 10/ customary dues.

Thomas Robinson assigns *Sarah Mahon* his servant to
William Reynolds of Chester County yeoman for six years
from this date.   Consideration £17: customary dues.

October 4th.

William and David McIlvaine assigns *James Corry* (a servant from Ireland in the ship William and Mary) to Wil-

liam Chambers of Lancaster County yeoman for three years from Sept. 16th 1746. Consideration £16 : customary dues.

Abraham Zimmerman in consideration of his passage from Holland paid to Benjamin Shoemaker indents himself servant to Casper Wistar of Phila. for five years from this date, customary dues.

Melchior Zimmerman in consideration of his passage from Holland indents himself servant to Casper Wistar of Phila. for eight years from this date to have customary dues.

Ursula Dicter in consideration of her passage from Holland paid by Casper Wistar of Phila. indents herself servant to the said Casper for seven years from this date, to have customary dues.

Ludwick Falkenstein in consideration of his passage from Holland paid by Richard Wistar of Phila. indents himself servant to the said Richard for eight years from this date, to be taught the trade of brass button making, customary dues.

Jacob Wetzell in consideration of his passage from Holland paid by John Williams of Monmouth county in East Jersey indents himself to the said John for three years from this date, customary dues.

Catharine Wetzell in consideration of her passage from Holland paid by John Williams of Monmouth county in East Jersey indents herself servant to the said John for three years from this date, customary dues.

Catharine Wetzell jr. in consideration of her passage from Holland paid by John Williams of Monmouth County in East Jersey indents herself servant to the said John for three years from this date to have customary dues.

James Maxfield assigns *Martha Hamilton* (a servant from Ireland in the ship Rundell) to William Allison of Lancaster County yeoman for four years from September 21st 1746. Consideration £14: 15/ customary dues.

William Lightfoot assigns *William Forster* his servant to Thomas Brown of Phila. brewer for the remainder of his time seven years from August 9th 1745, customary dues.

Darby Logan in consideration of £5 / paid for his use and at his request by William Hamilton of Phila. tanner indents himself servant to said William for three years and a half from this date, customary dues.

Robert Henry in consideration of £12 : paid William Blair for his passage from Ireland indents himself a servant to Michael McClenen of Lancaster County yeoman his Exc. for eight years from September 15th 1746, customary dues.

*Patrick M*c*Fagan* in consideration of £15 : paid William Blair for his passage from Ireland indents himself a servant to Samuel Sturgeon of Lancaster county yeoman his Exc. for four years from September 15th 1746, customary dues.

October 6th.

Maria Ramer in consideration of ten pistoles paid her father Christian Ramer indents herself apprentice to Isaac Roberts of Phila. bricklayer for seven years from this date, customary dues.

Alexander Boyd assigns *Abigail Edwards* (a servant from Ireland in the ship Pomona) to William Plackett of Trenton in West Jersey yeoman, for four years from Sept. 18th 1746, consideration £13 : customary dues.

George House and other overseers of the poor, &c. bind *Alexander Reddy* an orphan, apprentice to Samuel Garrigues of Phila. barber for thirteen years and four months from this date, to be taught to read and write, the trade of a barber and perruque maker and to have customary dues.

October 4th.

Mechior Zimmerman in consideration fourteen pistoles paid Benjamin Shoemaker for his passage from Holland indents himself servant to Casper Wistar of Phila. for nine years from this date, to have customary dues.

October 6th.

Martin Loughman in consideration of fifteen pistoles paid Benjamin Shoemaker for his passage from Holland indents

himself servant to Andrew Bierly of Lancaster baker for
four years from this date to have when free customary dues
and six pounds in money.

Cathrin Shreder in consideration nine pistoles paid Benjamin Shoemaker for her passage from Holland indents
herself servant to Hugh Hodge of Phila. for six years and
nine months from this date to have customary dues.

John Darrough in consideration £14: paid Neal McGowan
for his passage from Ireland indents himself a servant to
John Wood of Phila. county yeoman for eight years from
this date to be taught to read and write, and have customary dues.

William Henderson assigns *Fardy Gallaugher* (a servant
from Ireland in the ship Pomona) to Joseph Potter of Monmouth County East Jersey yeoman for four years and a
half from September 18th 1746. Consideration £14: 10/
customary dues.

October 7th.

Alexander Forster in consideration £15: paid for his
passage from Ireland indents himself servant to Isaac
Cooper of Gloucester County in West Jersey yeoman for
eight years from this date, to have customary dues.

Benjamin Burk assigns *Mary Hancock* (a servant from
Ireland in the Brig* Rebecca) to William Arbour of Phila.
tavernkeeper from Sept. 20th 1746. Consideration £13:
10/ customary dues.

Nathaniel Ambler assigns *Eustace Reddit* (a servant from
Ireland in the snow George) to Archibald Douglas of Phila.
taylor for four years from August 2nd 1746. Consideration
£17: 10/ customary dues.

RECORD OF SERVANTS AND APPRENTICES BOUND
AND ASSIGNED BEFORE HON. JOHN GIBSON,
MAYOR OF PHILADELPHIA, DECEMBER 5TH, 1772–
MAY 21, 1773.

[Compiled from the original Record Book, in the Manuscript Department of the Historical Society of Pennsylvania.]

List of Immigrant Vessels.

Date.	Vessel's Name.	Master.	Imported.	No.
May 12	Brig Connoly	Cain	Dublin	94
18	Snow Brittania	Eyres	Dublin	26
24	Brig Matty	Cochran	Glasgow	39
27	Ship Phenix	Gamble	Bristol	25
31	Brig. Dolphin	Hill	London	60
June 4	Ship Sally	Young	Bristol	11
4	Ship Rosanna	Coxe	London	2
4	Ship Carolina	Loxley	London	29
11	Ship Minerva	Faries	Newry	80
14	Brig. Charlotte	Montgomery	Newry	63
17	Brig Peggy	McKinsey	Belfast	118
July 2	Ship Jenny	McIlvaine	Londonderry	80
4	Snow Charlotte	Cap. Curtis	Waterford	81
6	Brig. Agnes	Cap. Living	Belfast	36
8	Shallopp	Tatler	New Castle	53
8	Ship Bettsey	Cap. McCutcheon	Newry	228
13	Snow Penn	Cap. McCaddon	Cork	81
Aug. 2	Ship Newry Assistance	Cuningham	Newry	87
3	Ship Jupiter	Capt Ewing	Londonderry	128
6	Ship Alex^r	Hunter	"	179
8	Hannah	Mitchell	"	182
20	Brig Sam	Burrows	Liverpool	27
23	Ship Sally	Osman	Rotterdam	196
31	Ship Caesar	Miller	London	5
Sep. 2	Snow Sarah	Curry	Dublin	115
2	Snow Sally	Stephen James	London	90
5	Ship Rea Galley	Robert Hunter	Isle Lewis	295
8	Brig Loniser	Kirkpatrick	Londonderry	46
9	Ship R^d Penn	T. All	London	4

Date.		Vessel's Name.	Master.	Imported.	No.
Sep.	17	Ship Rose	Robert George	Derry	150
	20	Ship Pennsy¹ Packet	Cap' Osborne	London	10
	20	Ship Catherine	James Sutton	London	53
	21	Snow Peggy	William Hastie	Glasgow	43
	21	Ship Brittania	James Peter	Rotterdam	307
	28	Ship Union	Bryson	Cowes	287
Oct.	4	Hope	Johnson	"	200

REGISTER.

December 5th 1772.

Robert George son of Joseph, apprentice to James Dickinson of Philadelphia.

Johan Casper Breadbaur last from Rotterdam, servant, to Jacob Barge, and by him assigned to Michael Swope of York.

Sophia Hehlman [April 18ᵗʰ 1772] assigned to John Snyder.

John Dickey son of Mary Herford, apprentice to James Cooper of Philadelphia.

Catherine Schoulgas last from Rotterdam, servant to Amos Wickersham of Philadelphia.

Johan Adam Fink last from Rotterdam, servant to Philip Flick of Philadelphia.

Johannes Romp last from Rotterdam, servant to Luke Morris of Southwark.

Elizabeth Prugel last from Rotterdam, servant to Christopher Sower jun' of Germantown.

Henry Scoup, servant assign'd by John Jones to Aquilla Jones of New Town Township.

George Wᵐ Baker last from Rotterdam, servant to Benjamin Shoemaker of Philad¹

Johannes Benner last from Rotterdam, servant to Henry Fancy of Providence Township, Philad¹ County.

Maria Saltes last from Rotterdam, servant to John Test of Woolwich Township.

John Kerlack Cooper last from Rotterdam, servant to Peter Purkus of German Town.

Jacob Henry Remp last from Rotterdam, servant to Charles Priors of Philad'

Barbara Eller last from Rotterdam, servant to Joseph Luken of Whitemarsh Township.

Johan Philip Kaltwasser last from Rotterdam servant to Patrick Gordon of New Providence Township.

Carolina De Pool last from Rotterdam, servant to Joseph Kaighin of New Town Township.

Jn° Zakerias Longebin last from Rotterdam, servant to Jacob Hinkle of Radnor Township

Nicholas Trautwine last from Rotterdam, servant to Charles Syng of Philad' and by him assigned to serve George Hinkle of Earl Township.

Weynand Rony last from Rotterdam, servant to John Blackledge of the Manor of Moreland.

Levi Burke [Feb. 20ᵗʰ 1771] assign'd to serve William Niles of Philad'

George Kerchner last from Rotterdam, servant to Thomas Moore of Philad' and by him assign'd to serve John Price of Lower Chichester.

James Yeaten assign'd by Capᵗ Seymour Flood to serve Ichabod Wilkenson of Salisbury Township.

Peter Schoulgas last from Rotterdam, servant to Jacob Snyder of Worcester Township.

Maria Elizabeth Leyfer last from Rotterdam, servant to Rachel Graydone of Philad' and by her assign'd to serve Jennet Marks of Philad'

Catherine Pepfher last from Rotterdam, servant to Rachel Graydon of Philad'

Barbara Sex last from Rotterdam, servant to Theodore Meminger of Philad'

John Phillips Miller last from Rotterdam, servant to John Pierce of Concord Township.

Murdock Patterson redemptioner, by Cunningham Sample of Fawn Township.

Michael MᶜMannis redemptioner, servant to Cunningham Sample of Fawn Township.

December 7th.

Henry Shuler last from Rotterdam, servant to George Clymer Esq' of Philad¹

Anna Catherine Elgert last from Rotterdam, servant to George Clymer Esq' of Philad¹

Edmond McDaniel last from Liverpool, servant to John Cottringer of Philad¹

John George Knobloch last from Rotterdam, servant to Richard Wister of Philad¹

Thomas Hall apprentice of William Davis Cooper deced. assigned with consent of the said Thomas Hall by Charles Rish administrater, to John Hall of Wilmington.

Daniel Cooper last from Rotterdam, servant to Martin Crider of the City of Phil* and assign'd by him to serve Milchor Shultz of Hereford, Bucks Co.

Mary Micklen with consent of her mother Mary bound an apprentice to John Druckenmiller and his wife Catherine.

Yost Willhelm Osterdaugh last from Rotterdam, servant to Adam Frischbach.

William Birch with consent of his Grand Mother Elizabeth Jackson bound an apprentice to John Patterson of Philad* whitesmith.

Maria Tomer last from Rotterdam, servant to Robert Bass of Philad¹

John Strautz son of Peter, apprentice to Jesse Row of Philad¹, House Carpenter.

Anna Eliz^a Habach last from Rotterdam, servant to Lawrence Bast of the Northern Liberties.

Christiana Tomer last from Rotterdam, servant to Joseph Moulder of Philad¹

John Freymouth last from Rotterdam, servant to Christopher Myrtetus of Philad¹

Arnold Peters last from Rotterdam, servant to John Dehuff of the Borough of Lancaster.

Philip Hortman last from Rotterdam, servant to John Heckiswillor of the Borough of Lancaster.

December 8.

Eliz^a Catherine Helman [Nov. 5th 1771] assigned by Jacob
Rote to serve John Pault of Vincent Township.

Coll McDonald with consent of his mother Henrietta apprentice to Jacob Binder of Philadelphia—Taylor.

Andrew Schoulgas last from Rotterdam, servant to Michael
Bishop of Lower Millford Township.

Conrad Schoulgas last from Rotterdam, servant to Michael
Bishop of Lower Millford Township.

Henry Schoulgas last from Rotterdam, servant to Michael
Bishop of Lower Millford Township.

Mandelena Schoulgas last from Rotterdam, servant to Michael
Bishop of Lower Millford Township.

Solenia Sweitzer last from Rotterdam, servant to Jacob Fries
of Upper Alloways Creek.

Catherine Elizabeth Elgert last from Rotterdam servant to
John Wilcocks of Philad^l

Johan Martin Koentzin last from Rotterdam, servant to Ben-
edict Dorsey of Philad^l

Martin Keylhauver last from Rotterdam, servant to Daniel
Burhhard of Passyunk Township.

John Fritzinger last from Rotterdam, servant to Henry Funk
of Philad^l and assign'd by him to Jacob Miller of Sads-
bury Township.

Henry Thiess last from Rotterdam, servant to Andrew Forsyth of Philad^l

Christiana Wilhelmina Thiess last from Rotterdam, servant to
Andrew Forsyth of Philad^l

Ernest Fritzenger and *Mary Elizabeth* his wife last from Rotterdam, servants to Benjamin Shule Malbro' Township.

December 9.

John McKee [Nov. 23rd 1771] under Indenture of Servitude
to Jonathan Paschall now cancelled, servant to Hugh
Torance of Neils Settlements, Rowan Co., N. C.

Mary Hymen [March 16th 1773] last from Rotterdam, servant to John Rub of Philad^l

Christian Rasor and *Elizabeth* his wife last from Rotterdam, servants to Jacob Fries of upper Alloways Creek, Salem Co., West Jersey.

John Holtz last from Rotterdam, servant to John Williamson of Newton Township.

John Smith with consent of his mother Deborah Poor, apprentice to Ralph Moore of Philad¹ Mariner

John William Meyer last from Rotterdam, servant to Jacob Winey of Philad¹

Henry Hartman last from Rotterdam, servant to Jacob Winney of Philad¹

Daniel Miller under Indenture now cancelled, last from Ireland, servant to John Rees of Pencaden hundred, New Castle Co.

Henry Weinheimer son of Henry, apprentice to Henry Keppele of Philad¹

Lena Samolt last from Rotterdam, servant to Dedimus Lewis of New Town.

John Miller last from Rotterdam, servant to John Vanlashe of Westnantmill.

Christopher Luger, servant to Wandel Zarban of Philad¹

Daniel Rise and *Ann Catherine* his wife last from Rotterdam, servants to Nicholas Burghart of Bristol.

Catherine Louks last from Rotterdam, servant to Thos. Nedrow of Bristol Township Philad¹

Juliana Louks last from Rotterdam, servant to Jacob Miller of Cheltenham Township

Anna Margaret Sonman last from Rotterdam, servant to Docᵗʳ Frederick Phili of Philad¹.

Jacob Hyer last from Rotterdam, servant to James Templin of East Nantmill.

Peter Powell last from Rotterdam, servant to Richard Templin of East Caln Township.

Eleanor Mubryan assign'd by James Taylor to Levis Pennock of West Marlborough.

Peter Rotenbergh last from Rotterdam, servant to Able Lippincott, Eavsham Township

December 10th.

Philip William Smith last from Rotterdam to Frederic Deeds
  of Philadelphia.

John George Pleifer last from Rotterdam, servant to William
  Hodge of Philad¹

Catherine Pouls last from Rotterdam, servant to Jacob
  Franks of Philad¹

John Sturgeon with consent of his Guardians Joseph Donaldson & Benjamin Fuller, apprentice to John Robertson ot
  Southwark, mariner.

John Jacob Bull last from Rotterdam, servant to William
  Rogers of Evesham Township.

Paul Huber,
Joanna Teresa his wife   } last from Rotterdam, servants
Anthony their son &   } to John Old of the Western
Joanna Mira their Daughter   } Districk, Berks County.

Jacob Ludwig Dise last from Rotterdam, servant to George
  Shafer of Philad¹.

Thomas Woollen apprentice [May 14ᵗʰ 1770] assign'd by Solomon White to Stephen Phipps of the City of Philad¹.

William Skinner with consent of his mother Rachael Warner
  apprentice to Jonathan Meredith of Philad¹ Tanner &
  Currier.

Jacob Ludwick Kershaw last from Rotterdam, servant to
  Philip Wager of Philad¹.

James Oliver last from Ireland, Indenture now cancelled,
  bound a servant to James McDowell of Oxford Township.

Neal Crossan last from Ireland, Indenture now cancelled,
  bound a servant to James McDowell of Oxford Township.

December 11th.

Frederick Steinhaur last from Rotterdam, servant to Mary
  Jenkins of Philad¹

John George Ruple last from Rotterdam, servant to John
  Carman of Northampton Township.

Jacob Fink last from Rotterdam, servant to Philip Mouse of Philad¹

Catherine Vandam last from Rotterdam, servant to John Luken, Surveyor General.

William Maxfield bound an apprentice by the Managers of the House of Employment to Jonathan Jones of Philadelphia, Saddle Tree maker.

Johann Gottlib Graff last from Rotterdam, servant to Samuel Howell Merchant of the City of Phil*

Jeremiah Driscoll [May 13ᵗʰ] Indentured to Abram Shelly now cancelled, by Thomas Tisdell of Philad¹

Hugh McDonald [May 7ᵗʰ 1770] apprentice assign'd by George Sharpless to Michael Canes of Philad¹

Peter Keller last from Rotterdam, servant to Dieterick Reise of Philad¹.

December 12th.

Johan Tyce Schnell last from Rotterdam, servant to William Staddleman of Lower Merion Township.

Jacob Diamond last from Rotterdam, servant to Godfrey Haga of Philad¹.

John Peter House last from Rotterdam, servant to Isaac Dorsten of Rock Hill Township.

John Roberts with consent of his next Friend William Burton, Bound an apprentice to Peter January of Phil*, cordwainer.

Wamert Oalwain last from Rotterdam, servant to Thomas Sinnickson, of Salem, Salem Co. Western Division of the Province of New Jersey.

Johan Yost Tamer last from Rotterdam, servant to Allen Moore of Phil*.

Maria Catherine Miller last from Rotterdam, a servant to Henry Haines of Phil*.

December 14th.

John Ulrick Lyell a servant to John Nixon of Philad*.

Mary Levers with consent of her mother Mary an apprentice to James Glenn of Philad*.

John George Tiger last from Rotterdam, servant to Christ[a] Forrer of Lampiter Township.

Anna Christiana Yeger last from Rotterdam, servant to John Breckbill of Strasburg Township.

Magdalen Yegar last from Rotterdam, servant to Christian Forrer of Lampiter Township.

Elizabeth Saneftien last from Rotterdam, servant to Hugh Roberts of Philad[l].

Theobald Cline [June 9th past] servant to George Wert of Phila.

Elizabeth Easman last from Rotterdam, servant to Charles Wist of the Northern Liberty

John Falconer apprentice, assign'd by William Ross to serve Richard Collier of Philad[a] Cordwainer.

Margery Broadley [Nov. 7th 1772] assigned by William Cochran to Robert Carson of Southwark.

Frederica Regina Hubner last from Rotterdam, servant to John William Hoffman of Philad[l]

Mary Martin redemptioner now cancelled, last from Ireland, a servant to William Weston of Philad[l]

December 15th.

John Sickfreid with consent of his mother Catherine signi-fied by Andrew Kesler her son-in-law, apprentice to Henry Cross of Philad[l] cordwainer.

William Green who was under an Indenture of apprentice-ship to Cornelius Cooper, now cancelled with consent of Parties & with consent of his Father Peter an apprentice to John Hannah of Philadelphia, Brush maker.

Henry Whitestick last from Rotterdam, servant to John Breckbill of Strasburgh Township.

Henretta Tick last from Rotterdam, servant to George Goodwin of Philad[l]

Catherine Will [Oct. 2[d] 1769] assigned by Charles Cham-berline to William Simpson Pextang Township.

John Rabjohn with consent of his Father bound an appren-tice to Philip Sinclair of Philadelphia, Taylor.

William Stevens [January 11ᵗʰ 1773] last from England servant to Ellis Newlin of Christiana Hundred.

December 16th.

Edmund Easy aged fourteen years, apprentice to Michael
Dawson by Managers of the House of Employmᵗ

Catherine Turniss with consent of her Father George apprentice to Adam Deshler of Whitehall Township.

Johan Adam Matzenbacher last from Rotterdam, servant to
Jacob Brown of Philadᴵ, Black Smith and assigned by
him to Adam Carver of Heidelberg township.

Margaret Maldrom with consent of her Father John, apprentice to Michael Davenport of Southwark, Cooper, and his
wife.

George Garnets servant bound before Thoˢ Lawrence assigned
by Peter Reeve to serve James Wharton of Philᴬ

Jacob Able with consent of his Father Matthias apprentice
to William Stots of Southwark.

December 17th.

Catherine Shaffer apprentice of Francis Lether [Jan. 10ᵗʰ
1772] by him assigned to George Myers of Reading.

Mary Shiekell with consent of her Father William apprentice
to Stephen Carmuk of Philadelphia.

William Sleving with consent of his Father Patrie Sleving
apprentice to Samuel Wright of Philadᴵ mariner.

December 18th.

Mary Hacket [May 14ᵗʰ 1770] servant assingn'd by Abraham
Shelly to Presly Blackiston of Philadᴬ

Jacob Weiscop last from Rotterdam, servant to John Stoner
Union Township.

John Duff with consent of his Father Michael, apprentice
to Robert Morris of Philadᴵ merchant.

Margaret Betts last from Rotterdam and with consent of
her husband John Fred^k, servant to Johan Geo. Fishback
of Manheim Township and by him assign'd to Abraham
Rife of Manheim Township.

Johan Fred^k Betts last from Rotterdam, servant to John
George Fishback of Manheim Township. and by him
assigned to Abraham Rife of Manheim.

John Justice Boltenfeld last from Rotterdam, servant to John
George Fishback of Manheim Township and by him
assign'd to Eronimus Hensilman of Manheim Township.

December 21st.

Arthur Caldwell aged eleven years, with consent of his
Father David, servant to Thomas Shields of Philadelphia.

George Peddle with consent of his Father Joseph, apprentice
to Joseph Master of Philad' cooper.

December 22d.

Thomas Knox last from Ireland, servant to Willian Carson
of Philadelphia.

William Wells with consent of his Father Philip, servant to
Robert Harper of Northern Liberties.

Philip Cake with consent of his Father Adam, apprentice to
Matthias Cake of Philad', Cooper.

James Hollen with consent of his Father John, apprentice to
Benj^m Town of Phil^a Coppersmith.

David Carr apprentice [Aug. 11th 1764] bound before Thos
Willing Esqr, assign'd by Margaret Hanson in Virtue of
a Power of Attorney from her husband Jonathan to
Thomas Penrose of Southwark.

Benjamin Smith to William Hay of Nottingham Township.

Maria Elizabeth Seibell last from Rotterdam, servant to Richard Wistar of Philadelphia.

December 23d.

John Cramp Junr with consent of his Father, apprentice to
Michael Kamper of Philad' Cedar Cooper.

Michael Harman last from Rotterdam, servant to William Will, Pewterer of Phila and by him assign'd to John Honts, Tanner on the other side Cunnewago Creek Settlement.

Mary Fowlo last from Ireland, servant to Robert M'Curley of Hallem Township.

Ann Scanlan [Oct. 20th 1772] servant assigned by William Ledtie to John Frazier of Philadelphia, mariner.

Elizabeth Margaret Hartman last from Rotterdam, servant to Henry Kepple Senr merchtt of Phila and by him assigned to Martin Lauman of the Borough of Lancaster.

Edward Swaine [August 5th 1772] servant assign'd by John Facey to Cornelia Cooper, Brushmaker of Phila.

December 24th.

Maria Elizabeth Folch last from Rotterdam, servant to John Fritz of Southwark.

Mary McCreary [May 15th past] assign'd by Thomas Nelson to Robert Nelson of Fair Manor.

Ludwig Tamer with consent of his mother Anna Elizabeth Tamer, apprentice to Nicholas Miller of Phila, Taylor.

Johannes Weighel last from Rotterdam to William Lawrence of Debtford Township.

Conrad Lambach last from Rotterdam to John Heister of Coventry Township

Anna Catherine Thillen last from Rotterdam, servant to Thomas Pryer of Philadelphia.

Eve Catherine Helffer last from Rotterdam, servant to John Musser of the Borough of Lancaster and by him assign'd to Christian Forrey, watchmaker, of Lampiter Township.

Clary Jongerbloed last from Rotterdam, servant to William Forbes of Philadl

Anna Maria Miller last from Rotterdam, servant to Thomas Prior of Philadl

Elizabeth Margaret Albach last from Rotterdam, servant to Daniel Burkhart of Passyunk Township.

Catherine Albach last from Rotterdam, servant to Rudolph
Feel of Moyamensing Towns[p.]

Barnard Michell last from Rotterdam, servant to Nathan
Garret of Upper Darby Township.

Jacob Nannetter last from Rotterdam, servant to John
Duncan, Hatter, of Phil[a].

December 26th.

John Jacob Spider last from Rotterdam, servant to Nathan
Levering of Roxbery Township.

And[w] Stilling last from Rotterdam, servant to Ristore Lippincott of Greenwich Township.

John Peter Ulrich [Jan[r] 27th 1773] last from Rotterdam,
servant to Henry Kemmerer of Philad[l] and by him
assign'd to Catherine Shetz in Lower Merion.

John Jacob Pifer last from Rotterdam, servant to Job Whit-
tell of Debtford Township.

James Reily last from Rotterdam, servant to Samuel Howell,
merchant, of Philad[l]

John William Finges last from Rotterdam, servant to George
Cooper of Philad[l] and by him assign'd to Christian Petre
of the Borough of Lancaster.

John Peter Finges last from Rotterdam, servant to Philip
Cauble, of Oversalford Township.

John Jacob Yerm last from Rotterdam, servant to Henry
Haines of Phil[a]

John Ward last from Ireland, redemptioner, to Thomas
Brown now cancelled, servant to Philip Price of Kingsess
Township.

Margery Breadley [November 7th & December 14th] to William Laidley of Philadelphia.

Thomas Prendergast last from Ireland, redemptioner, servant
to James Ross of Kingsess Township.

December 28th.

Charles Herter last from Rotterdam, servant to Matthias
Lendenbergher of Philad[l]

Jacob Kledi with consent of his Mother Mary Juker apprentice to Henry Oxbeeker of Stow Creek.

Michael Levy apprentice to Joseph Gavin of Phil* cordwainer, by the Managers of the House of Employment.

Archibald Brian [May 7ᵗʰ 1772] a negro assign'd by James Delaplaine to Mary Sindray of Phil*

Elizabeth Maxzeymour last from Rotterdam servant to John Vanderin of Roxbury.

Elizabeth Jung last from Rotterdam, servant to John Vanderin of Roxbury.

Leonard Hartranfth with consent of his Mother Susanna, apprentice to Henry Hyman of Philad¹, Taylor.

Henry Keyuts & ⎫ last from Rotterdam, servants to Wᵐ
Baltzar his son ⎭ Bryant near Trenton.

Catherine Elizᵉ Germane last from Rotterdam, servant to Christian Shade of Malborough.

John William Maxzeymour last from Rotterdam, servant to Leonard Karg of Lancaster and assign'd by him to Ludwick Lauman.

Philip Sewell aged seven years 20ᵗʰ November last, apprentice to Francis Springer of Phil* cordwainer, by the Managers of the House of Employment.

Maria Elizabeth Pfeifer last from Rotterdam servant to Jacob Hiltzheimer of Phil*

Christian Elizᵉ Pfeifer last from Rotterdam servant to Charles Lyan of Philad¹

Valentine Fingar last from Rotterdam, servant to Nathaniel Donald of Philad¹.

December 29th.

Ann Scanlan [October 20ᵗʰ 1772] servant assign'd by John Fraser to John Brown of Willis Town.

Thomas Hood with consent of his mother Mary, apprentice to Samuel Simpson of Philad¹ Cordwainer.

Elizabeth Becker last from Rotterdam, servant to John Peter of Phil*.

Pheebe Willis servant to John Burrough of Newtown.

Jane Williams last from Ireland, indenture of servitude now cancelled, servant to Thomas Hale of Phil[a]

Honor Sullivan last from Ireland, indenture of servitude now cancelled, servant to John Willson of Phil[a].

Richard Newman last from Galway, redemptioner to Thomas Brown now cancelled, servant to Michael Robinson of Phil[a].

John Heits last from Rotterdam, servant to Henry Kugger of Piles Grove.

John Matthias Dingas last from Rotterdam, servant to Daniel Drinker of Phil[a]

George Swartz last from Rotterdam, servant to Peter Dick of Phil[a].

Charles Miller bound before Tho[s] Willing Esq[r], apprentice assign'd by William Niles to David Jones of Philadelphia, cordwainer.

Maria Elizabeth Meyer last from Rotterdam, servant to Benjamin Olden of Phil[a].

Anna Margaret Konckerl last from Rotterdam, servant to Thomas Proctor of Phil[a]

Adam Stoll last from Rotterdam, servant to Charles Chamberlayne of Philad[a]

December 30th.

Anna Catherina Dingasey last from Rotterdam servant to Levi Hollingsworth of Phil[a]. and by him assigned to Henry Weaver of Strasburgh.

Gotfrid Pister last from Rotterdam, servant to Ludwig Kuhn of Phil[a] and assign'd by him to Henry Shoemaker of Windsor.

Ann Hall [Dec. 18th 1769] to William Walker of Warwick assigned by William Graham.

George Kisler last from Rotterdam, servant to Ludwig Kuhn of Phil[a]., assigned by him to Charles Shoemaker.

Hans George Schenediffer } last from Rotterdam, servants and *Dorothea* his wife } to Samuel Howell of Phil[a]

Adam Schenediffer aged two years with Consent of his Father John George, servant to Samuel Howell

Anna Maria Schenediffer aged four years with consent of her Father, servant to Sam¹ Howell of Phil*

Adam Shafer last from Rotterdam, servant to Ludwig Kuhn of Phil* and assigned by him to Henry Mullin of Windsor.

Simon Frickaver with consent of his mother Catherine apprentice to Peter Schreiver of Phil*. Butcher.

Michael Downs under indenture of servitude to John M*-Connell now cancelled, servant to Thomas Badge of Southwark.

Jacob Shearer last from Rotterdam, servant to John Beatler of Union Township.

Catherine Eli' Helfrigen last from Rotterdam servant to Charles Syng of Phil* and assigned by him to George Musser of Lancaster.

John Godfred Grafmayer last from Rotterdam, servant to William Lamburn of Kennet.

Anna Juliana Brey last from Rotterdam, servant to William Lamburn of Kennet Township.

John Burk under indenture of servitude to Thomas Brown now cancelled, to John Suber Middle Township.

William Short last from Ireland, servant to Saml. Talbot of New Town.

Lott Regan [Nov. 21ˢᵗ 1772] assigned by Samuel Caldwell to Zebulon Rudolph of Maryland.

Fredᵏ Fogle and
Catherin Barbara his
wife
} last from Rotterdam, servants to Jacob Paum of the Northern Libertys

Ludwig Henry Tiseman last from Rotterdam, servant to Benjamin Coultney of Phil* and assigned by him to Robert Park of Chester County.

Simon Jacob Bess last from Rotterdam, servant to Mary Jinkins of Phil*

Anna Elizabeth Pifer last from Rotterdam, servant to John Field of Phil*

Johan Henry Miffet last from Rotterdam, servant to Adam
  Foulke, and by him assigned to Adam Reigard of Lancaster.

December 31st.

Jacob Fress last from Rotterdam, servant to James Sparks
  of Philad¹

Henry Adam Maxzuymour last from Rotterdam servant to
  Anthony Groff of Phil ͣ

Maria Catherine Meyer last from Rotterdam, servant to
  Richard Bache of Phil ͣ

Mary Burn servant assign'd by Joseph Price to Martin
  Juges of Phil ͣ [July 20ᵗʰ last]

Anna Margaret Meyer last from Rotterdam servant to Jeremiah Warder of Philad¹

Nicholas Lederigh last from Rotterdam servant to John Baldwin of Phil ͣ.

Peter Henrickson [Feby. 6ᵗʰ 1772 Oct. 3ʳᵈ] assigned by
  Christopher Senclair to Frederic Burd.

John Frederic Orbel last from Rotterdam, servant to George
  Henry, at the same time assigned by him to his Father
  William Henry.

RECORD OF SERVANTS AND APPRENTICES BOUND
AND ASSIGNED BEFORE HON. JOHN GIBSON,
MAYOR OF PHILADELPHIA, DECEMBER 5TH, 1772–
MAY 21, 1773.

1773.

January 1ˢᵗ.

Hannah Moore under indenture of servitude to John
Hagan now cancelled, servant to Henry Starrett of Phil*.

James Karr with consent of his mother Mary, apprentice
to John Flinn of Phil* cabinet maker.

Anna Mary Famerin Junʳ with consent of her mother,
servant to George Smith of the Northern Liberties and his
wife.

January 2ᵈ.

Frederick Winter last from Rotterdam, servant to Jacob
Coblance of Bristol Township Phil*

Valentine Fingar last from Rotterdam, servant to James
Brinton of Pennsborough Township.

Peter Cellier aged twenty-one years and upwards, an apprentice to Wᵐ Shippen of Phil* Cooper.

George Smith Junʳ with consent of his father, apprentice
to Peter Cress of Phil*

January 4.

John Martin servant to John Raynolds cabinet-maker of
Phil*.

Mary Maxfield aged 12 years and six months, apprentice
to Andrew Bunner of Phil*. merchant by the managers of
the House of Employment.

John Chritⁿ Reineck last from Rotterdam, servant to
Michael Immel of Phil*.

James Woodward with consent of his Brother Thomas, apprentice to John Scattergood of the Northern Liberties Tanner and Currier, to be taught the business, found all necessaries and also allowed to go to night school during the time of his apprenticeship at the expense of his brother.

January 5.

Susanna Spaunin last from Rotterdam, servant to the Rev⁴ John Ewing of Phil*

Barbara Fordyth last from Rotterdam, servant to Francis Wade of Phil*.

Edward Bartholomew with the consent of his mother Mary, apprentice to George Wilson, hatter, of Phil*

January 6.

John Karla with consent of his Father Casper, apprentice to Peter Cooper of Phil* Cordwainer.

James Ford with consent of his Father Stephen, apprentice to Jacob Maag of Passyunk Township.

January 7.

Charles O'Connor [Nov. 12ᵗʰ 1772] servant assigned by James Whiteall to Thomas Moore of Phil*

George Taylor [May 14ᵗʰ 1769 before J. Jones Esqʳ] servant of Samuel Simpson to Amariah Farnsworth of Burden Town, New Jersey.

January 8.

John Nevell [June 3ʳᵈ 1771 & 11ᵗʰ Inst.] apprentice assigned by John Elmsly to John Handlyn of Phil*

Bartholomew Lyons [Sepᵗ 24ᵗʰ 1771] who was under an Indenture of Apprenticeship to Simon Fitzgerald late of Phil*. Cordwainer who has since absconded and by Virtue of an Order of the Mayors Court held the 5ᵗʰ of this Instant, cancelled, and with consent of his Mother Eleanor bound an apprentice to James Starr of Phil* Cordwainer.

Henry Weismiller last from Rotterdam, servant to George Ross of Phil* Butcher.

Conrad Undersee last from Rotterdam, servant to George Ross of Phil* Butcher.

Mary Lincoln servant assign'd by Jonathan Jones to Mary Pugh of Upper Merion. Phil* County

Mary Lincoln [aged five years and five months] servant, by her Father Thomas to Jonathan Jones and assigned by said Jones to Mary Pugh.

John Clark servant to John Marshall of Moyamensing.

January 9.

Thomas McDonald servant to William Richardson of Fawn Township.

January 11.

John Nevell [8th Inst] apprentice assing'd by John Handlyn to his Father Tho* of Phil*

Charlotte Tucker with consent of her Mother Elizabeth Fiddess, apprentice to Townsend White of Phil*

Joseph Bro with consent of his Mother Margaret Le Beauf, apprentice to Joseph Huddle of Southwark Cooper.

Ludwig Reineek } [Feby 23rd 1773] last from *and Maria Eliz^a his wife* } Rotterdam, servants to James Vaux of Providence Township.

John Christopher Haus last from Rotterdam, servant to Samuel Howell of Phil* merchant.

Paul Frederick Brunner last from Rotterdam, servant to John Rupp of Phil*

William Stephens [Dec. 15th last, past] serv^t assign'd by Elis Newlin to Eleazor Levi of New York City.

January 12.

Salome Albright a poor child aged eleven years, apprentice by Joel Zane and Joseph Thatcher Overseers of the Poor for the Northern Liberties to John Moyer, Tanner.

John Hanson servant to Andrew Moynihan of Phil*

James Manly servant assign'd by Matthew Conard to Robert Hopkins Jun* of Philadelphia.

January 13.

John Drinker with consent of his Father Edward apprentice to Bowyer Brooke of Phil* Boat Builder.

Isaac Wood with consent of his Father James apprentice to Bowyer Brooke of Phil* Boat Builder.

Patrick Taaffe [July 19th 1771] who was under Indenture to John Howard now cancelled, servant to James Lees of Phil*

John Mitchell
William Cleark
George Peters   servants to William Montgomery of Au-
John Flintham   gusta Co. in Virginia.
John Mills
William Farley

January 14.

Michael Farrel servants to W*m* Montgomery of Augusta
and *Owen Rogers* Co. in Virginia.

Anthony Auwor & last from Rotterdam, servants to Jo-
Dorothea his wife seph Mitchell of Tredeffryn

Duncan McArthur Junr with consent of his Father apprentice to James Fisher of Phil* Shopkeeper.

James McDonald redemptioner now cancelled, servant to John Scantlan of the Borough of Chester.

January 16.

John Connel last from Ireland redemptioner to Walter Marshal, servant to Robert Gray of Phil*

John Vicker who was under Indenture of Servitude, last from St. Croix, servant to Robert Turner of Phil*

Lewis Portia who was under Indenture to Samuel Penrose now cancelled, servant to Samuel Penrose of Kingcess Township.

January 18.

George Connelly who was under Indenture to Sam¹ Skillen now cancelled, with consent of his mother Elizabeth Rowen, apprentice to John Pollard of Phil*

Anthony Coupel aged 18 yrs. apprentice to Matthew Poller of Phil* Blacksmith.

Arthur Hurry with consent of his Father William apprentice to John McCalla of Phil*

January 19.

Elizabeth Till with consent of her sister Susanna apprentice to Wm Fisher of Phil*

Mary Mahoney [May 8th 1772] assigned by Robert Duncan to Charles White of Phil*

William Wright with consent of his mother Susanna apprentice to Enoch Hughs of Phil*

John Conrad Miffert ⎫
Maria Dorothy his wife & ⎬ servants to Jacob Morgan Junʳ of Phil*
Anna Cathe their daughter ⎭

Samuel Thorn with consent of his Friend Richard Marsh, apprentice to Joseph Marsh of Southwark.

John Conrade Miffert ⎫
Mary Dorothy his wife ⎬ assign'd by Jacob Morgan Junʳ to Jacob Morgan Esqʳ of Carnarven.
& Anna Cathe their Daughter ⎭

Jacob Lutz with the consent of his mother Catherine Cloe, apprentice to Jacob Reese of Phil*

Catherine Zauch with the consent of her Father Christian apprentice to John George Kemle of Phil* and his wife.

January 20.

Juliana Dinges last from Rotterdam servant to Davis Bleid.

Michael Lepp last from Rotterdam, servant to Lawrence Lepp of Phil*

William George Dorrington with consent of his mother Olane Skinner, apprentice to Robert Caruh of Phil*

January 21.

John Feierabend last from Rotterdam servant to Ludwig Kuhn.

Luke Coleman [March 24ᵗʰ 1773] who was lately under an Indenture of apprenticeship to James Buckcannan, apprentice to John Heller Cooper of Phil*

John Job aged three years and ten months with consent of his Mother Mary, apprentice to John White of Passyunck.

January 22.

Christopher Scott aged 17 years, apprentice by the Overseers of the Poor before John Lawrence Esqʳ the 11ᵗʰ February 1766 to John Hillard Cooper, which Indenture is now cancelled with consent of said Hillard and also of the Father Thomas Scott, apprentice by the managers of the House of Employment to David Soloman of Phil* Cedar Cooper.

Thomas Bell with consent of his Father James, apprentice to George Claypoole of Phil* cabinet maker

Elizabeth Margʳ Mackzeiner last from Rotterdam servant to William Bettle of the Northern Liberties.

Thomas Smith with consent of his mother Elizᵉ apprentice to Christel Bartling of Phil*

William Tracy last from Rotterdam, servant to John Kluig of the Northern Liberties.

Jane Mead who was under Indenture to Robert Otway now cancelled, servant to Charles Risk of Phil* and asign'd by him to Robert Park of West Caln Township

George Hollman servant to John Hollman of Plimoth Township

Ludwig Storch servant assigned by Wandle Zerben to George Baker of Norrington Township.

January 23.

Daniel Bakely with consent of his Father Christian, apprentice to John Stall of Phil*

Ludwig Storch [see 22ᵈ Instant] servant assigned by George Baker to Henry Summers of the Northern Liberties Philᵃ county.

John Strawcutter who was under Indenture to Fred. Verner now cancelled and with consent of his Father George, apprentice to Philip Worn of the Northern Liberties Black-smith.

Elisha Dawes [March 31ˢᵗ 1770] apprentice assign'd by William Johnson to John Prish of Philᵃ Bricklayer.

James Beudiker who was under an Indenture of apprenticeship to Daniel Wegmore which is last apprentice to John Hide Coster of Philᵃ

January 25.

John Myers a poor boy aged sixteen years apprentice to Richard Humphreys of Philᵃ

January 26.

Frederica Regina Hubner a servant assigned by John William Hoffman [Dec. 14ᵗʰ 1772] to George Hidle of Philᵃ

Jacob Catz with consent of his grandfather Martin Catz and his Stepmother Rosena, apprentice to Martin Besch of Philᵃ

Barbara Sexin [Dec. 5ᵗʰ 1772] assign'd by Theodore Meminger to John Wᵐ Hoffman of Philᵃ

January 27.

John Peter Ulrick [Dec. 26ᵗʰ 1772] who was a servant by Indenture to Cath. Slutz now cancelled, servant to William Hoffman of Dunker Town.

John Apps [May 20ᵗʰ 1771] aged twenty seven years and upwards, apprentice to Richard Ham of Philᵃ

John Hudson with consent of his mother Mary, apprentice to William Singleton of Southwark, Philᵃ County and his wife.

James Black with consent of his Father Daniel apprentice to Michael Brother of Philᵃ Silversmith

January 28.

Jacob Grub [Dec. 3ᵈ 1771] assign'd by Christʳ Rudolph to Matthew Grimes of Philᵃ

John Bickerton [Janʸ 1ˢᵗ 1770] assign'd by Matthew Grimls to serve Christian Rudolph of Philᵃ.

Joseph Armitage apprentice assign'd by James Worrel to his Father Benjamin Armitage of Bristol Township

Robert Hall with consent of his Friend James Carswell apprentice to Robert Allison of Sᵒwark.

Robert Leech with consent of his Father Duncan, apprentice to Robert Allison of Sᵒwark.

January 29.

John David Neef last from Rotterdam servant to Caspar Wistar of Kings County, N. Y.

Catherine Steel last from Rotterdam, servant to Caspar Wistar of Kings County, New York.

Rachel Chard a poor child aged ten years, apprentice by the Managers of the House of Employment to Thomas Bradford of Philᵃ.

January 30.

Charles Matthew Grill, servant assign'd by Detrick Reese to John Musser of Lancaster.

February 1.

Mary Founder [Feb. 28ᵗʰ 1771] servant assign'd by Joseph Williamson to Andrew Summers of Philᵃ

Jacob Knode with consent of his Father George, apprentice to Godfrey Gebler of Philᵃ black-smith.

February 2.

George Chard a poor child aged seven years apprentice by the Managers of the House of Employment to Edward Wells of Philᵃ Bricklayer.

John Mason servant to Joseph Year.

Stephen Solcher [Dec 4ᵗʰ 1771] servant assign'd by George Shepherd to Christopher Ludwig.

John Mitchell assign'd by Thomas Toole to John Lukins of Phil*

Christiana Frederica Hemphill last from Rotterdam servant to Samuel Rhoads Jun* of Phil*

Elizabeth Reinhold last from Rotterdam servant to Adam Hubley jun* of Phil* and assigned by him to Henry Keppele of Phil*

February 3.

Gislin Humphreys with consent of his Father John apprentice to Thomas Redman of Phil*

February 4.

John Jacob Misser last from Rotterdam servant to William Trautwine of the Northern Liberties.

Anna Maria Inglebold last from Rotterdam, servant to James Wallace of Phil* and by him assign'd to Daniel Clark of Maxfield.

Anthony Joseph Brazier [June 4ᵗʰ 1772] apprentice assign'd by Martin Fiss to Robert Hopkins jʳ of Phil*

Jacob Moser ⎫ last from Rotterdam servant to Jacob Diet-
and Catherine ⎬ rick of Waterford Township.
his wife ⎭

Mariah Barbara Hitz last from Rotterdam, servant to Christopher Dietrick of Waterford Township.

Tobias Hitz last from Rotterdam servant to Christopher Dietrick of Waterford Township.

February 5.

Bridget Rogers [May 9ᵗʰ 1772] servant assign'd by Joseph Johnson to Doctʳ Richard Farmer of Phil*

Richard Riddle with consent of his brother James apprentice to John King of Phil* House Carpenter

February 6.

Nicholas Izenninger with consent of his mother Sarah Rein hard apprentice to John Reinhard of Southwark Phil* County.

George Frederick Scheller [Sep' 33ᵈ 1771] servant assigned by John Rhor to Lewis Braihl of Philᵃ

Joseph Simmers apprentice assigned by Joseph Butler to Peter Robeson of Philᵃ

Casper Shibe last from Rotterdam, with consent of his Father John servant to George Kopper of Philᵃ

Sarah Moylan with consent of her Father Joseph, apprentice to Philip Worn of the Northern Liberties.

February 8.

Charles Miller last from Rotterdam servant to Matthias Meyer of Philᵃ

Margaret Barbara Fritz last from Rotterdam servant to Christian Derrick of Moyamensing Township

Johannes Fritz last from Rotterdam, servant to Christian Derrick of Moyamensing Township.

Catherine Larshin last from Rotterdam servant to Lawrence Upman of the Northern Liberties.

Maria Elizᵉ Larshin last from Rotterdam servant to Lawrence Upman of the Northern Liberties.

John May with consent of his Father William, apprentice to Samuel Read of Philᵃ Hatter.

February 9.

Michael Downs [Dec. 30ᵗʰ 1772] servant assign'd by Thomas Badge to Robert Magill of Philᵃ

Margaret Kelly who was under Indenture of Servitude to James Delaplaine now cancelled at request of Parties, servant to Daniel King.

John Magrath [July 22ⁿᵈ 1772 & March 15ᵗʰ 1773] servant assig'n by Catherine Curfiss Executrix to the Estate of Christian Curfiss dec'd, to John Hannah.

Elinor Fenn [Nov 28ᵗʰ 1771] servant assign'd by Jerimiah Mahony to Charles Mayse of Philᵃ

February 10.

Daniel Troy [Oct. 26ᵗʰ 1772] servant assign'd by Anthony

Fortune to Gamaliel Garrison of Manatan Precink Salem County.

Richard Newman [Dec. 29th 1772] who was under an Indenture of servitude to Michael Robinson apprentice to Stephen Shewell of Phil[a] Biscuit Baker.

February 11.

Jacob Harper with consent of his Father Peter apprentice to Christopher Binks of Phil[a]

John McClure with consent of his Father Robert, apprentice to William Green of Phil[a]

February 12.

Henry William Kemp last from Rotterdam, servant to John Williamson of Burlington.

James Maglathery with consent of his mother Elizabeth, apprentice to William Robinson of Phil[a] Taylor

Anna Marg[t] Meyer last from Rotterdam, servant to John Souder of Phil[a]

Jacob Krammer [Feb[y] 4th 1771] assigned by William Trautwine to Hugh Henry of Phil[a].

John Slour a free negro, servant to John Pyle of Brandywine Hundred.

February 13.

Michael Downs [9th Ins[t]] assign'd by Thomas Badge to Foster McConnell of Phil[a]

Mary Finley [Jan. 7th 1772] assign'd by John Adam Schwaab to George Benner of Middle Town.

William Evans with consent of his Mother Mary, apprentice to John Watkins of Warminster Township and his wife.

Patrick Weiargan apprentice assign'd by Patrick Farrel to Philip Moore of Phil[a] Merch[t]

Marion McDonald servant assigned by David Ireland to Robert Lumsden of Phil[a]

Gabriel Gosshaw [Sep[t] 20th 1771] servant assign'd by John Stienmetz to John Inglis of Phil[a].

February 15.

Neil Turner [Nov' 26th 1771] apprentice assigned by Jacob Van Sciver to Leonard Tweed of the Northern Liberties Cordwainer

Michael Caldwell servant to Thomas Bond Jun' of Phil*

Hannah Funks [Nov. 12th 1772] apprentice assign'd by William Morris to Archibald McIllroy of Phil*

John Vanwrinckle with consent of his Father Jacob Vanwrinckle, apprentice to Thomas Darrah of Phil* Sadler.

George Shrunk with consent of his Father Bernard, apprentice to Christopher Zimmerman of the Northern Liberties.

Samuel Kemble Jun' with consent of his Father apprentice to Tench Francis and Tench Tilghman of Phil* merchants.

February 16.

Philip Cooke [March 30th 1772] under Indenture to *Peter Mahrliz* now cancelled, servant to Daniel Barnes of Phil*

February 17.

Eleanor Campbell assigned by Daniel Meredith to her Father Arthur.

Jane Peacock [Feb' 27th 1771] apprentice assign'd by Jacob Graff to William Bispham of Blockley Township.

Mary Patterson with the consent of her mother apprentice to Jn° Burley of Upper Makfield Township.

Jacob Binder with consent of his Father Philip apprentice to George Heyl of Phil*.

Marion McDonald who was under an Indenture of Servitude now cancelled, servant to James Riddle of Southwark.

February 18.

Rebecca Fitch with consent of her mother Elizabeth Friar, apprentice to Edward Bonsall of Phil* House Carpenter.

Barnet Lawerswyler jun' with consent of his Father apprentice to Jacob Shreiver of Phil* Leather Dresser.

Charles O'Connor [January 7th 1778] assigned by Thomas
Moore tó James Starr of Phil^a Cordwainer.

February 19.

Joseph Nagle [Sep^t 30th 1772] apprentice assign'd by
Henry Felten to this Father John Nagle of Phil^a

Barbara Myardie [Oct. 6th 1772] assign'd by John Lawrence Esqr to John Ellet of Phil^a

James Thomas with consent of his Mother Elinor Thomas,
apprentice to John Moyer of the Northern Liberties and his
wife.

Mary Fitzgerald [March 17 1772] servant to Thomas
Thomson to William Moore of Phil^a

John Carins servant assigned by William Moore to
Thomas Thompson of Southwark.

February 20.

Margaret McKay with consent of her Father Robert, apprentice to Jedediah Snowden of Phil^a

Michael Downs who was under Indenture of Servitude
to Foster McConnell now cancelled, servant to Finley M^c-
Donnal of Southwark [Feby 13th 1773]

February 22.

Henry Gordon of full age, apprentice to William Hasle-
wood of Phil^a.

Jonathan Freicle last from Rotterdam, servant to John
Philips of Phil^a

Anthony Simeda, servant assigned by Casper Singar to
serve Anthony Pittan.

February 23.

Ludwig Reineck [Jany 11th 1773] who with his wife Mary
Elizabeth, servants to James Vaux, and assign'd by him to
John Soltar of Phil^a

John Bower with consent of his Father Thomas, apprentice to Morris Trueman of Phil^a

February 24.

Christian Kelpert, servant assign'd by David Waggoner to Jacob Kelpert [Oct. 3ʳᵈ 1772] of Germantown.

Grace Keen a free negro with consent of her grandmother Grace Roy, apprentice to James Thompsen of Oxford Township.

James Winters with the consent of his Father Patrick Winters, apprentice to Robᵗ Wickersham of Blockley Township.

February 27.

John Clark [Janʸ 8ᵗʰ 1773] assign'd by John Marshall to Michael Schwartz of Plumstead.

Henry Zimmerman [Janʸ 22ⁿᵈ 1772] assign'd by George Epley to Rudolph Heiber of Philᵃ.

Mary Bryan assign'd by John Little to Joseph Richardson [May 4ᵗʰ 1772] of Providence Township

David Altimus with consent of his Father Fredᵏ apprentice to Rudolph Neff of Bedford Township.

Michael Barry assign'd by Capᵗ David McCutcheon to John Hall of Philᵃ

Michael Farel [Jany 14ᵗʰ 1773] assign'd by James Starret to John Smith of Radnor Township.

March 1.

John Robinson with consent of his guardian Jonas Supplee, apprentice to Joseph Moore of Phila.

Philip Cook [Febʸ 16ᵗʰ past] who was under an Indenture of Servitude to Daniel Barnes now cancelled, servant to John Buckingham of the Northern Liberties.

Alexander Wilson, with consent of his mother Mary, apprentice to George Falker of Philᵃ Cordwainer.

John Bowland apprentice to John Parrish of Philᵃ Bricklayer.

John Hamilton servant to Henry Hill Esqʳ of Philᵃ

March 3.

Leonard Lutz apprentice to Henry Kurtz of Philᵃ

Christopher Stateback apprentice to Alexander Greenwood of Phil[a]

James Hall servant to Levy Marks of Phil[a] Taylor.

John Geary servant to Francis Trumbel of Southwark.

Elizabeth Bedley with consent of her Father Henry, servant to John Philips of Phil[a]

March 4.

Margaret Hall [bound by Robert Hardie and William Drewry overseers of the Poor before Thomas Lawrence Esq[r] May 2] assign'd by John Erwen to serve Robert Thomas of Upper Hanover Township.

Ann Hollowell with consent of her Mother Mary apprentice to Peter Sulter of Phil[a]

Adam Lear with consent of his uncle Martin Reinhart, apprentice to John Cress, of Phil[a] Blacksmith

March 5.

John Frider a Portuguese, apprentice to Christian Fiss of Phil[a]

Frederica Regina Hubner [Jan[y] 26th 1773], servant to Rosina Henizen of the Northern Liberties.

Jacob Trapple with consent of his Mother Sarah Ludgate, apprentice to Jacob Vansciver of the Northern Liberties, cordwainer.

March 6.

Jane White [Nov. 30th 1772] servant assign'd by Jn Harkins to Thomas Church of Limerick Township.

Frederic Castill ⎫
Francis Doyer ⎪ who were under an Indenture of Servitude to William Hasleton J[r] now
Telman Dresser ⎬ cancelled, to serve William Hasleton
Francis Belastein ⎭ Sen[r]

Barbary Brindle with consent of her mother Abagail, apprentice to Conrad Weaver of Bristol.

Anna Margaret Thomas [Sept. 20th 1771] servant assigned by John Stillwaggon to Adam Mullador of Passyunk.

William Wilkinson with the consent of his Mother Anna, apprentice to Thomas Paul of Lower Dublin Township.

Isaac Mc Alee with consent of his Father William, apprentice to James Armitage of Southwark.

John Wagg with consent of his Father John, apprentice to Michael Brothers of Phil*

March 8.

William Smith [Oct. 22^d 1772] who was under Indenture of Servitude to James Sutton, now cancelled, apprentice to Samuel Ruhard of Phil* cordwainer.

William Tuncks with consent of his Father William apprentice to Archibald M'Ilroy, peruke maker.

March 9.

John Creemer last from Rotterdam servant to John Souder of Deerfield Township.

Maria Magdelena Creemer last from Rotterdam to John Souder of Deerfield Township.

March 10.

John Campbel servant to Philip Jacobs of Racoons Creek, Jersey.

March 11.

Elizabeth Onongst with consent of her Mother Elizabeth, apprentice to Martin Weis of Phil^a

Abel Jeherd apprentice to Thomas Stroud of Brandewine Hundred.

March 13.

Robert Shoemaker with consent of his Father Benjamin, apprentice to Jonathan Dilworth of Phil* House-Carpenter.

William Murray with consent of his Father assign'd by Bernard Gratz apprentice to Alexander Henderson of Phil*

Edward Mc Glochlin aged sixteen years, apprentice to John Cox Marriner, of Phil^a.

Terrence Connoly servant to Christopher Dietrick of Waterford.

Nathaniel Raine with consent of his Father Samuel, apprentice to Jacob Godshalk of Phil[a] clock-maker.

March 15.

Thomas Cruise redemptioner to Jn° Dickson now cancelled, servant to Richard Porter.

John Magrath [Feb 9th 1773] servant assign'd by John Hannah to Cornelius Cooper of Phil[a]

March 16.

Margaret Campbell with consent of her mother Elizabeth, apprentice to William Bonham of Phil[a]

Joseph Nourse apprentice to Amos Stettele Esq[r] of Phil[a]

James Campbell with consent of his mother Mary apprentice to Andrew Philler of Phil[a] Cordwainer.

Henry Mang with consent of his step father Daniel Burkhart, apprentice to Thomas Search of Southwark, wheelwright.

Elizabeth M[c]Cauly with consent of her mother Rebecca Wessell, apprentice to Thomas Leiper of Phil[a] Tobacconist.

Mary Hymen, servant assigned by John Rupp to Christian Detterer [Dec. 9th 1772] of Rock Hill.

March 17.

Jn° Fred[k] Albright a servant [April 21st 1772] discharged from his servitude by his master John Zeller.

Mary Burman with consent of her Father Edward, apprentice to Rachel M[c]Cullough of Phil[a]

Rachel Burman with consent of her Father Edward, apprentice to Rachel M[c]Cullough of Phil[a]

Maria Elizabeth Folck assigned by John Fritz to John Summers of the Mannor of Moorland. [Dec. 13th 1772]

Margaret Ferguson [Nov. 4th 1772] assigned by Peter January to James Pyat of Derby.

March 18.

Neil M. Commaghill, servant to John Marshall of Moyamensing Township.

March 19.

Catherine Everding last from Rotterdam servant to Jacob
Dietrick of Phil[a]

March 20.

William Postlethwaite Heysham with consent of his Father
William, apprentice to Cop[l] John Souder of Phil[a]

Anna Maria Camberine assigned by Samuel Noble to
Matthew Keen of Oxford Township.

March 22.

Thomas Fitzgerald [May 30th 1772] who was under an Indenture of apprenticeship to Sebastian Muffler now cancelled, apprentice to Martin Noll of Phil[a] Baker, and his
wife Elizabeth.

Joanna Griffin assigned by George Wilson to Archibald
Gardner of Phil[a] [June 11th 1772]

Frederick Freile [Sep[t] 19th 1772] servant assigned with his
own consent by Ludwig Karcher to William Murray of
Cashasky in the Illinois.

March 23.

Samuel Land with consent of his mother Charity and of
Peter Turner his guardian, apprentice to Gunning Bedford
of Phil[a] House-carpenter

William Bowers [bound before J. Lawrence Esq[r]] apprentice assign'd by John Moody to Daniel Evans of Philadelphia, Blacksmith.

James Venall [Jan[y] 5th 1770] who was under an Indenture
of Servitude to Benjamin Fuller now cancelled, apprentice
to Francis Trumble of Southwark, Windsor, chair maker.

Anna Eliz[a] Habacki [Dec. 7th 1772] assigned by Margaret Past executrix of Lawrence Past, to Michael Steitz of
Back Creek Hundred.

March 24.

Luke Coleman [June 21ˢᵗ 1773] assigned by John Heller to Casper Schnyder of Philᵃ Cooper.

Joseph Clark Jr. with consent of his Father, apprentice to Jonathan Evans of Philᵃ Cooper.

John Souder with consent of his Father, apprentice to Matthias Gilbert of Philᵃ

March 25.

John Hamcher last from Rotterdam, servant to Sarah Davis of Stow Creek

Mary Elizabeth Hamcher last from Rotterdam, servant to John Duffield of Philᵃ

George Bartholomew with consent of his Brother Benjamin Town, apprentice to John Hood of Philᵃ

Michael Lepp [Janʸ 19ᵗʰ 1773] assigned by Lawrence Lepp to Frederick Frailey of Philᵃ

March 26.

Nicholas Gilbert aged 21 years, apprentice to Caspar Murath of Philᵃ chaise maker.

March 27.

Theobald Cline [Dec. 14ᵗʰ 1772] servant assign'd by George Wert to William McIlvain of Philᵃ

John Bignal a poor boy bound by a Majority of the Managers of the House of Employment to Jesse Williamson of Philᵃ

Charles Frederick Featherman last from Rotterdam, servant to Valentine Standley of Philaᵃ

March 29.

Charles Riggen [August 1ˢᵗ 1772] assigned by Robert Cooper to Alexander Rutherford of Philᵃ

George Thompson with consent of his Mother Margaret Lesley, apprentice to Philip Hayd of Philᵃ

Grace Buxton with consent of her Uncle James Coffer apprentice to Joseph Coffer of Gloucester

Godfrey Affler assigned by George Kner to Jacob Biderman of the Northern Liberties.

Maria Elizabeth Reineck who with her husband Ludwig, servants to James Vaux and at the expiration of their time servants to John Shea of Phil*

March 30.

Anna Spess Fisher last from Rotterdam servant to Frederic Boyer of Phil*

Arthur Thomas [April 30ᵗʰ 1770—J. Shoemaker Esqʳ] assigned by Thomas Naglee to Joseph Carr of Phil*

March 31.

John Miller assigned by Joshua Lampartee to John Bigler of Phil*

Emanuel Hyams servant to John Henry of Phil*

April 1.

James Cotter servant to Henry Weaver of Strasburg.

Charles Gotteil Hempel [Oct. 8ᵗʰ 1772] assign'd by John Ellwood to Martin Weis of Phil*

April 2.

John Butler servant to Anthony Fortune of Phil*

William Davis servant to John Quick of Oxford.

Richard Brown with consent of his Father George apprentice to Richard Masen of the Northern Liberties.

Robert Garret apprentice to Benjamin Griffit of Southwark.

Thomas Quill [Aug. 1ˢᵗ 1771] assign'd by Robert Greaver to James Willson of Piquay.

April 3.

John Collis [March 19ᵗʰ 1771] apprentice assign'd by John Bament to David Ware of Phil*

Charles Godleib Hempel [April 1ˢᵗ 1773] servant assign'd by Martin Weis to David Shafer of Philᵃ

John Sheppard with consent of his Father Josiah apprentice to Richard Inkson of Philᵃ mariner.

April 5.

Jacob Awalt with consent of his Father John apprentice to Frederick Walter of Philᵃ bricklayer.

Juliana Winey [Dec. 31ˢᵗ 1771] assign'd by Catherine Carpenter to William Moulder of Philᵃ

James West apprentice to Thomas Hough of Philᵃ cooper.

William Arnell Junʳ with consent of his Father apprentice to John Piles of Philᵃ House Carpenter.

Thomas Rogers with consent of his Father Joseph apprentice to Jacob Young of Philᵃ

William Reeburg with consent of his mother Mary Mossor, apprentice to Thomas Redman of Philᵃ Tin Plate worker.

Henry Roark servant to Jonathan Adams of Philᵃ

Hans George Schenediffer } [Dec. 30ᵗʰ 1772] servant as-
and Dorothy his wife   } sign'd by Samuel Howell to
Gilbert Rodman of Bensalem.

Adam Schenediffer [Dec. 30ᵗʰ 1772] servant assign'd by Samuel Howell to Gilbert Rodman of Bensalem.

Anna Maria Schenediffer [Dec. 30ᵗʰ 1772] servant assigned by Samˡ Howell to Gilbert Rodman of Bensalem.

April 6.

John Albert Junʳ [Mar. 12ᵗʰ 1771] apprentice assign'd by Christian High to John Rudle of Philᵃ Taylor.

April 7.

Griffith Owen with consent of his mother Elizabeth Owen, apprentice to Jacob Godshalk of Philᵃ clock-maker.

Margaret Sadleigh [Febʸ 22ⁿᵈ 1772] assign'd with her own consent by Thomas Masturman to William Lawrence of Deptford.

April 8.

Elizabeth Warner with consent of her mother Hannah, apprentice to Joseph Jenkins of Philᵃ House Carpenter.

April 10.

Henry Liz apprentice to Adam Stone of Philᵃ Butcher.

Elizabeth Jones with consent of her Father Thomas, apprentice to John Joseph and Hannah his wife of Philᵃ

April 12.

Johann Frederick Fetterman last from Rotterdam servant to Martin Kreider of Philᵃ

John McKay [Oct. 27ᵗʰ 1772] assigned by Charles Mears to his Father Hector MᶜKay of East Nottingham, Chester County.

Dan Bristol with consent of his Father Hezekiah apprentice to Robert Warrill of Philᵃ cordwainer·

Godlip Figely servant assign'd by Henry Funk to Abraham Kinsey of Philᵃ

April 13.

Joseph Monney servant to Jacob Tryne of Passyunk.

John Frierabend [Janʸ 21ˢᵗ 1773] assign'd by Ludwig Kukn to Reverend Frederick Muhlenberg of Heidelberg Township.

Henry Sharick [Nov 22ⁿᵈ 1771] who was under an Indenture of Servitude to William Jenkins now cancelled, servant to George Seasholtz of Goshahoppen Philᵃ

Alice Bryan assign'd by Peter Nowland to John Murray of Providence Township, Philᵃ

Samuel Moss with consent of his Father Isaac apprentice to Charles Stow of Philᵃ Tayler.

Amarias Coxe [Novemʳ 23ʳᵈ 1771] assign'd by William Willmore to Henry Cary of Philᵃ

William May servant to John Reynolds of Philᵃ

April 14.

John Milner Junr [Octr 10th 1770] who was under an Indenture to Thomas Low, cancelled by the Mayors Court with consent of his Father, apprentice to Samuel Barrow of Phil^a watchmaker.

John Rowan [Octr 25th 1771] assign'd by Presley Blackiston to Jacob Peters of Phil^a cordwainer.

Anna Cath. Thillen [Decr 24th 1772] assign'd by Charles Pryer to Michael Croll of Upper Salford.

Margaret Bacon servant to Lawrence Fagan of the Northern Liberties.

William Musgrove with consent of his Father Matthew, apprentice to Wm Williams of the Northern Liberties.

Leonard Hartranfft [December 28th 1772] assign'd by Henry Hyman to Godfrey Haga of Phil^a.

Dennis Kough assign'd by Capt Noel Todd to Bryan O'Harra of Phil^a.

Frederick Fox with consent of his step mother Eliz^a Fox, apprentice to Conrad Alster of Phil^a Cordwainer.

Edward Harper assign'd by Capt Noel Todd to Christopher Collis of Phil^a.

Archibald McSparran with consent of his Uncle Archibald, apprentice to George Hyle of Phil^a Leather Breeches maker and skinner.

John Edwards assign'd by Capt Edward Spain to Henry Neal of Phil^a

James Davie assign'd by Capt Edward Spain to Henry Neal of Phil^a

RECORD OF SERVANTS AND APPRENTICES BOUND
AND ASSIGNED BEFORE HON. JOHN GIBSON,
MAYOR OF PHILADELPHIA, DECEMBER 5TH, 1772–
MAY 21, 1773.

1773.

April 15th.

Maria Catherine Mifflin with consent of her Father
George, apprentice to Jacob Waggner of Phil* cooper.

Betty—Mulattoe [March 21ᵁ 1772] assign'd by Samuel
Moore to Samuel McClure of Southwark.

John Zinn apprentice to Richard Porter, Tallow Chandler,
before Isaac Jones Esqʳ Mayor by Joseph Warner and
Isaac Cathrall, Overseers of the Poor, the Indenture now
cancelled, apprentice to George Wack of Phil* Cordwainer
by the Managers of the House of Employment.

Owen Carney & } servants to William Montgomery of
William Dodd } Augusta Co, Virginia.

Luke Haley servant to Wᵐ Montgomery of Augusta
County, Virginia.

John Burns servant to Bernard Sweeny of Augusta
County, Virginia.

John Harrold, servant to Edward Cather of Augusta Co.
Virginia.

Thoˢ Brown servᵗ to Edward Cather of Augusta Co. Va.

April 16th.

Sarah Colford servant assign'd by Anna Margaret Menge,
Executrix to the Estate of Henry Menge dec'd to John
Menge of the Northern Liberties.

Alexander Duguid apprentice to Richard Armit of Phil*.

Thomas Marshall servant to Wᵐ Montgomery of Augusta
County, Va.

Thomas Mayfield & } servants to Barnard Sweeny of Au-
Daniel Montgomery } gusta County, Virginia.

John Murphy servant to Edward Cather of Augusta Co.

Joseph Aydelott apprentice to Peter January of Phil[a]
cordwainer.

April 17th.

Michael Hitts apprentice to George Cooper, Skin Dresser
of Phil[a].

Gertrude Shoemaker last from Rotterdam, servant to Edward Penington of Phil[a].

Martha Murray }
Francis More } servants to James Taylor of Shippens-
Mary Nichols } burgh Cumberland Co.
Mary Humphreys }

Sarah Frazier } servants to James Taylor of Shippens-
Judith Conner } burgh Pa.

Susannah Thompson servant to James Taylor of Shippensburgh.

Benjamin Bankson apprentice to Samuel Burge of Phil[a]
Distiller.

Sophia Quinn a poor child aged about six years apprentice
to James Nevil of the Northern Liberties by the Managers
of the House of Employment.

Elizabeth Clarke servant to Robert Bill of Phil[a].

John Chambers with consent of his Mother Mary Chambers, apprentice to Caspar Souder of the Northern Liberties
of Phil[a] cordwainer.

Henry Fox with consent of his Step-Mother Eliz[a], Apprentice to Jacob Brand of Phil[a] cedar-cooper.

Jeremiah Bourgeois with consent of his Father John, apprentice to Frederick Hitner of Phil[a].

April 20th.

Richard Stacy with consent of his uncle John Tolly, apprentice to Levy Marks of Phil[a].

Michael Haley apprentice to John M[c]Cullouch in Ireland,

the Indenture being lost, apprentice to Hugh M°Culloch of Phil⁴ Merch⁴.

Samuel Milward assign'd by Noel Todd to William Peerson of the Northern Liberties Phil⁴.

Daniel M˓Michael with consent of his Mother Mary, apprentice to George Way, coach maker of Phil⁴.

Thomas Cummings with consent of his Father John, apprentice to Stephen Phipps of Phil⁴ Taylor.

April 22d.

Henry Creber with consent of his Father, apprentice to George White of Phil⁴ Taylor.

James Lavers with consent of his Mother Mary, apprentice to Edward Bonsell of Phil⁴.

Catherine Blanck last from Rotterdam by Joseph Pemberton of Phil⁴.

Levin Harmanson with consent of his mother Sabia Jestor signified by his Uncle John Harmanson apprentice to Robert Loosely of Phil⁴.

Matthias Kemp with consent of his Father Christian apprentice to Jacob Sivevell of Phil⁴.

Peter Weller with consent of his Mother Mary, apprentice to George Way of Phil⁴ Coach-Maker.

Luke Coleman [Janʸ 21ˢᵗ 1773] assign'd by John Keller to Chamless Allen of Phil⁴.

Mary Mitchell with consent of her Father John Mitchell, apprentice to Jonathan Newhouse of New Britain Township and his wife.

Mary M˓Ilroy who was under an Indenture of Servitude to Andrew Porter now cancelled, servant to Charles Prior of Phil⁴.

April 23rd.

James Kegan assign'd by James Cooper to John Wilcocks.

April 24th.

James Enoss with consent of his Father and Mother apprentice to John Martin of Phil⁴.

April 26th.

Elizabeth Waggoner with consent of her Father Frederic, apprentice to Benjamin Davis of Phil⁴ and his wife.

Ann Canjumtach [Dec' 21ˢᵗ 1768—I. Jones Esq'] assign'd⁴ by Nicholas Barkow to Thomas Bishop.

Hugh Owen last from Liverpool, apprentice to Jonathan Meredith of Phil⁴ currier.

Robert Mortimer who was under an Indenture of Servitude to Jacob Fletcher for his passage from Liverpool now cancelled, apprentice to Jonathan Meredith of Phil⁴ Currier.

April 28th.

Ann Oquener [May 18ᵗʰ 1772] to Guy Johnson of Albany.

John Hasleton assigned by Isaac Jones to Samuel Brusster of the Northern Liberties.

Thomas Yardlay with consent of his father, apprentice to Sam¹¹ Brusster ship carpenter of the Northern Libertys.

Daniel Bakely with consent of his Father Henry, apprentice to George Furback of the Northern Liberties of Phil⁴.

Paul Cooper with consent of his Father David signified by a letter to Reuben Hains, apprentice to Uriah Woolman of Phil⁴.

Robert Cowell servant to Edmond Milare.

James Belfour servant to Archibald Graham of Frederic County, Virginia.

George Schnitzer [April 22ᵈ 1772] under Indenture to George Cooper, apprentice to Matthias Sherman of Phil⁴ cordwainer.

William Filliston servant to Archibald Graham of Virginia.

April 29th.

Adam Rifly with consent of his mother Anna Marg', apprentice to Michael Graff of the Northern Liberties, Tanner and Currier.

Elizabeth Horean with consent of her Father William apprentice to John Halzer of Phil⁴ and his wife.

William Becket under Indenture to James Cooper now cancelled, paid for his passage from Liverpool, servant to James Starr of Phil*.

April 30th.

Christiein Brandt last from London, servant to Joseph Potts.

Francis Cooper [Nov. 29th 1771] under Indenture to Ephraim Faulkner now cancelled, apprentice to Robert Patterson of Phil*.

Charles Gleckner last from London to Israel Morris, and assign'd by him to Sam¹ Morris Jun' of Phil*.

John Gerard Meyer last from London.

John Fred. Rintleman.

John Miller last from London, servant to William Allison of Phil* Sugar Baker.

Peter Doyle with consent of his Father James, apprentice to Philip Druckinmiller of Phil*.

Godfrey Gibower last from London, servant to Robert Parrish of Phil*.

Daniel Fegan with consent of his Father Patrick, apprentice to Martin Juges of Phil* Cabinet maker.

Hugh Fegan with consent of his Father Patrick, apprentice to William Martin of Phil*.

May 1st.

Elizabeth Frazier with consent of her mother, apprentice to William Hodge and his wife Eleanor of Phil*.

Fred Bosserman* last from London, servant to Francis Hopkinson of Phil*.

William Wood servant assign'd by David McCutcheon to George Correy of New London Township.

William Connoly a poor boy bound by a majority of the Managers of the House of Employment to Patrick Farrel of Phil* Cooper.

Charles Alexander with consent of his mother Eve Lurke, apprentice to William Pierson of Kensington Phil*.

John Woodrow last from London and with consent of his Friend William Norton, apprentice to John Balderston Jun*ʳ* of Solbury Township.

William Nick with consent of his Father, apprentice to Philip Druckenmiller of Phil*ᵃ* Taylor.

Simon Weyland servant to James Conpaid of Phil*ᵃ*.

Edward McQuillen last from Ireland assign'd by Hugh Blair to Aaron Ashbridge of Goshen, Chester Co.

Meredith McGown servant assign'd by Cap*ᵗ* William McCullough to James Paker of Uchland Township.

John Puriol last from London, servant to Andrew Beckman of Phil*ᵃ*.

Anthony Koneg last from London to William Logan Esq*ʳ* of Phil*ᵃ*.

Nathan Riffet with consent of his Father Nicholas apprentice to William Tolbert of the Northern Liberties Taylor.

Catherine Calaker servant assign'd by Captain David McCuctheon to John Evans of Phil*ᵃ*.

Rachael Walker assigned by William McCulloch to Walter Shea of Phil*ᵃ*.

Ann Murphy assigned by William McCullough to George Stanforth of Princeton, New Jersey.

May 4th.

Ann Murray assign'd by Jo*ˢ* Cooper to James Logan of Phil*ᵃ*.

Henry Marrier last from London by Richard Rundle of Phil*ᵃ* servant to him with consent of his Father.

Samuel Low servant to James Lees of Phil*ᵃ*.

Robert Biggart last from Ireland by James Blaxton of Chester Township.

Margaret McKivan assign'd by William McCullough to Patrick Bevin of Southwark.

Daniel McEvoy under indenture of servitude to William McCullough now cancelled, last from Ireland, servant to James Stewart of Phil*ᵃ* and assigned by him to William Rerion of the Northern Liberties.

Jane Blair assign'd by William M°Cullough to Job Fallows of Ashe Town, Chester County.

Clemens Manypenny assign'd by William M°Cullough to Job Fallows of Ashetown.

William Honeyman with consent of his Father, apprentice to Robert Smith of Phil^a Hatter.

Samuel Smart under Indenture of Servitude to William Thompson for his passage from Ireland now cancelled, apprentice to Robert Kennedy of Phil^a.

May 5th.

Conrad Undersee under Indenture of Servitude to George Ross now cancelled, servant to George Kastner Whitpain Township.

Adam Mc Connell assign'd by Hugh Blair to John Smith of Lower Chichester.

Patrick Tagert assign'd by Hugh Blair to John Smith of Lower Chichester.

John Peter Gable last from London, to Reuben Hains of Phil^a and assigned by him to W^m M°Clay Esqr of Sunberry, Northumberland County.

James Sweeney [July 13th 1772] assign'd by John O'Bryan to his Father Dennis Sweeney, of Carlisle.

John Francis Gonder last from London, servant to Michael Lapp of East Whiteland Township, Chester Co.

Mary Mc Gee servant assign'd by Capt Willm M°Cullough to Benjamin Lightfoot of Reading.

Henry Conrad Boger last from London, to Levis Lohren of Phil^a.

Sarah Smart assign'd by William Thompson to John Shurman of Phil^a.

Jacob Hoober with consent of his Father Rudolph apprentice to John Rouch of Phil^a Skinner.

Thomas Riddle last from London servant to William Cliffton of Southwark.

Margaret Mc Cloud assign'd by William M°Cullough to George Ranken of Phil^a.

Patrick Hile assign'd by William M°Cullough to James Fullton of Phil".

George M°Gillis assigned by William M°Cullough to Selwood Griffin of Phil".

May 6th.

David Clarke with consent of his Brother John, apprentice to Francis Tremble of Phil" cabinet-maker.

James Loughlin last from Ireland, under Indenture to John and James Luke now cancelled, servant to William Alleson of Phil".

John M°Ivers last from Ireland, under Indenture to William M°Cullough now cancelled, servant to John Steel of North Carolina.

Mary Huthinson assign'd by William M°Cullough to Samuel Shoemaker Esq' of Phil".

Mary Donnan assigned by William M°Cullough to Jacob Miller of the Northern Liberties.

Esther Piles with consent of her Guardian John Wheelbank of Lewis Town, apprentice to Hannah Donaldson of Phil".

John Doyle assign'd by David Hoops to William Dibley of Phil" [Oct. 20ᵗʰ 1772].

John Yourt last from Ireland, under Indenture to William Thompson now cancelled, to William Donnell of Phil".

John Menge with consent of his Mother Margaret, apprentice to Jacob Weaver of the Northern Liberties, Tanner and Currier.

May 7th.

Patrick Keith to Benjamin Davis of Phil".

John Graham aged seven years, with consent of his Mother Mary, apprentice to Isaac Coran of Phil" Tavern keeper.

John Henry Miller last from London with consent of his Mother Dorothea, apprentice to Thomas Penrose of Southwark, ship-carpenter and mast-maker.

Christina Barbara Danderin last from Rotterdam to Tho⁣* Penrose of Southwark.

Daniel Rourke assign'd to John Inglis of Phil⁣*.

John Hart servant to Charles Gibbs of Maryland.

Cornelius Durre [Nov. 18ᵗʰ 1772] servant assign'd by Archibald M⁣ᶜElroy to William Blythe of Phil⁣*.

James Kite assign'd by Joseph Volam to John Goodwin of Phil⁣*.

Jeremiah Merryfield
William Hartley
William Vaghorne ⎫ Assign'd by Joseph Volams to Abram
John Bragg   ⎬ Kinsing of Phil⁣*.
John Davies   ⎭

May 8th.

Charles Warner with consent of his father Joseph apprentice to Benjamin Hooton of Phil⁣*.

Henry Howard with consent of his father Peter, apprentice to Joseph Warner of Phil⁣*.

John Mannen with consent of his Father, apprentice to John Fox of Greshem Township.

Richard Orcle assign'd by Seymour Hood to Joseph Lachet of Wrights Town.

William Simmer assigned by Seymour Hood to Samuel Meredith of Phil⁣*.

Robert Powell assign'd by Seymour Hood to Edward Wells of Phil⁣*.

Daniel M⁣ᶜA Nully servant assign'd by Captain William M⁣ᶜCullough to Jacob Richardson of Upper Merion Township.

Thomas Hobbs Redemptioner to Seymour Hood, now cancelled, last from Bristol, servant to John Brown of Willis Town.

James Porter a servant assigned by William Thompson to John Hanna of Phil⁣*.

Thomas Watson servant assign'd by Captain Seymour Hood to John Britton of the Northern Liberties Phil⁣*.

Peter Blatchly last from Bristol, Redemptioner to Captain Seymour Hood now cancelled, servant to James Sharswood of Phil*.

May 10th.

Mabel M< Cartney assign'd by William M<Cullough to John Hopkins, Salisbury Township.

John Ponsler with consent of his Father Ludwig apprentice to Henry Sheatz of White marsh Township.

Joshua Johnston [Henry Harrison Esq' Mayor] assign'd by Thomas Hough to William Milner of Phil*.

Isabella Hansen apprentice to Eliz* Hamen of Phil*.

William Hopkins servant assign'd by Captain Joseph Volans to Benjamin Cathrall of Newtown.

James Beere with consent of his Father Jonathan apprentice to John Fuss of Phil* Sailmaker.

John Bell assigned by Seymour Hood to Stephen Watts Esq' of Phil*.

William Hind assign'd by William M<Cullough to John Aiken of Pencader.

James Carr with consent of his Father William, apprentice to Richard Parmer of Phil* Joyner and chair maker.

Anthony Coupal [Jan' 18th 1773] assign'd by Matthew Potter to Jacob Ritter of Phil*.

Aaron Jayne under Indenture of Servitude to Seymour Hood cancelled, servant to Andrew Buckhard of Phil*.

Mary Fitzgerald [Feb' 19th 1773] servant assign'd by James Whitehood by order of William Moore to William Elton of Phil*.

May 11th.

Ann Ellis assign'd by Hugh Blair to Michael Troy, Paxton township.

William Tully assign'd by Seymour Hood to William Brown of Phil*.

Thomas Grames assign'd by Samuel Moore to George Ranken of Phil*.

Mary Fitzgerald assign'd by William Elton to James Taylor of Shippensburgh.

Jacob Moser and } assign'd by Jacob Dietrick to Adam
Catherine his wife } Erbe of Phil[a].

Margaret Allison servant to James Taylor of Shippensburgh.

John Watkins to Jacob Dedrick of Waterford.

Eleaner Armstrong to James Taylor of Shippensburgh.

Thomas Sopp who was under Indenture to Seymour Hood now cancelled, servant to Samuel Bringhurst of Germantown.

Richard Russell assign'd by Seymour Hood to Richard Johns of Dedford.

Henry Kaise last from London servant to Israel Morris Junior of Phil[a] and by him assign'd to Sam[l] Morris Jun[r] of Phil[a].

Jane Wilson servant assigned by Captain Noel Tod to William Patterson of Turbel.

Lawrence Byrne servant assigned by Cap[t] Noel Tod to Michael Troy of Sunburry.

May 12th.

Nathaniel Anster assigned by Henry Gest to Pem Robinson of Phil[a].

Thomas Harlin assign'd by William Austin to Aaron Brown of Pittsgrove.

Owen Daniel with consent of his Father Henry, apprentice to Anthony Billig of Phil[a].

John Williams [June 24th 1771] apprentice assign'd by Archibald Fisher to Thomas Shortell of Phil[a].

Joseph Garwood with consent of his Father William apprentice to Bowyer Brooke of Phil[a].

Mary Fitsgerrald [May 22nd 1772] under Indenture of servitude to Rob[t] Miller now cancelled servant to William Golden of Phil[a].

John Hall under Indenture to James Lilly for his passage from Ireland now cancelled, servant to John Care of Phil[a].

Jean Gray servant assign'd by Robert Dunlap to Fargust
Purdon of Phil[a].

May 13th.

Simeon Fortiner [T. Jones Esq[r]] apprentice assign'd by
Harry Robinson to Israel Hollowell of Phil[a].

Philip Verner [Nov. 20th 1772] assign'd by Henry Keppele
jun[r] to John Crush.

Margaret Randle assign'd by William McCullough to John
of Phil[a].

Mary McCardle assign'd by William McCullough to Peter
Howard of Phil[a].

Ann Fitsgerrald under Indenture of Servitude to Noel
Todd is discharged and set free.

James Conner under Indenture of Servitude to James
Crawford now cancelled, to William Henry of George Town.

John Smith last from London servant to John Steinmetz
of Phil[a].

George Black to Samuel Blackwood of Deptford Township, Maryland.

May 14th.

Harry Korr with consent of his Father William apprentice
to Samuel Jarvis of Phil[a] House Carpenter.

Daniel Trimby assign'd by Seymour Hood to Joseph White
of Bristol.

George Brooks assign'd by Seymour Hood to John Merrick
of Falls Township.

Marg[t] Crawford [June 2nd 1772] assign'd by William
Adcock to James Lukens of Phil[a].

Abram Outen with consent of his friend Thomas Cliftton,
apprentice to John Hamilton of Phil[a] Mariner.

Thomas Raine apprentice assigned by Thomas Parsons to
Simon Sherlock, ship carpenter of Southwark.

Thomas Davis last from Bristol, redemptioner to Seymour
Hood now cancelled, servant to Peter Biggs of Phil[a].

Nicholas Hand son of Jeremiah assigned by John Guest
apprentice to John Hood of Phil[a] cordwainer.

May 15th.

Joseph Garr last from London servant to Richard Gibbs of Bensalem Township.

Francis Kelley servant assign'd by Alexander Cain to David Jones of Phil'.

John Dunn servant assigned by Cap' Alexander Cain to William Cartir of Phil'.

Robert Dougherty with consent of his Father Richard apprentice to Martin Juges of Phil' carver and gilder.

John Thomas assign'd by Joseph Volans to Richard Collins of Newtown.

John Meloy under Indenture of Servitude to James Boyd now cancelled, servant to Harman Fritz.

Sarah Gillis under Indenture to Alexander Cain now cancelled, to John Hoskins of Burlington.

William Kelly last from London, servant to Samuel Griscom House-carpenter of Phil'.

Robert Davis last from London, to Jacob Waggoner of Blockly Township, Phil'.

May 17th.

Catherine Woster with consent of her mother, apprentice to Nicholas Brum of the Northern Libertys.

Conrad Seyfert with consent of his Father Anthony apprentice to William Mentz of Phil' bookbinder.

Hannah Graydon assign'd by Seymour Hood to Samuel Read of Phil'.

Maria Turmucl last from London, servant to Jacob Graff of Phil'.

May 18th.

John Sebastian Clinesmith servant to Anthony Forten of Phil'.

Timothy Culley servant assign'd by Captain Alexander Cain to Thomas Norris of Merion.

John Perry under Indenture of Servitude to Thomas Jann now cancelled, apprentice to Richard Tittemary of Southwark.

John Stock servant assign'd by Cap' Seymour Hood to Daniel Bender of Phil*.

John Church servant assigned by Captain Seymour Hood to Jacob Giles jun' of St. George's Parish Baltimore.

Andrew Clinesmith last from London, servant to Michael Bishop of Lower Millford.

May 19th.

Edward Giddons servant assign'd by Captain Seymour Hood to Thomas Wharton Sen' of Phil*.

Sarah Neilson a servant assign'd by Hugh Blair to James Hinchman of Woolwich.

John Walsh ⎰ Assigned by Alexander Cain to James
Patrick Morgan ⎱ Black of Kent in Maryland.

Margaret Mushell with consent of her mother Catherine Sifert, apprentice to Israel Hallowell of Phil*.

Hugh Heffernon servant assign'd by Captain Alexander Cain to Simon Shurlock of Southwark.

Thomas Reily ⎰ assign'd by Richard Eyres to Robert
Patrick Crosby ⎱ Callenden of Meadheton.

Sybella Leyfert with consent of her Father Anthony apprentice to Robert Bell of Phil*.

Nicholas Smith servant assign'd by Richard Eyres to Philip Flich of Phil*.

John Kinshalle servant assigned by Richard Eyres to George Goodwine of Phil*.

Thomas Murphy servant assign'd by Alexander Cain to Joshua Bunting of New Jersey.

Sarah Dunlap assign'd by Elizabeth M'Neil to Joseph Rhoads of Southwark [Aug 1ᵃ 1772].

John Misbell Hope a poor child bound by the Managers of the House of Employment apprentice to John Lefeavor of Worcester Township, Phil*.

William Dunn assigned by Seymour Hood to George Haywood of Wesham, Burlington, New Jersey.

William Gray redemptioner to John and James Luke now cancelled, servant to Robert Craig of Dunegall Township.

James Ferris servant assigned by Alexander Cain to John
Supplee of Blockley, Phil[a].

Thomas Robinson servant to Seymour Hood, now cancelled, and servant to Thomas James.

Mary Murphy assigned by Alexander Cain to George
Stevenson of Carlisle.

Anne Delaney servant assign'd by Richard Eyres to Thomas
Cully of Christiana.

May 20th.

William Ward last from Bristol servant to James Brenton
of Pennsbury.

Rebecca Beech [July 8th 1772] assign'd by Caspar Sneevely
servant to Jacob Barge of Phil[a].

Nicholas Dell [June 17th 1772] discharged and set free
from his Master James Dalton.

Samuel Jobson with consent of his Father apprentice to
Samuel Noble of the Northern Liberties Tanner and Currier.

Christopher Leonard	*Andrew Moore*
Samuel Jackson	*Matthew Stoys*
Thomas M[c]*Hugh*	*Alexander Cook*
John Quinn	*John Byrn*
James Smyth	*James Mahoney*
John Burnett	*James Davis*
Simon Owens	*James Magrath*
John Field	*John Bolton*
Lawrence Phillips	*Thomas Keating*

servants to Alexander Cain, and by him assign'd to James
Ray of Little Britain.

Robert Conyers assign'd by Alexander Cain to James Ray
of Little Britain.

Mary Carney ⎫ servants to Alexander Cain and by
Jane Kelly ⎬ him assign'd to James Ray of Little
Esther Murphey ⎭ Britain.

Christopher Jourdan servant of Richard Eyre by him
assigned to John Oudenheimer of Phil[a].

Barbara Ferdysh [Jan. 5th 1773] assign'd by Francis
Wade to Frederick Phile of Phil[a].

William Sharpe servant of Alexander Cain, by him assigned to Joshua Cooper.

Lawrence Phillips under Indenture of Servitude to Alex[r]
Cain, servant to James Ray of Little Britain.

Bridget Hefferin last from Dublin to John Hannum.

Andrew Moore under Indenture of Servitude to Alex[r]
Cain now cancelled, apprentice to Robert Severly of Phil[a]
cordwainer.

Daniel Fennell servant of Alexander Cain assigned to William Dungan of New Britain.

Jane Nelson servant of Richard Eyres assigned to William
Reese of Newtown.

May 21st.

Francis Kane	*Sarah Godfrey*
James Gibson	*Christopher Reilly*
Ignatius Keating	*John Wilkinson*
Gabriel Lount	*John Biggs*
Margaret Kelly	*Nicholas Ready*
Rose Duffy	*Mary Gill*

Servants of Richard Eyre and by him assigned to David
and Thomas Fulton of Nottingham.

John Caton ⎫ servants of Richard Eyres, by him
John Molloy ⎬ assigned to David and Thomas Ful-
William Stewart ⎭ ton of Nottingham.

Patrick Maginnes redemptioner to Alex[r] Cain for his passage from Ireland now cancelled, servant to Peter Off of
Blockly Township, Phil[a] Co.

George McAllister servant of Richard Eyres by him assigned to Henry Graham Esq[r] of Chester.

Aaron Thempson with consent of his Father, apprentice to
Samuel Pancost of Phil[a] House-carpenter.

William Davis servant to Seymour Hood by him assigned
to Samuel Harrold of Buckingham.

William Athens servant of Seymour Hood by him assign'd
to Charles West of Deptford, New Jersey.

A LIST OF GERMAN EMIGRANTS, 1773.—Rupp's "Collection of Thirty Thousand Names of Immigrants to Pennsylvania" gives the arrival at the port of Philadelphia, 18th September, 1773, of the ship "Britannia," James Peter, master, from Rotterdam *via* Cowes, with two hundred and fifty passengers. Of this number one hundred and eighteen names are given. Bradford's *Journal* of 29th September contains the following advertisement:

"GERMAN PASSENGERS.

"Just arrived in the Ship Britannia, James Peter, Master.

A number of healthy GERMAN PASSENGERS, chiefly young people, whose freights are to be paid to *Joshua Fisher* and *Sons* or to the Master on board the Ship lying off the Draw-bridge."

Among the recent accessions to the Historical Society of Pennsylvania is an original manuscript endorsed: "Germans Landed from on board the Britannia 11 mo: 2ᵈ 1773," evidently prepared by an employé of Messrs. Joshua Fisher & Sons, which gives the names of fifty-three passengers, with the amount of their passage-money and expenses due. This list is particularly valuable as it gives the names of several males, females, and children not given by Mr. Rupp, and should be compared with his by all interested. We make a *verbatim* copy of the names:

Andreas Keym	£26. 7.—	
Lena Bekker, his wife . . .	22. 2.—	
Expenses, 16 days	1.12.—	£50. 1.—
Hendrick Soneau	20.15.—	
Dorothea, his wife	20.11.—	
Expenses	1.12.—	42.18.—
Johann Fredrick Camerloo . .	23.15.—	
Anna, his wife	22. 1.—	
Expenses	1.12.—	47. 8.—
Simon Martz,		
Ann, wife,		
Anna Margaretta, daughter.		
Expenses	2. 8.—	
Augustinus Hess	19. 1.—	
Maria, wife	18.19.—	
Anna Margᵗᵗᵃ daughter . . .	19. 4.—	
Expenses	2. 8.—	59.12 .—
Jacob Schott, } . . .	17. 1.—	
Anna, wife }		
Expenses	1.12.—	18.13.—
Christophel Schwer, } . .	50. 7.—	
Anna, wife }		
	1.12.—	51.19.—
John George Kunkell, }		
Anna, wife, } . . .	41. 5.—	
Catherina, daughter }		
Expenses	3. 4.—	44. 9.—

Jacob Steyheler.	. . . .	£19.19.—	
Catharina, wife .	. . . .	17.18.—	
Expenses .	. . . . .	1.12.—	£39. 9.—

Bernard Schmit,
Margaretta, wife,
Turgen, son, . . . 61. 5.—
Catharina, daughter
Expenses . . . . . . 3. 4.— 64. 9.—

Andreas Otto, } . . . . 41. 7.—
Sophia, wife }
Expenses . . . . . . 1.12.— 42.19.—

John Dan¹ Roth, } . . . . 49. 8.—
Anna, wife }
Expenses . . . . . . 1.12.— 51.

Jacob Wanner, } . . . . 20.15.—
Maria, wife }
Expenses . . . . . . 1.12.— 22. 7.—

Dan¹ Spees, } . . . . 38.17.—
Anna, wife }
Expenses . . . . . . 1.12.— 40. 9.—

Dan¹ Spees, Junr, } . . . . 36.17.—
Anna, wife }
Expenses . . . . . . 1.12.— 38. 9.—

Christian Habert, } . . . . 43. 4.—
Anna Maria, wife }
Expenses . . . . . . 1.12.— 44.16.—

Andreas Kirch,
Anna Maria, wife, } . . . 44. 9.—
Maria Eliz^a, daughter
Expenses . . . . . . 2. 8.— 51.17.—

Jacob Zwytser, } . . . 42. 7.—
Johanna Barbara, wife }
Expenses . . . . . . 1.12.— 43.19.—

Conrad Foltz, }
Susanna, wife, } . . . . 51.—.—
Maria, daughter
Expenses . . . . . . 2. 8.— 53. 8.—

William Schwatz, } . . . 35.16.—
Anna Maria, wife }
Expenses . . . . . . 1.12.— 37. 8.—

Christian Nell . . . . . 20.— —
Expenses . . . . . . 16.— 20.16.—

Johann Jeremiah Snell	.	.	.	£24.19.—	
Expenses	.	.	.	16.—	£25.15.—
Gerrett Benengé	.	.	.	23.11.—	
Expenses	.	.	.	16.—	24. 7.—
Antᵛ Guerin	.	.	.	21. 3. 6	
Expenses	.	.	.	16.—	21.19. 6
Pierie Mullott	.	.	.	21.—.—	
Expenses	.	.	.	16.—	21.16.—
Gerturia Vogelesang	.	.	.	17.18.—	
				16.—	18.14—

The following memorandum is appended to the list: "Sundʳʸ at H. Haines; 1 Frying Pan; 1 large Iron Pot; Scales & Weights; some Flour, abᵗ a week; some salt Beef; some Barley & Rice; a chest belonging to G. Vogelesang. 1 barˡ Bread will last near 2 weeks."

LIST OF ARRIVALS PER "PENNSYLVANIA PACKET," 1775.

[Copied from the original manuscript in the collection of the Historical Society of Pennsylvania.]

A List of Serv^ts Indented on Board the Pennsylvania Packet Capt. Peter Osborne for Philadelphia the 15th day of March 1775.

TRADESMEN'S NAMES AND TRADES.

1. Ed^w Beaton, Cordwainer,	20.4.	Sold to Restore Lippincott	£18.
2. Thos Watkins, House Carpenter,	21.4.	" W^m McMullin	
3. John Thomas, Smith,	26.4.	" Thos Mayberry	£20.
4. Thos Martin, Taylor,	23.4.	" Geo Dilhorn	£20.
5. Richd Noxon, Peruke Maker,	25.4.	" Arch^d Burns	£17.
6. Moses Hains, Jeweler,	24.4.		
7. Moses Jacobs, do	22.4.		
8. Wm Edwards, Painter,	36.4.	" Samuel Ridley	£20.
9. James Vanlone, Watchfinisher,	17.5.	" Elijah Clark	£21.
10. Benj. Boswell, Baker,	15.7.	" Michael Bishop	£18.
11. Wm Mitchell, Stone Mason,	21.4.	" Thos Mayberry	£20.
12. John Wallis, Baker,	21.4.		
13. John Row, do	21.4.	Sent to Samuel Rowland	
14. Wm Dickerson, Butcher,	25.4.		
15. Danl Deffoe, C & Watch Maker,	24.4.		
16. Wm Avery, Taylor,	21.4.	John Martin	£20.
17. Paul Courtney, Plasterer,	23.4.		
18. Saml Le Count, Printer,	24.4.	Sold to Enoch Story	£20.
19. Wm Hayes, Hair Dresser,	15.7.	" Dr Benjamin Rush	£24.
20. James Russel, Stone Mason,	24.4.	Thos Mayberry	£20.
21. John McCann, Cab^t Maker & Joyner,	22.4.	Matthew Hand	£20.
22. Wm Gray, Wool comber,	21.4.		
23. John Ames, Hatter,	27.4.		
24. John Graves, Peruke Maker,	37.4.		
25. Wm Chase, Cordwainer,	23.4.	William Ross	£19.
26. John Haynes, Hair Dresser,	22.4.	Enoch Story	£20.
27. Robert Hayard, Carpenter,	22.4.	Hollingsworth & Mullins	£23.16.

NO TRADES.

28. Thos Dunning, Labourer,	15.7.	Geo P. Beckham	
29. Richd Peplow, do	18.5.	Thos Joseph Pool—Gilpin	
30. Thos Thompson, do	15.7.	Charles, Ann Pool Pryor	£19.
31. James Lover, do	15.7.	Isaiah J. Robb, Charles Hughes	
32. Wm Basley, Clerk,	33.4.	John Read	
33. Wm Brown, Labourer,	15.7.	Wm Prince Gibbs	
34. Valentine Ruly, Groom,	16.5.	Wm Temple	
35. John Foster, Cl & Bookkeeper,	30.4.	Thos & Peter Robinson	
36. Wm Longwood, Groom,	23.4.	J. Vandegrist	£20.
37. Geo Warren, Labourer,	14.7.	do	£24.
38. John Longan, Husbandman,	19.5.	Peter Cline	£19.
39. Wm Harrison, do	23.4.	Robert Verree	£20.
40. Jno Humble, do	21.4.		
41. Geo Woodford, do	21.4.	Thos Mayberry	£20.
42. John Crabb, Groom,	22.4.	Wm Logan	

LISTS OF FOREIGNERS WHO ARRIVED AT PHILA-DELPHIA, 1791–1792.

CONTRIBUTED BY LUTHER R. KELKER, ESQ.

[The following certified lists of foreigners who arrived at Philadelphia, 1791–1792, are additional to those printed in Pennsylvania Archives, Second Series, Vol. XVII.]

LIST OF PASSENGERS ON BOARD THE SHIP "PHILADELPHIA PACKET," EDWARD RICE, MASTER, FROM AMSTERDAM. PHILA. JANY. 18, 1791.

Marie Jacobs.	Barnhard Driesbach & wife.
Henry Richards.	John Gottfrieden Markt.
Sussaneh Koam.	Abral Geerman.
J. G. Meyers, his wife & two children.	John Valentine.
	Jacob Whitcomb.

I do hereby certify that the above is a true list of Passengers on board of the above ship under my command.

EDWARD RICE.

HIS EXCELLENCY THOMAS MIFFLIN ESQ.
        GOVERNOR OF THE COMMONWEALTH OF PENNSYLVANIA.
SIR

I take the liberty to transmit to your Excellency the Lists of Names of German Passengers who arrived at this Port from June 30th 1791 to June 29th 1792, and were permitted to Land agreeably to Law.

I am with the greatest respect, your Excellency's most obedient and very humble Servant

PHILADELPHIA July 9, 1792   LEWIS FARMER,
                Register of German.

LIST OF PASSENGERS, WHO ARRIVED IN THE BRIGANTINE "MARY" FROM AMSTERDAM AT THE PORT OF PHILADELA. JUNE 30th 1791.

Stephanus Clauss.	George Ernst Fries.
Johannes Balde.	Regina Dorethea Heningin.
Johan Henry Balde.	William Balde.

I do hereby certify the above being a True List of the Passengers on sailing Vessel above mentioned.

K. FITZPATRICK.

A LIST OF GERMAN PASSENGERS ON BOARD THE SHIP "DIANA," OZIAS GOODMAN, COMMANDER.

Heinrick Jullig.
Dorothea, his wife.
George Peter, ⎤
Henrick, ⎬ 3 children.
Parble, ⎦

———

Peter Grall.
Barbara, his wife.
Catharina, ⎤
Georg, ⎥
Peter, ⎬ 4 children.
Barbara, ⎦

———

Daniel Guntar.
Anna Margaret, his wife.
Daniel, ⎤
Hans Daniel, ⎥
Catharine, ⎥
Caroline, ⎬ 7 children.
Hans Jacob, ⎥
Hans William, ⎥
Conrad, ⎦

Conrad Schmeltzer.
Margaret, his wife.

———

Francis Rame.
Catharine, his wife.
Frederick, ⎤
John Daniel, ⎬ 2 children.

———

Daniel Stier.
Catharine, his wife.

———

Catharine Marg^t. Rippart.
George, ⎤
Christian, ⎥
Catharine, ⎥
Elizabeth, ⎬ 6 children.
Margaret, ⎥
Sophia, ⎦

———

Casper Hein.
Margaret, his wife.
Peter, ⎤
Hans, ⎬ 3 children.
Lewis, ⎦

Jacob Snell.
Sophia, his wife.
Joh. Henry, ⎫
Catharine, ⎪ 4
Hano Mary, ⎬ children.
Jacob, ⎭

Peter Blanch.
Dorothy, his wife.
Sophia, ⎫
Margaret, ⎬ 3 children.
Magdalene, ⎭

George More.
Catharine, his wife.
George, ⎫ 3
George Henry, ⎬ children.
Peter, ⎭

Daniel Weisborin.
Barbara, his wife.
Laurens, their child.

Magdalena Eidelmeinin.
Magdalena, her child.

Christina Weisbornin.
Margaret, her child.

Michel Bauer.
Catharine, his wife.
Philip Jerry, ⎫
Philip Jacob, ⎪
Hans Michael, ⎬ 5 children.
Catharine Debora, ⎪
Hans Peter, ⎭

Peter Durenburgh
Eliza, his wife.
Solima, ⎫
Philip, ⎪ 4
Jerry Frederick, ⎬ children.
Hans Jerry, ⎭

Salima van der Gros.
Urelina, her child.

Margaret Rippart.
Lewis, ⎫
Martin, ⎪ 4
George, ⎬ children.
Jacob, ⎭

Christian Woltz.
Catharine, his wife.
Christian, ⎫
Catharine, ⎪ 4
Regina, ⎬ children.
Maretia, ⎭

George Sifz.
Anna Elizabeth, his wife.
Hans Jerry. ⎫
Catharine Eliza. ⎪ 4
Hans Jacob. ⎬ children.
Maria Magdalene. ⎭

George Henry Mortel.
Catharine, his wife.

Martin Rapp.
John George, his son.

Peter Durenbaugh.
Margaret, his wife.
Hans Jerry, }
Magdalene, } children.
———
Joh Gettinger.
Johan Titius.
Fred*. Granram.
Carl Granram.
Valentine Weindling.
George Klein.
George Wolf.
Joh. Christⁿ. Weinmuller.
Christian Fritz.
Nichol Hang.
Johanna Jost.
Nichol Hauter.
Nicholas Schworer.
Theobald Schmidt.
Jacob Raith.
Conrath Schultz.
Johan Lewis Urban.
Catharina Wagnarin.

Joh Justus Kersten.
Charl Fred. Huguenin.
Georg L. ramur.
Johan Matthias Simon.
Joh Hoehn.
Frantz Arforg.
Carl Hendᵏ. Schmadhtaha.
Joh Leonard Bloeser.
M. Schneider.
Phl Ander-man.
Georg Fred. Krauss.
Dan Fred Ley.
Loisa Linnerin.
Susan Mertlen.
———
Fred Brecheisen.
Catharine, his wife.
Frederich, }
Catharine Eliza, } 3 children.
Johan George, }
———
Barbara Weindling.

I do certify the within being a True List of the Passengers on board my ship. Witness my hand this tenth day of August 1791.

OZIAS GOODWIN.

LIST OF PASSENGERS ON BOARD THE SHIP "PHILADELPHIA PACKET" FROM AMSTERDAM.

Ph. Jac. Bretry.
Jacob G. Pofie.
Jacob Stohr.
J. Fred. D. Fanholtz.
Ant. Hartmann.
J. G. Hartzog.
Salamarina Hartzog—wife.

George Hartzog.
Frederick Hartzog.
Coen Jutter.
J. J. Hause.
Francis Hause, wife.
Jacob Hause.
Francisco Hause.

Barbara Hause.

J. I. Hadelmaker.

J. S. Eder.

G. C. Lux.

Elizabeth Herman.

J.P.Echhard, *Cabin Passenger.*

I do hereby certify the within Being a True List of the Passengers on board my ship. Witness my hand this twenty-third day of August 1791.   EDWARD RICE.

PASSENGERS ON BOARD THE SHIP "FAIR AMERICAN," CAPT. BENJAMIN LEE, FROM AMSTERDAM, ARRIVED IN PHILADELPHIA, 12 SEPTEMBER 1791.

Georg Ludwig Anschutz.

Catharine Elizabeth Anschutz.

Johan George Anschutz.

Christian Anschutz.

Elizabetha Anschutz.

Dorothea Anschutz.

Johan Jacob Anschutz.

Heinrich Jully.

Catharina Barbera Jully.

Maria Magdalena Jully.

Heinrich Jully.

Adam Jully.

Johann Jacob Günther.

Maria Barbara Günther.

Jacob Günther.

Johanna Günther.

Frantz Breiner.

Friederich Weirzsäcker.

Johan Martin Klein.

Maria Magdalena Schmucken

Margarethe Schmucken.

Peter Koch.

Johan Wilhelm Versbach.

Wilhelm Versbach.

Conradt Lysinger.

Jacob Hermann Hein.

Anne Catharine Hein.

Margaretta Phillippina Hein.

Bernhart Hein.

Catharine Phillipin Guntzing.

Johana Elenberger.

Maria Elenberger.

Elizabeth Elenberger.

Magdalen Elenberger.

Friederich Hiun.

Friederich Jonas.

Anna Maria Jonas.

Johan Wilhelm Jonas.

Phillippina Jonas.

Jacob Jonas.

Ann Catharina Jonas.

Juliana Jonas.

Heronomus Ecker.

Henrich Gölzen.

Phillipp Linder.

Phillipp Bosler.

Johan Jacob Hartmann.

Christian Kutscher.

Jacob Mesmer.

Johanna Ginder.

Elizabeth Ginder.

Frederick Ginder.
Anne Marie Ginder.
Johanna Louisa Ginder.
Johanna Ginder.
Casper Fallen.
Peter Fallen.
Anna Catharina Fallen.
Mietzie Josephs.
Gustav Frederic Goetz.
Johan Christov Geil.

Johan Peter Diring.
Adam Henrich.
Jacob friederick Roller.
Johan Bernhardt Schüler.
Johan Gotfried Dieterich.
Scintje Obisan.
Caroline Christiana Gainer.
Phillip Schimper.
Bernhart Schulles.

Cabin Passengers.

Christopf Ludwig Albertz.
Maria Catherina Albertz.
Maria Dorothea Bronner.

Johann Jacob Bronner.
Christian Godfried Elsacher.

I do hereby certify, the above being a True List of all the Passengers on board the Ship within mentioned.

Witness my hand this thirteenth day of September 1791.

B. LEE.

Joh. G. Nertwig and Elizabeth Netwig.
John George Dickhout.
Anna Clara Dickhout.
Peter Bare with wife and two children, Peter Catharine & Catharina.
Casper Hill.
John Steim Strauel.
Jacob Echternoel.
Charles Bosbishel.
Nicholas Hoffman.
Andrew Schneider.
Cornelius Barthemel.
Abraham Kelder.
—— Dichman.
John Muller.

Cor. Gott Saur.
Joh. Hen Hugel.
G. Wm Hugel.
Mart Browner.
John Morgenthal.
John Cappers.
John Cline.
George Notting.
Catharine Meyer.
Mar Strooms.
Paul Smith.
Philip Schmidt.
Died. Petts.
Andreas Egternoel.
Nic Leigle.
Christian Cable & wife, Christian & Mary.

Frederick Snyder.
John Valentine Heir.
Elizabeth Schmitt.
John Ostreith.
John Peter Kern.
Ant° Bousorum.
Philip Stubenitzhe.
John Peter Blende.
Gen⁺ Schlicht.

John Mason, with wife & two
    children, Mary, Joseph
    George Mechil.
Andrew Screros.
Charles Egternoel.
John Roon.
Lamber Roberson.
Barhout Butlinger, wife &
    daughter Margarethe.

I do hereby certify this to be a True List of the Passengers on Board the Ship Pallas, under my command, September 27, 1791.

CHARLES COLLINS.

A LIST OF PASSENGERS BROUGHT OVER IN THE SHIP "VANSTOPHORST" FROM AMSTERDAM, JAMES PORTER, MASTER.

John W. Starag Pᵗ (?)
John Conrad Brun.
Friederich Duisbe.
John H. Rosenburg.
Daniel Carboum.
Elizabeth Carboum.
Daniel Carboum.

Charles Carboum.
Maria Elizabeth Carboum.
Maria Susanna Carboum.
Maria Margarethe Carboum.
Simon Hipple.
Addam   "

These are to certify, the above being a True List of the Passengers on Board my Ship.   Philadelᵃ. October 22. 1791.

JAMES PORTER.

LIST OF GERMAN PASSENGERS, WHO ARRIVED IN THE SHIP "PHILADELPHIA PACKET" CAPT. EDWARD RICE, FROM AMSTERDAM, PHILADELPHIA APRIL 26, 1792.

Henry frantz Henstead.
Jacobina Colpin.

Tuniss Tunece.

A List of Passengers by the Ship "Betsey Rutledge"
from Hamburg, Danl. McPherson, Master.

Freiderich Wilhelm Kung-
oldt.
Freiderich Ludwig Albert.
Johann Christian Bartel.
Johann Christian Loehr.

Johann Christopher Lange.
Carol Schumaker.
Johann Dedrich Smith.
George Rex his wife Maria
& one child.

I do hereby Certify that the above are the names of all
the Passengers on Board the Vessel above named. Philad⁴
May 25ᵗʰ 1792.
Dan'l. McPherson.

List of Passengers on board the Ship "America," William
Campbell Master last from Amsterdam.

Mrs. Pet van Hage & 3 child-
ren.
Christⁿ Strohm & wife.
John Strohm.
Barbara Strohm.
Elizabeth Strohm.
George Hoff & wife & 4
children.
Philad⁴ 29ᵗʰ June 1792.

J. E. D. Himroth.
Heronemus Lesh.
J. V. D. Muhlen.
Anthony Regel.
Casper Zollinger & wife & 2
children.
Benjamin.

William Campbell.

List of Passengers & Servants by the Brig "Union" from
Hamburg arrived the 28ᵗʰ day of June 1792.

Johan Valentine Schel-
lard.
Martha Elizᵇ Schellard.
Johan Jurgen Schel-
lard.
Peter Andre Langan-
hargen.
Carl Harbermeier.
Christian Adeler.
Caterina Elizᵇ Casterins.

} Passengers paid.

Johan Francis
Christian 5
years old.
Johan Hendrick
Daniel 3 years
old.

} Children.

Johan Wilhelm Storck.
Christo Cloudy.
Christian Henderick Lando-
wick.

James Dryburgh.

LISTS OF FOREIGNERS WHO ARRIVED AT PHILADELPHIA, 1791–1792.

CONTRIBUTED BY LUTHER R. KELKER, ESQ.

To His Excellency Thomas Mifflin Esquire,
     Governor of the Commonwealth of Pennsylvania.

SIR: I take the Liberty to Transmit to your Excellency the Lists of Names of German Passengers who arrived at the Port of Philadelphia from August 13th to September 25th | A: C: | I further more add that nothing Occurred in the Proceedings of my Office which wants any alteration.

I have the Honor to be
with the greatest respect
Your Excellency's most Obedient
and Very Humble Servant
LEWIS FARMER *Register of*

PHILA Nov. 1st 1792   *German Passengers.*

EN; LIST VAN DE MANSCHAFT IN HETT SCHIEF DE FRAU CATHRINA CAPT. HENDRICK TRAUTMAN GEKOMMEN VON HAMBURG GEDISTENNT (?) NA. PHILADELFE MET PASSASIERIN.

Her Berze unt sein frau und Kindt.

Dochter alt 26 Jahr	1 Person
Hiarigette alt 26 Jahr	1 dito
Mars° Peamor mit Frau and Sohn	3 dito
Jacob Evars alt 29 Jahr	1 dito
Friedrick Oldwick Westfall	1 dito
Johann Loraun alt 22 Jahr	1 dito
Westfallen unt Frau und 4 Kinder	6 dito
Johan Hendrick Olsen alt 29 Jahr	1 dito
Hendrick Tiel alt 20 Jahr	1 dito
Friedrich Scheÿder mit sein Frau	2 dito

Stubbe mit Frau und 5 Kinder . . . 7 persons
Linderman mit Frau und 2 Kinder . . . 4 dito
Anna Leimslack 38 Jahr . . . . 1 dito
Johan Bonsa 28 Jahr . . . . . 1 dito
Melgert Qwans mit Frau und 2 Kinder . . 4 dito
Johan Schmelsen mit Frau und 2 Kinder . . 4 dito
Johan Bauer mit Frau . . . . . 2 dito
Danniel Wittschief mit Braüt . . . . 2 dito
Jochim Ritter mit Frau und Kindt . . . 3 dito
Johan Wittschief unt Braüt . . . . 2 dito
Johan Sparer mit Frau und 2 Kinder . . 2 dito ?
Hendrik Dirks alt 32 Jahr . . . . 1 dito
Michel Broan alt 24 Jahr . . . . 1 dito
Johan Gasan alt 30 Jahr . . . . . 1 dito
Franz Bronstedt alt 22 Jahr . . . . 1 dito
Johan Somerfeldt alt 28 Jahr . . . . 1 dito
Martien Tiel und Sohn 8 Jahr . . . . 2 dito
Margretha Casiens und Sohn 3 Jahr . . 2 dito
Paul Husing alt 34 Jahr . . . . . 1 dito
Christienn Schroder alt 42 Jahr . . . 1 dito
Johan Bohr Mestar mit Frau und Kindt . . 3 dito
Cathrine Kromron alt 22 Jahr . . . . 1 dito
Peter Pien alt 28 Jahr . . . . . 1 dito
Jochim Piole alt 37 Jahr . . . . . 1 dito
Christina Tempel alt 32 Jahr . . . . 1 dito
Hans Schultz alt 25 Jahr . . . . . 1 dito
Johann Mosemann alt 34 Jahr . . . . 1 dito
Johann Waggner mit Frau und Kindt . . 3 dito
Carlel Dell mit Frau . . . . . 2 dito
Pieter Holtz mit Frau . . . . . 2 dito
Jochim Lorentz mit Frau . . . . 2 dito
Christina Westen mit 3 Kinder . . . 4 dito
Peter Bokkendall mit Frau und 2 Kinder . . 4 dito
Hans Beyter mit Frau und Kindt . . . 3 dito
Jochim Hagemann mit Frau und 2 Kinders . 4 dito
Jochim van Netten alt 44 Jahr . . . . 1 dito
Martin Schaeffner alt 24 Jahr . . . . 1 dito

Pilip Ekhart alt 24 Jahr . . . . . 1 person
Johan Reymers – alt 23 Jahr . . . . 1 dito
Johann Kramer alt 42 Jahr . . . . 1 dito
Johan Hagh mit Frau und 2 Kinders . . 4 dito
Paul Schütt alt 32 Jahr . . . . . 1 dito
Franz Schmitt mit Frau und Kindt . . . 3 dito
Jochim Pingel mit Frau und 5 Kinders . . 7 dito
Claus Koppman mit Frau und 5 kinders . . 7 dito
Clas Hipner mit sein Braut . . . . 2 dito
Anna Catherine Stieffen . . . . . 1 dito
    Torbann alt 20 Jahr . . . . . 1 dito
    Helmke mit Sohn alt 5 Jahr . . . 2 dito
    Beyter . . . . 1 dito
    Rasch und Bruder . . . . . 2 dito
    Siek . . . . 1 dito

    August 3, 1792.

LIST OF PASSENGERS ON BOARD THE SHIP " RAINBOW," RICHARD
SALTER, MASTER, FROM AMSTERDAM, 1792.

Henry Bart.	Nichols Guddermouth.
Cethnet Bart.	Catharine Guddermouth.
Casp Kuhnzick.	Hans Gudermouth.
Ann Kuhnzick.	Lau^r Gudermouth.
Cathnet Kuhnzick a child.	Philip Gudermuth.
Barr Bart.	Nichlos Gudermuth.
Margret Bart.	Dorety Gudermuth *child*.
Cathrine Bart.	Johan Zittle.
Cathrine Bart.	Barbry Zittle.
Johann Bart.	Johann Zittle.
Hein. Bart.	Nichlos Zittle.
John Tungent.	Elizth Zittle.
Barbry Tungent.	Geo. Zittle.
Anne Susannye Tungent.	Gertrute Zittle.
Cath. Tungent.	John Geo. Zittle a child.
Susanne Tungent.	William Walter.
Barbry Tungent.	Margret Walter.
Niclos Tungent a child.	Susana Walter.

Jacob Walter.
Peter Walter.
Johanna Walter a child.
Michel Marten.
Nicholus Burkhart.

PHILADA. Sept. 7, 1792

Johanna Gudemuth.
Catharine Hartmannia.
Law' Schleising.
B. G. Schneek.
John M Senft.

RICHD SALTER

LIST OF ALL THE PASSENGERS ON BOARD THE SHIP "COLUMBIA," CAPT. WM. MALEY.

Andres Hennisch.
George Storck.
Phillipp Geist.
Henric Nerthwein.
Georg Nenzenhoeffer.
Franz Dunne.
Conrad Weigand.
Conrad Ekhart.
Christian Fahler.
George Weistenbach.
Hartmann Scheer.
Johan Schirmer.
Anna Schirmer, his wife.
Conrad Schirmer, his son.
Fetter Emig.
Ludwig Schewkel
Anne Elisabeth, his wife.
Anna Catharine, his daughter
Kunigunda Simonin.
George Albrecht.
Heinrick Albrecht.
Catharine Müller.
John Wernet Esert.
Marie Magdalene, his wife.
Gabriel Ament.
Joseph Knobelbasch.
Michel Dobler.

Valentin Ekhart.
Frederic Freutley.
George Meyer.
Christopher Brume.
Wilhelmine Fiehr.
Ludwig Riedy.
Christina Schildin.
Felter Fischborn.
Adam Schetzel.
Adan Euer.
Christine Dilleman.
Elisabetha Dilleman.
Catherine Rotterin.
Elisabetha Heidlinger.
Matthieu Grunnenwald.
John Meyer.
Anne Marie Meyer, his wife.
John Adam, his son.
Nicholas Hetterrich.
Eva Elizabeth Hetterich, his
    wife.
John Adam, his son.
Casper Werner.
Margretha Werner, his wife.
Conrad Werner and } his
John Werner   } sons.
John Larch.

John Oblinger.
Barbara, his wife.
Christian, his son, 13.
Narbara, his daughter, 12.
John, his son, 10.
Carl, his son, 8.
Jacob, his son, 3½.
Lorenz Hoffman.
Louis Ducomena.
Hennes Roulett.
Frederic Pitscher.
Narbara, his wife.
Frederic, his son.
Barbara, his daughter.
Abraham, his son.
Rodolph Pitscher.
Maria Margaretha, his daugh-
 ter.
Jacob Hug.
John Prussel.
Catherina, his wife.
Jacob Felmy, his son,
John Müller.
Andrae Müller.
Jacob Müller.
Jacob Gerster.
John Gerster.
Martin Gass.
Heinrich Scheffers.
Christian Burger.
Barbara Würtz.
Elisabetha Keller.
Michel Schnertzinger.
Samuel Gentsch.
Ludwig Koch.
Frederick Geiler.
Jacob Knapp.

George Preisach.
Catharina Schallerin.
Petter Werner.
Philip Strohe.
John Hartmann.
Narbara, his wife.
Anne Marie, his daughter, 11
 years.
Elizabetha, his daughter, 8
 years.
Narbara, his daughter, 5
 years.
Nicholas, his son, 3 years.
Margaretha, his daughter,
 ½ year.
Daniel Nast.
George Renner.
Dorothee Reissenach.
Philip Emee.
Wilhelm Kohler.
George Nauer.
Charlotta, his wife.
Charlotta & }
Narbara,   } his daughters.
Jacob Naue.
Christina, his wife.
Jacob, his son.
Daniel Daw Nieda.
Christoph Shmitt.
John Shmitt.
Narbara Hammin.
Frederic Erbes.
Magdalina Pfeiffe
 Beutomüller.
Ferdinant Loewenstern.
John Muller.
Louisa Ellenberger.

George Ludwig.

George Ludwig, his son.

Magdaline & } his daughters
Catharina,

John Weiss.

Maria Notemius.

Gottliebe & } his daughters.
Frederika,

Heinrich Huckard.

Wendelina Dormick.

Catharine Lexin.

George Weimann.

John Gast.

Marie Eilserin.

Jacob, her son.

Caroline Hochstein.

Jacob Schuster.

Margarethe Baldin.

Dorothee Rohrscheid.

Petter Oymer.

Sept. 8, 1792.

Frederic Schneider.

Jacob Klein.

Phillip Frey.

Michel Zeyley.

Catharina Grüninger.

Barbara Wacherin.

Andres Barthels.

Justus Barthels.

George Schiebelhuth.

Henriet Dugenhart.

Nicolas Schmitt.

Frantz Petter Remann.

Jacob Wibbeling.

Ludwig Mierg.

John Van Grünningen.

Conrad Seypart.   }
John Keller. |
Jacob Frey.   } Americans.
John   Gottlieb Berg-|
      mann.   }

LIST OF PASSENGERS ON BOARD BRIG "HENRICUS," CAPT.
MARTIN JAYER, FROM AMSTERDAM. PHILADELPHIA, SEPT. 22,
1792.

1—J o h a n n e s Theodorus
  Bartlain.
2—George Schutz.
3—Margarethe Schultz.
4—Johannes Anspach.
5—Christine Sachsen.
6—her child 4 weeks old.
7—Catharine Damen.
8—Sibella Damen.
9—Godfrey Rerch.
10—Johann Schmaltz.

11—Johannes Rude.
12—Johannes Grebill.
13—Nicholas Miller.
14—frederich Walder.
15—Christine Striekler.
16—Johannes Reiffendorff.
17—Peter Reiffendorf.
18—frederick Brunt (?)
19—George Kraust.
20—Philipp Dalen.
21—Margarethe Dalen.

22—Nicholaus Dalen.
23—Barbara Herstien.
24—Jacob Ebel.
25—Jacob Nickolaus.
26—Gertrout Eaberten.
27—Phillipine Zerwüne.
28—Christina Otenheimer.
29—Margarethe Becker.
30—Carl Hollenberger.
31—Wilhelmina Hollenberger.

32—Anna Bolman.
33—Catharine lefiber.
34—Raatje lefieber.
35—Rooje van Aaken.
36—Carolina Gotie.
37—Alepin de lentunte.
38—George Struckler.
39—Bernard Spier.
40—Christian Ernst Lax.

Americans.

Johannes Haslein.
August Braun.
September 22, 1792.

Wendel Serwin.
Christⁿ Schneider.
MARTIN JAGER.

LIST OF PASSENGERS ON BOARD THE BRIG "MARTHA," CAPT. EBENEZER HOYT, FROM AMSTERDAM.

Mr. Charles Whanbert, Cabin Passenger.
Charles Lewis Baumann, Steerage do
Heinrich Abelmann,   do   do
Hermann Diedrich Biemar   do   do
Franz Lasser,   do   do
                Bohe Bohlens | American—
Sept. 22, 1792   EBENR HOYT.

LIST OF PASSENGERS ON BOARD THE SHIP "FAME," CAPT. ALEXR. FRASER, FROM ROTTERDAM.

Barbara Jungedius.
Andrew Schusler.
Eliza Schusler & two children
Nicholas Schleyger.
Ann Margaret Schusler.
Margaret Schusler.
John Stuff.
John Frederick.
Valentine Schusler.

Eliza Godmaning.
John Schlough.
Andrew Zehn.
Catharine Margaret Trunking.
Catharine Uring.
George Schiever.
Christopher Hofnagel.
Andreas Dieterick.

John Beum & his wife Beum
& one child.
John Beyer.
Casper Zuler.
John Quilman.
Balzar Hartmann.
Valentine Beyer.
John Beyer.
John Keitznor & his wife &
two children.
Nicholas Juger & his wife
Anna Marie one child.
Dolly Woodmakerin.
John Schanbergen.
Christian Hoffman.
John Hoffman.
Nicholas Loresch & his wife
& one child.
Melchoir Hock & his wife.
Ann Margarethe Hock.
Michal Hock.
Henry Hock.
Valentine Hock.
Casper Hock.
John Andrew Hock.
John Ziner & his wife.
John Ziner Jun'.
Ann Margarett Ziner.
Zigmond Zener.
Catherin Zener.
Eberharden Zener.
John Zener.
John Zener.
Nicholas Jordon & his wife.
Eliza Jordon.
Ann Margarett Jordon.
John Jordon.

Dorothy Jordon.
Susan Jordon.
Henry Jordon.
John Merchelin & his wife.
John Merchelin, Jun'.
Christian Merchelin.
Ann Junkin.
John Mum.
Valentine Vatholt.
Casper Vatholt.
Dorothy Vatholt.
Maria Vatholt.
Ann Richterin.
Andrew Krumlich.
John Neuman.
Margarett Burgedin & one
child.
Catharin Croming.
Jacob Slayger.
William B. Euler.
Ann Catherin Euler.
Berder Slauch & his wife.
John Slauch.
John William Slauch.
John Riticher & his wife.
Catharin Riticher.
John Riticher.
Eva Evertine.
Margarett Hartmann.
George Junger & wife.
Barbara Junger.
Casper Junger.
John Sleygar & wife.
Catharin Sleygar.
Valentine Sleygar.
Michael Hincken.
Andrew Scherck.

John Adam Beum.
Christian Bonnet.
Eliza Moedine.
Barbara Lossin & child.
John Wytzel & his wife.
John Wytzel.
Conrad Wytzel.
John Anton Brand.
Conrad Killman.
Antron Truppertin.
John Ludwig Giphart.

Sept. 23, 1792.

Christian Frederick.
John David Kesler.
Christopher Walker.
Ludwig Simmons & his wife
  Eve.
John Simmons.
Frederick Simmons.
Peter Simmons.
Melchoir Simmons.
Gabriel Simmons.
Catherin Simmons.

PASSENGER LIST OF THE SHIP "ELIZABETH," WHICH ARRIVED AT PHILADELPHIA IN 1819.

[Copied from the original in the Library of the Historical Society of Pennsylvania.]

We the undersigned : I, M. Adams, Captain of the Ship Elizabeth on one part, and we the passengers on the other part do obligate ourselves—

First, We the passengers to take our passage with the above mentioned Capt. Adams to Philadelphia in North America, and to conduct ourselves as good passengers ought to do, quiet and orderly, and to be satisfied with the food mentioned at foot as per agreement with the Captain, and with regard to water and other provisions, to follow the Captain's directions as he shall find necessary through long passage or other circumstances.

Second. We agree to take our passage on the following conditions, viz. to pay

For those who are able to pay in Amsterdam for each person man or woman 180 fr.

Children under four years of age are free—

From four to twelve years to pay 90 fr.

From twelve years and older to pay 180 fr.

For those who are not able to pay here or only in part, the passage to be

Children under four years of age free

From four to twelve years 95 fr.

From twelve years and older 190 fr. and 200 fr. as specified.

Those who have to pay their passage in America shall be obliged to do so in ten days after their arrival. No passenger shall be allowed to leave the vessel in America without leave from the Captain and in particular those as have not paid their passage money. Should any one of the passengers die on the voyage, the family of such person shall be obliged to pay his passage, if such decease took place on more than half the distance of the voyage, but should the person die this side half the distance, the loss of the passage shall fall to the Captain.

In return I, M. Adams obligate myself to carry these passengers to Philadelphia, to accommodate them with the necessary comfort and give them daily the here below mentioned proportion of victuals—children not to receive anything.

Sunday—one pound Beef and half pound Rice,

Monday—one pound Flour,

Tuesday—one half pound Pork with pease,

Wednesday—one pound Beef and barley,

Thursday—like Tuesday,

Friday—like Monday,

Saturday—like Wednesday,

One pound Butter, one pound Cheese, six pounds Bread, per week.

One glass Gin and three quarter gallons Water per day.

There shall also be on board a sufficiency of Vinegar to cleanse the vessel and for the refreshing the passengers. To all this we bind ourselves with our persons and property.

Witness VAN OLIVIER & Co.

AMSTERDAM, 4 May, 1819.

Names	Number of Persons	Freight	Passage Money	Paid here	To be Paid in Philada
George Michael Huetter, ...	6	5 fr.	900 fr.	900 fr.	
Henry Roedel,.................	10	9	1620.	1620.	
Michael Idler,...............	6	6	720.	720.	
Magdalena Strählin, ...	1	1	180.	180.	
Frederick Walber (?)	4	3	540.	540.	
John Frederick Betzold,.......	1	1	180	100	80 fr.
John Frederick Speiser, ...	1	1	190	50	140
Francis Krucker,.............	1	1	190	60	130
John Henry Wilk, ...	1	1	190	30	160
Henry Luttell, ...	1	1	200	21	179
John Andrew Ammon,........	1	1	170	170	
V. P. Myersott (?)	1	1	150	150	
Xavier Streuber (?)	1	1	160	160	

Names	Number of Persons	Freight	Passage Money	Paid here	To be Paid in Philada
George Henry Bute, ...	1	1 fr.	200 fr.		200 fr.
Jean Louis Kemser, ...	1	1	200		200
George William Miller, ...	1	1	200		200
S. T. Van de Graff, ...	2	1½	290	120 fr.	170
Philip Fr. Leisaten, (?)	1	1	200		200
George Eberle, ...	1	1	190		190
Carl Ollie...................	1	1	200		200
John Frederick Schuhardt, ...	1	1	200		200
Carl Rommel, ...	1	1	190	50	140
John Sautter, ...	1	1	200		200
—— Tomber (?)...............	1	1	200		200
Henry Geiger	1	1	200		200
Conrad Neinstein, ...	7	6	760		760
Jacob Frederick Maechtle,.....	1	1	190		190
Anton Hanhaussen, ...	1	1	190		190
John Henry Burg,.............	1	1	190		190
George Francis Klee, ...	1	1	190		190
John Jacob Keppel, ...	1	1	190		190
John George Heugel, ...	1	1	190		190
Barbara Schwasen (?).........	1	1	190		190
Barbara Etlung,..............	1	1	190		190
John Fuchs, ...	1	1	200		200
John Kücherer, ...	1	1	200		200
Barndina Hulsing,............	1	1	200		200
Barbara Jundt,...............	1	1	190		190
Magdalena + Langin, ...	1	1	190		190
Rudolph + Hagmann, ...	1	1	190	70	120
Elizabeth Hensin, ...	1	1	190		190
—— Maria Steinman,.........	1	1	190		190
Carl Lebold, ...	1	1	200		200
Jacob Stark, ...	1	1	200		200
Michael Haag, ...	1	1	180	180	
John George Hauser, ...	1	1	200		200
John George Weber,..........	1	1	200		200
Seligmann Zimern, ...	1	1	170	170	
Jacob Fuchs, ...	1	1	190		190
Jacob Adolt,.................	1	1	200		200
John Leonard Gieser..........	1	1	190		190
Barbara Lang, ...	1	1	190		190
J. M. Schüle, ...	1	1	180		180
George Peter Gieser, ...	1	1	190		190
John S. Kline, ...	1	1	180	120	60
Henry Steinman, ...	1	1	180	170	10
Jacob Breitenbücher, ...	1	1	180	180	
Christina + Keim, ...	1	1	190		190
John George Gundt, ...	1	1	180	180	
Frederick Seitz, ...	1	1	180	180	
F. Lennig,...................	3	2½	700	700	
Carl Schuele, ...	1	1	190		190
John Schmitt, ...	1	1	180	180	
John Haas (?)	3	2½	425	425	
Reichard Saltzer, ...	5	3	510	510	
William A. Diecken, ...	1	1	160	160	
Anna Melinger, ...	1	1	180	180	

Names	Number of Persons	Freight	Passage Money	Paid here	To be Paid in Philada
Ludwig Reiff,...............	1	1 fr.	200 fr.		200 fr.
Conrad Kegel, ...	1	1	200		200
Augustin Wandel,...........	1	1	200		200
John George Reiner,.........	1	1	200		200
Christian Frederick Reinhold,..	1	1	200		200
Adam Gelhart...............	1	1	200		200
John Frederick Guedeman,....	1	1	200		200
Anton Vanbun, (?)...........	1	1	200		200
Jacob Frederick Lehmann, ...	1	1	200		200
Xavier Vanbun,.............	1	1	200		200
Gottfried Schink, ...	1	1	200		200
Henry Hofer, ...	1	1	170	170 fr.	
Gottfried Straub.	1	1	200		200
Caspar Walber (?) ⎫ Simon Walber (?) ⎬.......... Jacob Walber (?) ⎭	3	3	570		570

MISCELLANEOUS LISTS

GERMAN FAMILIES :—The following list of German families, arrived at Philadelphia, appears in an advertisement in Henry Miller's *Staats Bote* of February 9, 1758, and will be helpful for genealogical purposes. The translation was made by the contributor, R. G. Swift.—

The following German families and a couple of unmarried persons, are now in this city ; all held for their passage from Holland, and desiring to bind themselves out for the same ; they are in present need ; they hope to find their friends and would like to emigrate to free themselves of indebtedness to *Willing and Morris* as they themselves are unable to pay, since they (W. & M.) are willing to give credit either to their friends or themselves if they bind themselves out.

Johannes Hobart, joiner, born in the Chur Maynz, town of Lembach ; *wife*, Maria Elisabetha Kettelin, from Langenkandel in Zweibruck.

Johann Jacob Müller, peasant, of Dierdorf, town of Dirnbach ; *wife*, Margreta Elisabetha Thomas.

Johann Wilhelm Kaper, peasant, born in Grafschaft, Dierdorf, town of Potterbach ; *wife*, Annagir Hoffman, town of Werkbach.

Johannes Müller, peasant, born in Chur-Pfaltz, town of Bretzen ; *wife*, Anna Elisabetha Sandpöffer, from Anspach, town of Bürgenhausen.

Johann Müller, peasant, born in Hesse Darmstadt, Herrschaft Itter ; *wife*, Anna Maria Müller (no town given).

Eva Schleichart, needlewoman, born in Elsass, town of Lembach (single).

Joseph Bläs, tailor, Chur Maynz, town of Burtzele ; *wife*, Dorothea Kartz, born in Elsass, town of Lembach.

Bastian Dauber, peasant, Hesse Cassel district of Marburg, town of Leidehoffen ; *wife*, Anna Elisabetha Litt, born in Braunselseischen, town of Oberhofen.

Johan Derbald Hauck, peasant, born in Zweybruck, town of Hunbach ; *wife*, Barbara Schunckel, town of Hassen.

Johann Jacob Albrech, peasant, born in Zweybruck, town of Langenkandel ; *wife*, Anna Maria Nirland, Landau.

Johann Philip Bott, peasant, born in Elsass, town of Fachbach ; *wife*, Anna Maria Malonc, born in the town of Kruszbach.

Johann Kobbeloch, linen weaver, Zweybruck, town of Langenkandel ; *wife*, —— Seyler, town of Vörlebach.

Anna Catharina Rosz, born in Zweybruck, town of Langenkandel (single).

Johann Georg Hoch, peasant, born in Zweybruck, town of Bürlebach ; *wife*, Maria Dorothea Baur, born in Elsass, town of Lembach.

Jeremias Algeyer, peasant and vine dresser, born in Kirchheim on the Necker ; *wife*, Elisabetha Margaritha Schäf, born in Guglingen.

Johann Nicholas Albrech, peasant and vine dresser, born Kirchheim on the Necker ; *wife*, Christina Krausz, born in Leham.

Johannes Westermeyer, maker of wooden shoes, Elsass, Köllendorf ; *wife*, Adilga, from Fischback, Elsass.

Johann Georg Schäfer, musician, from Pfaltz, district of Lindenfels ; *wife*, Elsa, born in Clembad, Chur Pfaltz.

R. G. SWIFT.

LIST OF SERVANTS who sailed from Dublin February 25th 1746/7 on the Euryal, and arrived at Philadelphia April 11th.

Catherine Gainer,	Elizabeth Dunn,
Catherine Durcum,	Eleanor Dwier,
Catherine Whitehead,	Catherine Dwier,
Celia Byrne,	Mary Fling,
Hannah Row,	Mary Brady,
Margaret Poor,	Mary Mucklerow,
Catherine Cane,	Elizabeth Fox,
Margaret Connor,	Dorothy Jones,
Mary Whelan,	Margaret Traynor,
Eleanor Hanlan,	Mary Williams.

Passengers aboard the *Mary* who arrived in
Philadelphia in November, 1743.

John Ulrick Hagenbuck, Wife and 3 childⁿ. aged 12-11-2
Felix Rebsamen   do & 6   do   do   12-11-7-3-5-½
John Rueg   do & 5   do   do   11-7-4-2-½
Jacob Rueg   do & 3   do   do   18-12-11
Rudolf Epprecht   do & 6   do   do   20-18-14-12-7-4
Henry Angst
Elizᵗʰ. Angst   do

INDEX OF SHIPS

INDEX OF NAMES

Bakely (cont.)
Daniel 202, 223
Henry 223
Baker, George 202, 203
George Wm. 181
Henry 11
Hester 11
Margaret 11
Nathan 11
Nehemiah 54
Patrick 102
Phebey 11
Rachell 11
Rebecca 11
Samuel 11
Balde, Johan Henry 241
Johannes 241
William 241
Balderston, John Jr. 225
Baldin, Margarethe 253
Baldwin, John 109, 196
Balffs, Marcus 44
Ball, John 11
Ballenhorst, Margaret 42
Bament, John 216
Banbury, James 15
Banc, Ingebar 5
Banister, Elizabeth 38
Bankson, Benjamin 221
Bard, Peter 101
Bare, Catharina 245
Catharine 245
Peter 245
Barge, Jacob 181, 234
William 109, 110
Barkow, Nicholas 223
Barnard, Robert 97
Barnes, Daniel 208, 210
Elizabetha 90
John 83
Barnett, Robert 80
Barret, John 97
Barrett, Richard 112
Barrow, Rebecca 11
Samuel 219
Barry, Michael 210
Bart, Barr 250
Cathrine 250
Cethnet 250
Hein. 250
Henry 250
Johann 250
Margret 250
Bartel, Johann Christian 247
Barthels, Andres 253
Justus 253
Barthemel, Cornelius 245
Bartholomew, Edward 198
George 215
Mary 198
Bartlain, Johannes Theodorus 253
Bartling, Christel 202
Barton, Joseph 102
Bartow, Thomas 58
Basley, Wm. 239
Bass, Robert 183
Bast, Lawrence 183
Bates, [?], Thomas 14
Batsford, Edward 14
Battin, Francis 154
Battle, Anne 121
Bauer, Catharine 242
Catharine Debora 242
Hans Michael 242
Hans Peter 242
Johan 249
Michel 242

Bauer (cont.)
Philip Jacob 242
Philip Jerry 242
Baumann, Charles Lewis 254
Baumgarten, George 44
Baur, Maria Dorothea 261
Beakes, Abraham 20
William 20
Beardsly, Alexander 11
Margaret 11
Mary 11
Beasy, William 25
Beatler, John 195
Beaton, Edw. 239
Beatty, Daniel 81
Beaumont, John 92
Beck, John Valentine 52
Becker, Elizabeth 193
Margarethe 254
Becket, Mary 11
William 224
Beckham, Geo. P. 239
Beckman, Andrew 225
Becktell, Jacob 66
Bedford, Gunning 163, 214
Bedley, Elizabeth 211
Henry 211
Beech, Rebecca 234
Beere, James 229
Jonathan 229
Beer(s), Andrew 114, 155
Begg, Patrick 124
Behman, John 148
Nathaniel 148
Beitel, Maria 53
Belastein, Francis 211
Belfour, James 223
Beliteg, Pasco (or Pasro) 8
Bell, James 202
John 59, 88, 143, 229
Robert 233
Thomas 202
Beltshire, John 15
Benck, Maria 5
Bendall, Davies 78
Bender, Daniel 233
Benenge, Gerrett 238
Benner, George 207
Johannes 181
Bennet, Elizabeth 28
Rebecca 24
William 24, 28
Benson, John 157
Robert 22
Benzet, James 168
Benzien, Anna Benigna 47
Anna Maria 47
C. T. 47
Christel 47
Bergman, Henry 44
Bergmann, John Gottlieb 253
Berndt, Gottlieb 41
Bernhard, Wenzel 41
Berr, Jacob Jr. 169
Berry, James 81
Richard 90
Berze, Her 248
Besch, Martin 203
Bess, Simon Jacob 195
Bestitraser, Richard 17
Bettle, William 202
Betts, John Fredk. 190
Margaret 190
Betty, Anne 146, 150
Betzold, John Frederick 258
Beudiker, James 203
Beum, John 255
John Adam 256

Beutomuller, Magdalina Pfeiffe 252
Bevan, Richard 132
Bevin, Patrick 225
Beyer, Anna Maria 45
Anna Rosina 42
Frederick 46
John 255
Maria 42
Valentine 255
Beyter, ____ 250
Hans 249
Bickerton, John 204
Biddle, John 96
Biderman, Jacob 216
Biefel, John Henry 37
Rosina 37
Bieg, Elizabeth 42
Biemar, Hermann Diedrich 254
Bierly, Andrew 179
Biggart, Robert 225
Bigger, Peacock 133
Biggs, John 235
Peter 231
Bigler, John 216
Bignal, John 215
Bikker, Michael 83
Biles, Charles 22
Elizabeth 21
George 21
Johanah 21
Johannah 21
John 21
Mary 21
Rebecca 21
William 21
Bill, Robert 221
Billger, Daniel 82
Billig, Anthony 230
Binder, Catherine 43
Jacob 184, 208
Philip 208
Bingham, Mary 75
William 75
Binke, Sarah 15
Binks, Christopher 207
Biorsson, Lars 3
Laurence 3
Birch, Alexander 56
William 183
Birchfield, Samuel 68
Bird, William 174
Birnbaum, Joachim 41
Bischoff, Ann Catherine 35
David 35
Bishop, Michael 184, 233, 239
Thomas 223
Bispham, William 208
Bitterlich, J. G. 40
Black, Daniel 203
Elizabeth 61, 128
George 128, 231
James 203, 233
Robert 61
Blackhouse, Richard 93, 95
Blackiston, Presly/Presley 189, 219
Blackledge, John 182
Blackshaw, Alice 25
Jacob 25
Martha 25
Mary 25
Nathaniel 25
Phebe 25
Randulph 25
Blackwood, John 156
Samuel 231
Blair, George 144, 145

268

270

Gill, John 63
  Mary 235
Gillan, Hugh 151
Gillaspy, John 67
Gillcrest, James 71
  John 71
Gillis, Grove 125
  Sarah 232
Gimmile, Matthias 48
Ginder, Anne Marie 245
  Elizabeth 244
  Frederick 245
  Johanna 244, 245
  Johanna Louisa 245
Ginney, William 22
Giphart, John Ludwig 256
Girtie, Simon 107
Givings, Mary 159
Givings (?), Mary 159
Glaire, George 25
  Issabel 25
Glancy, Darby 112
Gleave, Matthew 61
Gleckner, Charles 224
Glenn, James 187
Godfrey, Sarah 235
Godmaning, Eliza 254
Godshalk, Jacob 213, 217
Goetje, Anna Barbara 37
  Peter 37
Goetz, Gustav Frederic 245
Goff, Edward 54, 135
Gold, George 42
Golden, William 230
Golkowsky, George Wenzeslaus
  46
Gollohan, Mary 93
Golzen, Henrich 244
Gonder, John Francis 226
Gonele, James 73
Good, Lawrence 64, 65
Gooding, George 15
Goodman, Ozias 241
  Stephen 169
  Walter 137
Goodwin, George 188
  James 153
  John 102, 228
  Ozias 243
Goodwine, George 233
Goohegan, Hugh 144
Gordon, Barbara 92
  Henry 209
  Patrick 182
Gorman, Dennis 108
  Mathew 105
Gory, John 150
Gosshaw, Gabriel 207
Gotie, Carolina 254
Gottier, James 107
Gottschalk, Jahn Jurg 173
  Matthias Gottlieb 40
Govett, Joseph 86
Grabs, Anna Mary 37
  John Godfrey 37
Graeme, (Dr.) Thomas 66
Graff, Gertrude 45
  Jacob 208, 232
  Johann Gottlib 187
  John Michael 45
  Michael 223
Grafmayer, John Godfred 195
Graham, Archibald 223
  George 120
  Henry 235
  James 115
  John 227
  Mary 227

Graham (cont.)
  William 194
Grall, Barbara 241
  Catharina 241
  Georg 241
  Peter 241
Grames, Thomas 229
Granner, John 156
Granram, Carl 243
  Fredk. 243
Grant, Robert 154
Gratz, Bernard 212
Grave, Jacob 114
  Jacob Jr. 114
  Thomas 115, 116
Graves, John 239
Gray, Jean 231
  John 115, 123
  Robert 200
  William 233
  Wm. 239
Graydon, Hannah 232
Graydon(e), Rachel 182
Greaver, Robert 216
Grebill, Johannes 253
Green, Ann 135
  Barthol. 17
  Peter 188
  Pyramus 101
  William 188, 207
Greenaway, Robert 21, 24
Greene, John 17
  Margaret 17
  Thomas 17
  (Dr.) Thomas 133
Greening, Elizabeth 38
  James 38
Greenland, Frances 25
Greenless, Margaret 93
Greenway, John 162
  Rob 17
  Robert 12
  William 150
Greenwood, Alexander 211
Grenan, John 65
Greville, Allmer/Aylmer 106
Griffin, Jane 90
  Joanna 214
  Joseph 90
  Selwood 227
Griffit, Benjamin 216
Griffith, Daniel 59
  Susan 10
Griffith(s), Thomas 32, 81,
  118, 141, 142, 148
Grill, Charles Matthew 204
Grim, George 94
  Phetha 94
Grimes, Barnaby 83
  Mary 77, 169
  Matthew 204
Griscom, Samuel 232
Groen, John George 44
Groeszer, Margaret 43
Groff, Anthony 196
Gromell, James 166
Gross, Andrew 44
Grove, Richard 16
Grub, Jacob 204
Grubb, Emanuel 103
  Jacob 82
  Peter 82
Grube, Bernhard Adam 40
Gruendberg, Helena 43
Grunewald, John Henry 48
  Ludwig C. 52
Gruninger, Catharina 253
Grunnenwald, Matthieu 251

Guddermouth, Catharine 250
  Nichols 250
Gudemuth, Johanna 251
Gudermouth, Hans 250
  Laur. 250
Gudermuth, Dorety 250
  Nichols 250
  Philip 250
Guedeman, John Frederick 260
Guerin, Anty. 238
Guerry, Mary 120, 176
Guest, Henry 18
  John 231
  Mary 17, 18
Guion, George 135
Gundt, John George 259
Guntar, Anna Margaret 241
  Caroline 241
  Catherine 241
  Conrad 241
  Daniel 241
  Hans Daniel 241
  Hans Jacob 241
  Hans William 241
Gunther, Jacob 244
  Johann Jacob 244
  Johanna 244
  Maria Barbara 244
Guntzing, Catharine Phillipin
  244
Guthry, James 123
  John 76
Gwinop, George 17
Gyger, Christopher 81
  Frederick 67

-H-

Haag, Michael 259
Haas (?), John 259
Habach, Anna Eliza. 183
Habacki, Anna Eliza. 214
Haberecht, Gottfried 33
  Rosina 33
Haberland, Anna Helena 41
  George 33
  Joseph 46
  Juliana 43
  Michael 33, 41
Habert, Anna Maria 237
  Christian 237
Hackabuck, Margaret 72
Hacket, Mary 189
Hadelmaker, J. I. 244
Haensel, John C. 44
Haga, Godfrey 187, 219
Hagan, John 197
Hagemann, Jochim 249
Hagenbuck, John Ulrick 262
Hagh, Johan 250
Hagmann, Rudolph 259
Haidt, Catherine 47
  J. Valentine 47
Haines, H. 238
  Henry 187, 192
  Samuel 30, 31, 32
Hains, Moses 239
  Reuben 223, 226
Hale, Thomas 194
Haley, Derby 15
  Joseph 43
  Luke 220
  Michael 221
Hall, Ann 194
  David 27

274

280

McKoun (cont.)
 John 138
McLaske, Arthur 78
McLaughlan, Philip 132
McLaughlin, Charles 115
 Hugh 119
 John 109
McLene, Hector 62
McMahon, Morgan 90, 141
McMannis, Michael 182
McMeen, William 64
McMichael, Daniel 222
 Mary 222
McMinn, John 79
McMollin, Thomas 155
McMullan, John 116, 117
McMullin, Wm. 239
McNalton, Elizabeth 133
McNeal, Arthur 167
McNeil, Elizabeth 233
McNemee, William 121
McNormara, Jonathan 70
McPherson, Danl. 247
McQuillen, Edward 225
McSparran, Archibald 219
McSwiney, Charles 122
McVaugh, James 119
McVea, Duncan 118
McVeagh, Martin 151
 Matthew 164
McWhirter, George 166

-M-

Maack, Jacob 139
Maag, Henry 213
 Jacob 198
Maans, Martha 43
Mabane, Alexander 144
Mack, John Martin 33
Mackleduff, Joseph 83
Mackzeiner, Elizabeth Margr.
 202
Maclay, John 102
Maddin, Stephen 74
Maddock (Madock), Henry 9
Maechtle, Jacob Frederick 259
Magill, Robert 206
Maginnes, Patrick 235
Maglathery, Elizabeth 207
 James 207
Magner, Anthony 97, 167
 Barbara 97
Magrah, Honour 160
Magrath, James 234
 John 206, 213
Magrogan, Mary 72, 142
Mahan, James 63
 John 61
Maher (?), Roger 57
Mahon, Sarah 176
Mahoney, James 234
 Lawrence 86
 Mary 201
Mahony, Jerimiah 206
 Paul 129
Mahrliz, Peter 208
Maine, Alexander 94
Maldrom, John 189
 Margaret 189
Maley, (Capt.) Wm. 251
Malin, Randall 152
Malone, Anna Maria 261
 Michael 145
Maltimore, Anne 160

Man, Robert 65
Manie, Francis 111
Manly, James 200
 Sarah 269
Mann, Anna 45
Mannen, John 228
Mansson, Hans 3
Manypenny, Clemens 226
Marckusson, Carl 2
Marjorum, Elizabeth 20
 Henry 20
Markill, John 64
Marks, Jennet 182
 Levy 211, 221
Markt, John Gottfrieden 240
Markusson, Lars 2
Marlay, John 61
Marley, Manus 54
Marlton, John 15
Marrier, Henry 225
Marsey, Tho. 9
Marsh, Richard 201
Marshal, Walter 200
Marshall, Frederick von 52
 Hedwig Elizabeth von 52
 John 16, 199, 210, 214
 Joseph 173, 201
 Thomas 220
 (Capt.) Thos. 59
Marten, Michel 251
Martin, Hannah 16
 John 147, 197, 222, 239
 Margery 16
 Mary 16, 188
 Rachell 16
 Sarah 16
 Tho. 16
 Thomas 59, 143
 Thos. 239
 William 224
Martz, Ann 236
 Anna Margaretta 236
 Simon 236
Masen, Richard 216
Masland, Hugh 9
Masner, John G. 44
Mason, Abram 68, 89, 90
 Benjamin 67
 George Mechil 246
 John 204, 246
 Joseph 68, 246
 Mary 246
Massey, White 93, 98
Master, Joseph 190
Masturman, Thomas 217
Matchet, Richard 164
Mather, Joseph 26
 Rechard 14
 Richard 29
Mathewes, Jeane 12
Mathews, Hugh 118
 John 129
 Robert 129, 150
Matsson, Hindrich 2, 3
Matthieson, Christopher 44
 Nicholas 44
Matzenbacher, Johan Adam 189
Maux, Jacob 86
Maxfield, James 177
 Mary 197
 William 187
Maxzeymour, Elizabeth 193
 John William 193
Maxzuymour, Henry Adam 196
May, John 206
 William 206, 218
Mayberry, Thos. 239
Mayfield, Thomas 221

Maylan/Maylon, William 82
Mayow, Elizabeth 15
 Helen 15
 John 15
 Martha 15
 Philip 15
Mayse, Charles 206
Mead, Jane 202
Mealy, Walter 105
Mearns, Hugh 117
Mears, Charles 218
Meath, Dominick 60
Meehan, Edward 104
Meenagh, Hugh 127
Mehone, John 15
Mein, Agnes 59
Meinung, Abraham 34
 Judith 34
Meisser, Henry George 48
Melinger, Anna 259
Meloy, John 232
Meminger, Theodore 182, 203
Mendenhall, Aaron 80
Mendinhall, Moses 16
Menge, Anna Margaret 220
 Henry 220
 John 220, 227
 Margaret 227
Mentz, William 232
Mentzinger, George E. 49
Merchelin, Christian 255
 John 255
 John Jr. 255
Merck, John Henry 44
Meredith, Daniel 208
 Jonathan 186, 223
 Samuel 228
Merkly, Christopher 44
Merrick, John 231
Merryfield, Jeremiah 228
Mertlen, Susan 243
Mesmer, Jacob 244
Mestar, Johan Bohr 249
Meurer, John Philip 36
Meyer, Adolph 35, 36
 Agnes 45
 Anna Margaret (Margt.) 196,
 207
 Anne Marie 251
 Catharine 245
 Eve Mary 39
 George 251
 Jacob 44
 John 251
 John Adam 251
 John Gerard 224
 John Michael 33
 John S. 44
 John William 185
 Maria Catherine 196
 Maria Dorothea 36
 Maria Elizabeth 194
 Mary M. 53
 Matthias 206
 Philip 44
Meyerhoff, Magdalena 43
Meyers, J. G. 240
Michael, John 67
Michéll, Barnard 192
Michler, Barbara 37
 John 37
Micklen, Mary 183
Micon, John 99
Mierg, Ludwig 253
Miers, Charles 171
Miffert, Anna Cathe. 201
 John Conrad(e) 201
 Maria (Mary) Dorothy 201

Miffet, Johan Henry 196
Mifflin, George 220
  Johnathan/Jonathan 93, 98
  Maria Catherine 220
  Thomas 240, 248
Miksch, Anna Johanna 35
  John Matthew 48
  Michael 35
Milare, Edmond 223
Milcom, Ann 20
  Grace 20
  Jane 20
  Mary 20
Miller,_____ 180
  Alexander 74
  Andrew 75
  Anna Maria 191
  Charles 194, 206
  Daniel 185
  Dorothea 227
  George William 259
  Henry 45, 67, 261
  Isabelle 103
  Jacob 184, 185, 227
  James 73
  Johanna D. 45
  John 185, 216, 224
  John Henry 34, 227
  John Phillips 182
  Maria Catherine 187
  Nicholas 191, 253
  Paul 164
  Richard 117, 155
  Robt. 230
  William 59
Mills, John 200
Milner, John 219
  John Jr. 219
  Jos. 8
  Rachell 8
  Ralph 8
  Robt. 8
  Sarah 8
  William 229
Milward, Samuel 222
Mingo, Magdalena 43
Misser, John Jacob 205
Mitchell,_____ 180
  Abraham 125, 140
  Gabriel 153
  James 71, 120, 122
  John 200, 205, 222
  Joseph 200
  Mary 222
  Thomas 137
  Wm. 239
Mode, Jane 27
  Margery 27
Moedine, Eliza 256
Moehring, John M. 52
Moeller, John Henry 37
  Joseph 36
  Rosina 37
Mogdridge, Hannah 21
Moland, John 144
Molenex, James 14
Molinex, James 29
Molloy, John 235
Monaghan, Patrick 66
Monk, Jacob 163
  John Conrad 162
Monney, Joseph 218
Monroe, John 104
Montgomery,_____ 180
  Archibald 168, 174
  Daniel 221
  Patrick 120
  William 200, 220

Moode, William 55, 57
Moods, William 101
Moody, John 214
Mooney, John 73
Moor, Elinor 166
  James 63
  John 56
  Julian 170
  Mary 165
Moore, Alexander 143
  Allen 187
  Andrew 234, 235
  Charles 55, 94
  Danl. 22
  Edward 32
  George 87
  Hannah 197
  Hugh 63, 92
  James 154
  John 17, 18, 75, 133
  Joseph 210
  Mary 18
  Philip 207
  Quintin 90
  Ralph 185
  Richard 18
  Samuel 220, 229
  Thomas 182, 198, 209
  William 98, 127, 229
Moorey, Thomas 153, 154
Moos, Niel 52
Moran, Patrick 125
Mordick, Peter 42
More, Catharine 242
  Francis 221
  George 242
  George Henry 242
  Peter 242
Morgan, Alexander 148
  Anne 16
  Benjam. 16
  Elizabeth 7
  Jacob 201
  Jacob Jr. 201
  James 107
  John 105, 106
  Joseph 16, 154
  Latin 61
  Patrick 70, 233
  Samuel 170
  William 7
Morgenthal, John 245
Morhardt, Christina 46
Morin, Daniell 15
  Miles 15
Morn, John 157
Morrin, John 71
Morris,_____ 261
  Anthony Jr. 68, 107
  Israel 224
  Israel Jr. 230
  James 20
  John 30, 31, 32
  Joshua 74, 138
  Luke 181
  Morris 63
  Patrick Fitts 170
  Robert 189
  Saml. Jr. 224, 230
  Thomas 138
  William 69, 132, 208
Morrison, John 78, 123
Morrough, Patrick 120
Mortel, Catharine 242
  George Henry 242
Mortimer, Robert 223
Morton, James 104
  William 20

Mosemann, Johann 244
Moser, Catherine 205, 230
  Jacob 205, 230
Moss, Isaac 218
  Samuel 218
Mossor, Mary 217
Moulder, Joseph 183
  William 217
Mouse, Philip 187
Moyer, John 199, 209
Moylan, Joseph 206
  Sarah 206
Moynihan, Andrew 200
Mozer, John 37
  Mary Philippina 37
Mubryan, Eleanor 185
Mucklegun, Thomas 145
Mucklerow, Mary 262
Muecke, Catherine 37
  John Michael 37
Mueller, John 49
  John B. 42
  John Jacob 34
  Joseph 41
  Verona 41
Muensch, John 44
Muenster, Anna 52
  John 38
  Melchior 44
  Michael 42
  Paul 52
  Rosina 38
Muffler, Sebastian 214
Muhlen, J. V. D. 247
Muhlenberg, (Rev.) Frederick
  218
Mullador, Adam 211
Mullan, Thomas 56
Mullen, Charles 133
  Thomas 133
Muller, Andrae 252
  Anna Maria 261
  Catharine 251
  Jacob 252
  Johann 261
  Johann Jacob 261
  Johannes 261
  John 245, 252
Mullin, Henry 195
Mullott, Pierie 238
Mulvay, John 106
Mum, John 255
Mumma, Samuel 67
Murath, Caspar 215
Murdoch, William 67
Murdock, William 69, 100
Murphey, Esther 234
Murphy, Ann 225
  Edward 137
  Elinor 165
  James 112
  John 60, 221
  Mary 234
  Robert 106, 111
  Thomas 233
Murray, Ann 225
  Charles 121
  Garret 150
  John 218
  Martha 221
  Mary 72
  Richard 116
  William 212, 214
Murrough, John 77
  William 57
Musgrove, Matthew 219
  William 219
  William Jr. 106

Mushell, Margaret 233
Muske, Richard 15
Musser, George 195
  John 191, 204
Myardie, Barbara 209
Myers, George 189
  John 203
Myersott (?), V. P. 258
Myles, Bartholomew 104
Myrriall, James 14
Myrtetus, Christopher 183

-N-

Nagle, John 209
  John Jacob 44
  Joseph 209
Naglee, Thomas 216
Nannetter, Jacob 192
Nast, Daniel 252
Naue, Christina 252
  Jacob 252
Nauer, Charlotta 252
  George 252
  Narbara 252
Neal, Edward 132
  Henry 219
  John 71, 166
Nedrow, Thos. 185
Neef, John David 204
Neelson, Andrew 146
Neff, Rudolph 210
Neild (or Wild), John 8
Neilhock,_____ 44
Neilson, Sarah 233
Neinstein, Conrad 259
Neisser, Augustine 33
  George 33, 39
Nell, Christian 237
Nellson, Gerard 119
Nelson, Jane 235
  Robert 191
  Thomas 191
Nenzenhoeffer, Georg 251
Nerthwein, Henric 251
Nertwig/Netwig, Elizabeth 245
  Joh. G. 245
Nesmith, Arthur 154
Netherwood, Cornelius 14, 28
Neubert, Daniel 36
  Hannah 36
Neuman, John 255
  Regina 46
Nevell, John 198, 199
Nevil, James 221
Newhouse, Anthony 58, 93
  Jonathan 222
Newlin, Ellis 189
Newman, Jacob 77, 115
  Richard 194, 207
Nicholas, Anthony 158
  Edward 32
Nicholls, Joseph 147
Nichols, Mary 221
Nicholson, Joshua 156
  Margery 58
  William 75, 89, 91
Nick, William 225
Nickolaus, Jacob 254
Nickson (see Nixon)
Nieda, Daniel Daw 252
Nieke, George 38
  Johanna E. 38
Nield, John 22
Niels, Karin 5

Niels (cont.)
  Margaretha 5
  Sigri 4
Nielsen, Lorenz 48
Nihil, Edmund 97, 147
  Maurice 97, 147
Nile, Tobias 160
Niles, William 182, 194
Nilsen, Jonas 37
  Margaret 37
Nirland, Anna Maria 261
Nitsche, Anna M. 43
Nitschman, Martin 42
Nitschmann, Anna 53
  David 41
  David Sr. 47
  (Bishop) David 33, 34, 38
  Emanuel 52
  John 41
  Juliana 41
  Rosina 34, 41
Nixdorf, John G. 38
Nixon, Eliz. 8
  Frederick 8
  James 8
  Jane Margery 8
  John 8, 187
  Joseph 8
  Margery 8
  Mary 8
  Nehemiah 8
  Thom 8
  Thomas 16
  Thomas Jr. 16
  William 101
Noble, Samuel 214, 234
  Thomas 39
Noll, Elizabeth 214
  Martin 214
Noorington, Thomas 86, 139
Norley, Mary 106
Norrington, Thomas 150
Norris, Isaac 60
  Thomas 232
Norton, Elizabeth 134
  William 225
Notemius, Frederika 253
  Gottliebe 253
  Maria 253
Notten, Faith 16
Notting, George 245
Nourse, Joseph 213
Nowell, Stephen 16
Nowland, Peter 218
Noxon, Richd. 239
Nuernberg, Dorothea 43
Nusz, Helena 43
Nuttall, Ralph 25

-O-

Oalwain, Wamert 187
O'Barr, Daniel 115
  David 116
Oberlin, John F. 52
Obisan, Scintje 245
Oblinger, Barbara 252
  Carl 252
  Christian 252
  Jacob 252
  John 252
  Narbara 252
Obourn, Joseph 142
O'brien, Cormick 81
Obryan, Christopher 71

Obryan (cont.)
  Grace 71
O'bryan/O'Bryan, John 109, 110,
  226
O'Connor, Charles 198, 209
O'Daniel, Daniel 130
  John 173
Odenwald, John M. 44
O'Donnell, John 138
Oertel, Elizabeth 43
Oerter, Christian F. 38
Off, Peter 235
Ogilby, Patrick 152
Ogelthorpe, General 34
O'Hanly, Bridget 119
O'Hara, Bryan 59
O'Harken, Edmund 117
O'Harra, Bryan 219
O'Hassan, Patrick 116
Ohneberg, George 37
  Susan 37
O'Kell, George 161
Okely, John 36
  William 36, 47
O'Kill, George 59, 72, 117,
  155, 156, 158, 169
O'lanshalin, Teddy 63
Old, John 186
Olden, Benjamin 194
Olffson, Jon 4
Oliver, James 186
  Van 258
  Winnifred 32
Ollendorf, Carl 48
Ollie, Carl 259
Ollringshaw, Henry 49
Olofsson, Mats 3
Olsen, Johan Hendrick 248
Oluff, Britha 4
  Elie 5
  Sigrij 4
Oluffson, Lars 4
O'Mullan, Bryan 120
  Daniel 142
  Mary 121
O'neal/O'Neal, Francis 72, 101
O'Neal, John 117
Oneal, Patrick 157
O'Neil, Ferdinando 143
  Neal 148
O'Neill, Francis 144
Onion, Stephen 69, 70
Onongst, Elizabeth 212
Opitz, Carl 42
  Maria E. 43
Oquener, Ann 223
Orbel, John Frederic 196
Orcle, Richard 228
Orevan, Shebe 15
Orley, Catherine 91
Ormsby, Clevell 113
  Lawrence 110
O'Rogherty, James 116
Ortlieb, John 44
Osborne, (Capt.) 181
  (Capt.) Peter 239
Osbourn, Jonas 138, 139
  Samuel 106
Osburne, Thomas 32
Osman,_____ 180
Osterdaugh, Yost Willhelm 183
O'Stevin, Laughlin 74
Ostreith, John 246
Ostrum, Andrew 38
  Jane 38
Otenheimer, Christina 254
Otto, Andreas 237
  John Matthew 44

283

Potts (cont.)
Joseph 224
Thomas 141
Pouls, Catherine 186
Pourdey, John 166
Powel, Robert 106
Powell, Bryan 156, 157
David 30, 31, 32
Evan 32
John 32
Joseph 35
Martha 35
Mary 55
Peter 185
Samuel 35, 55
Thomas 32, 112
William 112
Power, Clement 119
Pownall, Abigail 19
Elizabeth 19
Ellenor 19
George 19
Rachel 19
Reuben 19
Sarah 19
Prawll, John 94
Preeson, William 10
Preisach, George 252
Prendergast, Thomas 192
Presoner [?], John 9
Presser, Martin 44
Price, David 100
James 32
John 80, 182
Joseph 196
Philip 192
Thomas 100
Priessing, Jacob 44
Printz,_____ 2
Prior, Charles 222
Thomas 191
Priors, Charles 182
Prise, Isacher 93
Prish, John 203
Pritchard, Richard 150
Pritchit, Thomas 60
Proctor, Thomas 194
Prugel, Elizabeth 181
Prussel, Catherina 252
Jacob Felmy 252
John 252
Pryer, Charles 219
Thomas 191
Pryor, Ann Pool 239
James 111
Puff, Valentine 174
Pugh, Mary 199
Purcell, James 175
Purdon, Fargust 230
Puriol, John 225
Purkus, Peter 181
Purslow, John 21
Pyall, George 85
Pyat, James 213
Pyewell, Mary Catherine 160
William 160
Pyle, John 207
Pyrlaeus, John C. 34

-Q-

Quant, Thomas 124
Quick, John 216
Quigley, Owen 80
Quill, Thomas 216

Quilman, John 255
Quin, Hugh 158
Quinland, George 70
Quinn, David 15
John 234
Sophia 221
Quirk, Dennis 127
Qwans, Melgert 249

-R-

Rabjohn, John 188
Rachinor, Mary 92
Radcliff, Mary 110
Raine, Nathaniel 213
Samuel 213
Thomas 231
Raith, Jacob 243
Rame, Catharine 241
Francis 241
Frederick 241
John Daniel 241
Ramer, Christian 178
Maria 178
Ramsburger, Anna 43
Ramur, Georg L. 243
Randle, Margaret 231
Ranken, George 226, 229
Rankin, William 102-114
Ransted, Joseph 7
Rapine, Nicholas 170
Rapp, John George 242
Martin 242
Rasch,_____ 250
Rascher, Henry 33
Rasor, Christian 185
Elizabeth 185
Ratclife, Edward 14
James 14
Mary 14
Rachell 14
Rebecca 14
Richard 14
Rauch, Christian Henry 34
John H. 52
Rawle, Francis Jr. 16
Francis Sr. 16
Ray, James 149, 234, 235
Raynolds, John 197
Read, John 11, 239
Samuel 110, 117, 153, 206, 232
Ready, Nicholas 235
Reardon, Daniel 76
Dennis 166
John 58, 72, 129, 136, 143, 166
Reay, Jane 161
Rebsamen, Felix 262
Rebstock, Margaret C. 43
Recey, Elizabeth 144
Rechards, Bridget 10
Hannah 10
John 10
Susan 10
Reckiner, Mary 91
Redderberg, Linet 46
Reddit, Eustace 179
Reddy, Alexander 178
Redman, George 160
Joseph 170
Thomas 205, 217
Redmond, Michael 63
Reeburg, William 217
Reed, (Capt.) 11

Rees, Ann 10
John 10, 185
Mary 10
Phebe 10
Rees 10, 32
Rich. 10
Sarah 10
Reese, Detrick 204
Jacob 201
William 235
Reeve, Joseph 82
Peter 189
Reeves, John 13
Regan, Lott 195
William 103
Regel, Anthony 247
Reichard, David 37
Elizabeth 37
Reidel, Frederic 33
Reif, Conrad 84
Peter 170
Reiff, Ludwig 260
Reiffendorff, Johannes 253
Peter 253
Reigard, Adam 196
Reiley, Farrel 152
James 90
Reilly, Christopher 235
Reily, James 192
Owen 149
Thomas 233
Reincke, Abraham 39
Sarah 39
Reineck, John Chritn. 197
Reineck/Reineek, Ludwig 199, 209, 216
Mary (Maria) Elizabeth 199, 209, 216
Reiner, John George 260
Reinhart, Martin 211
Reinhold, Christian Frederick 260
Elizabeth 205
Reise, Dieterick 187
Reiser, Bernard 148
Reissenach, Dorothee 252
Reiter, Philip Christian 49
Remann, Frantz Petter 253
Remp, Jacob Henry 182
Rennare, Borje Hakenson 4
Rennell, Samuel 16
Renner, Anna C. 43
George 252
John G. 42
Repslagare, Olff Swenson 4
Rerch, Godfrey 253
Rerion, William 225
Reside, Robert 94
Reuecdot, James 93
Reuss, Magdalena E. 41
Reutz, Magdalen 37
Matthew 37
Rex, George 247
Maria 247
Reymers, Johan 250
Reynolds, James 120
John 27, 218
Samuel 58
William 176
Rhoads, Adam 113
Joseph 233
Samuel 111
Samuel Jr. 205
Rhor, John 206
Rice, (Capt.) Edward 240, 244, 246
Elizabeth 35
Owen 35